RECORDING
AMERICA'S
PAST

RECORDING AMERICA'S PAST

*An Interpretation of the Development
of Historical Studies in America
1607–1884*

By

DAVID D. VAN TASSEL

THE UNIVERSITY OF CHICAGO PRESS

Library of Congress Catalog Number: 60-14404

THE UNIVERSITY OF CHICAGO PRESS, CHICAGO 37
Cambridge University Press, London, N.W. 1, England
The University of Toronto Press, Toronto 5, Canada

© *1960 by The University of Chicago. Published 1960*
Composed and printed by THE UNIVERSITY OF CHICAGO
PRESS, *Chicago, Illinois, U.S.A.*

To the memory of
HOWARD KENNEDY BEALE

Preface

The history of American historiography is a rapidly expanding field of study. Articles, monographs, and biographies of historians have been produced in great number in recent years as students of our country's history survey and summarize what has been done, how it was accomplished, and what remains to be done. The studies to appear thus far have been of a biographical or a topical nature. The biographical approach places major emphasis on an analysis of the historian's work in conjunction with his life, as did Michael Kraus's pioneering studies, among the most valuable of which is *The Writing of American History* (1953), and the classic *Marcus Jernegan Essays in American Historiography* (1937), edited by William T. Hutchinson. The topical approach analyzes what successive historians have written about a specific event, phase, or facet of history; for example, Hugh Hale Bellot's *American History and American Historians* (1952) and Thomas J. Pressly's *Americans Interpret Their Civil War* (1954). But no one has treated the subject of historiography chronologically in an attempt to examine the whole range of American historical studies. Aside from filling a gap in American historiography, such an account would seek an answer to a question long puzzling—how did historiography develop in a country made up of a people on the move, whose story is one of successive breaks with the past and outspoken commitment to the future?

My purpose in this essay is to survey American historiographical endeavor in the years between 1607 and 1884 in an attempt to discover why American historical studies developed as they did. For instance, what contribution was made by the often maligned and more often forgotten local historian? Why did historical societies so soon appear in frontier communities? And what was the impetus for the writing of the popular history of a territory, a state, or a village?

Since my concern is with trends and causes, I have not attempted to analyze the work of any single historian unless it might explain or illustrate a trend, nor have I attempted a detailed analysis of interpretations of specific events or phases of history, a task best left to the specialist.

The terminal date for this study, 1884, a traditional one, is particularly apt because it was the year in which Justin Winsor published the first volume of his *Narrative and Critical History of America*, a monumental summary and a culmination of all previous work done in American historiography. It was the year that trained historians took over the job of recording America's past by organizing the American Historical Association. The date 1884 marks both a culmination and a fresh beginning in the writing of American history. The new historians, who pridefully traced their intellectual ancestry to the disciplines of German universities, were inclined to ignore, or at least underestimate, the debt they owed to the contributions of earlier generations of American historians. An account of the development of historiography in America will right an old imbalance and may contribute to an understanding of one facet of our national heritage.

Acknowledgments

This book is the end product of all the interest, knowledge, and inspiration given to me by many fine people on the staffs of the manuscript divisions of the Visconsin State Historical Society, the Pennsylvania Historical Society, the New York Public Library, the New-York Historical Society, the Massachusetts Historical Society, the Princeton Library, the Yale Library, and the Harvard Library. My thanks are due to Charles Scribner's Sons for allowing me to use their archives and to the Council of the American Historical Association for permission to delve into the association's unpublished records.

For their cogent criticisms and helpful suggestions about form and content of all or parts of the manuscript, I am especially grateful to Professors Glyndon Van Deusen, Vernon Carstensen, Robert A. Divine, Michael Kraus, Thomas Pressly, Otis A. Pease, and William T. Hutchinson, as well as to my patient but critical parents, Etta May and Walter R. Van Tassel.

Above all else, I am permanently indebted to three people who contributed to this work from its beginning: to Merle Curti for his continuous inspiration, encouragement, and guidance, and to whom this study owes its inception; to William B. Hesseltine, whose rigorous criticisms and organizational suggestions did much to shape this book; and lastly to my wife Helen, for seemingly endless clerical and editorial labors, the temporary respite from which may be more welcome than the gratitude I gladly offer here.

Although much in this book is a result of the help of others, I alone am responsible for the views and interpretations it expresses.

Contents

Contents

PART ONE

Colonial Origins of Local History
1607–1776

---

1 COLONIAL PROMOTION: GENESIS OF
AMERICAN HISTORY, 1607–30

During the sixteenth century exciting things were happening in the field of historical scholarship, but they were of little interest then to anyone but students and theologians. Brilliant and dedicated men laboriously developed the rudiments of critical scholarship and searched out and carefully preserved old documents, the materials for future histories. The people of Europe, engrossed in momentous current events, took little note of these accomplishments.

But in 1588 England became a serious competitor in the race for territory in the New World when the Queen's Navy successfully seized dominance of the seas from Spain. A few men of business and some ambitious politicians, looking to the building of an empire, engaged in vigorous efforts to interest their countrymen in the investment possibilities of the New World. Europeans clamored for and eagerly read accounts of the fascinating new land across the ocean and the wonders revealed by the adventurers who explored it. Narratives about the New World were not written by scholars but—far more exciting— by sea captains and explorers. This was a field for men of vigor, not for theologians, least of all for historians.

The earliest documents we have concerning the history of America are travel accounts and promotion tracts which bear little resemblance to contemporary European historical scholarship, just as historical writing produced in the colonies differed greatly from the study of long-range trends which preoccupied European historians.[1]

But in Europe scholars were moving away from a set plan of history in which individuals had little influence and played subordinate roles. The Renaissance not only renewed interest in the unearthing of Greco-Roman antiquities but marked a return to a humanistic view of world history. This emphasis, while it did not eliminate the Providential interpretation of causa-

[1] George P. Gooch, *History and Historians in the Nineteenth Century* (New York: P. Smith, 1949), pp. 1–3.

[1]

tion, served to make original sources more important than they had once seemed to early chroniclers. Religious disputations during the Reformation increased the value placed on primary sources and forced some historians to be more critical of the validity of the sources they used. Both Catholic and Protestant scholars examined and exposed myths contained in church history. Secular historians attempted to lay the myths of national and European history. Polydore Vergil, in his *Anglica historia* (1533), proved to his own satisfaction that the legend of the founding of England by Brutus, a Trojan, was without foundation in fact. His work helped to establish a new standard for critical historiography in England. Jean Bodin in 1566 argued that the long-accepted periodization of Western civilization into four empires was based upon biblical revelation and without much concern for observed facts.[2] By the opening of the seventeenth century, when Francis Bacon worked diligently on his history of the reign of Henry VII, and Sir Walter Raleigh, in the Tower chamber, labored on his history of the world, one view of history was generally accepted by English scholars. History, they felt, should be studied for its own sake; the causes of historic events were to be sought in the human record. God's plan might still be discerned by the historian, and history might be dedicated to the glory of God, but as an immediate cause the Divine Hand was less conspicuous.[3] John Dryden, in mid-century, asserted his agreement with Bacon's view of history: "God, it is true, with his divine providence overrules and guides all actions to the secret end He has ordained them; but in the way of human causes, a wise man may easily discern that there is a natural connection betwixt them. . . . The laws of history, in general, are truth of matter, method and clearness."[4]

The English historian no longer had to follow the fixed scheme laid down by a formal philosophy, religion, or tradition; nevertheless, he was not entirely free to make what he would of his findings. He held a fixed assumption about human nature that served to make history of some immediate utility to the present. Human nature, to him, was alike in all times and places, so that "like counsels will probably succeed the like events," and men were to be encouraged to learn from the examples of the past.[5] The true historian, unlike the annalist who simply recorded events in chronological order, was duty bound to discover the nature of God's plan insofar as it was revealed in the past and to draw lessons for the present from the text of human experience.

[2] R. G. Collingwood, *The Idea of History* (New York: Oxford University Press, 1956), pp. 57–58.

[3] Charles Firth, *Essays, Historical and Literary* (Oxford: Clarendon Press, 1938), pp. 42–44.

[4] John Dryden, "On History and Biography," in Robert Chambers (ed.), *Cyclopaedia of English Literature* (Edinburgh, 1841), I, 498.

[5] Francis Bacon, "On Uses of Knowledge," in Chambers (ed.), *Cyclopaedia*, I, 243.

This was the idea of history that justified the seventeenth-century historian's demand to be heard.[6]

Although many of the men writing about America held the same assumption, it is important to emphasize for an understanding of American historiographical development that they were, by and large, not trained historians. The foundations of historiography in America were laid by men vitally interested in the immediate effect of their written work. Richard Hakluyt and Samuel Purchas were not intent on serving the cause of history but were interested in gathering all useful information about America to serve and promote the interests of Englishmen in the new-found land.[7] In 1584, at the behest of Sir Walter Raleigh, Hakluyt himself wrote such a pamphlet to persuade Queen Elizabeth to support and encourage colonization in the New World. Having described the resources to be exploited and the opportunities for commerce, Hakluyt argued that Spanish colonies were the source of Spain's strength but that her hold on them was weak and her claim to the North Atlantic coast of America by discovery was less valid than England's (and further proscribed by the Papal Bull of 1494).[8]

The men whose accounts laid the basis for the study of history in America wrote as best they could about the things people in the Old World wanted to know: what routes to sail; how long the crossing might take; what difficulties were to be met; the condition and location of harbors and rivers; details of the climate, plant life, and minerals; descriptions of the natives and how to get along with them or outwit them; and the kind of political and economic organization most effective in operating a colony.[9]

Because these accounts dealt with the recent past and the writers were not attempting to interpret what had happened or leave a record of events, they did not draw on contemporary documents or on the traditions of historical scholarship. In fact, it was not until the eighteenth century that an American student of history utilized European scholastic techniques. Every colony accumulated historical material, oblivious to the trends and traditions of European historical scholarship, just as opponents of James I and Charles I hammered out the so-called Whig interpretation of English history without regard

[6] For some indication of a similar philosophy of history in the colonies see Jarvis M. Morse, *American Beginnings* (Washington, D.C.: Public Affairs Press, 1952), pp. 1–3, 12–14, 30, 40, 106, 110–19, 246–48. Kenneth Murdock has a good account of the philosophy of history current in colonial New England in chapter iii of *Literature and Theology in Colonial New England* (Cambridge, Mass.: Harvard University Press, 1949), pp. 67–97.

[7] Richard Hakluyt (ed.), *Divers Voyages touching the Discouerie of America and the ilands adiacent* (London, 1582).

[8] Hakluyt, *Discourse on Western Planting*, ed. Leonard Woods and Charles Deane ("Maine Historical Society Collections, Documentary Series," Vol. II [Cambridge, Mass., 1877]).

[9] Samuel Purchas, *Hakluytus Posthumus; or Purchas, his pilgrimes, contayning a history of the world in Sea voyages and Lande-trauells, by Englishmen and others* (5 vols.; London, 1625–26); George B. Parks, *Richard Hakluyt and the English Voyages* (New York: American Geographical Society, 1928).

[3]

for the growing currents of critical scholarship.[10] At the same time an embattled Parliament was seeking to maintain its integrity against the "divine right of kings" by discovering support for "the historic rights of Englishmen" in the documents and precedents of the past, the English colonists, under the necessity of making reports, defending policies, and promoting their settlements to attract new settlers and investors, set the patterns for written history in America. These early reports, tracts, and apologias fostered the interest of local historians in American social and economic history, geology, and cultural anthropology.

Colonial historiography fulfilled specific needs to meet particular conditions. Only the New England colonies developed a strong interest in regional history. To a great degree the individual requirements of the various colonies were similar during comparable periods of growth. In the early years the colonies lacked settlers and supplies, and men like Edward Winslow and John Smith wrote at length of these needs. The colonies supplied information to English readers eager to hear of adventure in the strange new world. Colonial historians defended Separatism, Puritanism, and Quakerism in the colonies and boasted of missionary prowess among the savages of a "howling wilderness." Contradicting these claims were numerous accounts of the colonists' wars with the Indians. Historical narratives in the early colonial period of America were not written to preserve a complete record of past events but to fulfil specific purposes.

Some authors sought to promote the colony in which they had an interest and to counter false reports which might deter prospective investors and settlers. William Wood's *New England's Prospect* (1634) was written to "enrich the knowledge of the mind-travelling Reader, or benefit the future Voyager,"[11] because "there hath beene many scandalous and false reports past upon the Country, even from the sulphurious breath of every base ballad-monger."[12] The anonymous author of *A Relation of Maryland in 1634* intended to show that Maryland of all the colonies had the most advantages to offer settlers. He pointed out the proud fact that "this colony hath arived to more in six months, than Virginia did in as many yeeres."[13] The land was so bountiful that within six months of settlement the young colony was able to send a shipload of corn and salt fish to New England.[14]

The first writings produced by the English colonists were for the most part of a promotional nature. Tracts, pamphlets, and broadsides were printed in London for an English audience, for those who were curious about the New

[10] Herbert Butterfield, *The Whig Interpretation of History* (London: G. Bell & Sons, 1931).

[11] William Wood, *New England's Prospect* (London, 1634), p. 1.

[12] *Ibid.*, p. 2.

[13] "A Relation of Maryland, 1635," in Clayton Colman Hall (ed.), *Narratives of Early Maryland* (New York: Charles Scribner's Sons, 1910), p. 77.

[14] *Ibid.*, p. 75.

World, and for those who were potential colonists. This material was circulated in translation throughout most of the Western world under the auspices of such men as Theodore DeBry, Levinus Hukius, and Jan DeLaet.[15]

The promoter-historians combined exciting eyewitness narratives and geographical and natural description. Many of the authors were prominent actors in the scenes that they chronicled. They used this opportunity to defend their own actions, particularly the stands that they had taken, as did Lord De-La-Warre when he explained to the Council of Virginia in London the reason for his short stay (1610–11) as governor of the colony: "I perceive, that since my coming into England, such a coldnesse and irresolution is bred in many of the Adventurers that some of them seeke to withdraw those paiments, which they have subscribed towards the Charge of the Plantation, and by . . . making this my returne the colour of their needlesse backwardnes and unjust protraction."[16] He left the colony, he said, for reasons of health; he had contracted the flux, gout, and scurvy. But at the time of his departure the other colonists luxuriated in health and prosperity. After giving a brief account of what occurred in Virginia during his short stay, the governor reported that there remained in the colony nearly two hundred men in good health and well supplied.

Many of the books written by Captain John Smith, including *A Map of Virginia* (1612) and *The Generall History of Virginia* (1627), served in part to justify his actions in Virginia. Smith had a fervent desire to lead further expeditions to the New World and he was far more anxious to impart information about and to stir interest in the exploration and colonization of the new continent than to clear his name of charges brought against him or to hurl epithets at his enemies. What self-justification there is, is a deviation from his great purpose—persuading settlers to embark for the colonies.

The early histories insist that the great trials and hardest part of colonization confronted the first settlers; latecomers would reap the harvest and "at ease labour for their profit." Captain John Smith's *True Relation*, written a year after landing in Virginia and a year before the great "starving time" of 1609, described "such famin and sicknes, that the living were scarce able to bury the

---

[15] For a comprehensive collection of these tracts, see Peter Force, *Tracts and Other Papers Relating to the Origin, Settlement and Progress of the Colonies of North America to 1776* (4 vols.; Washington, D.C., 1836–46), hereinafter called *Force Tracts;* and John Franklin Jameson (ed.), *Original Narratives of Early American History* (18 vols.; New York: Charles Scribner's Sons, 1907–17). An excellent discussion of many of these tracts may be found in Jarvis Morse, *American Beginnings*, pp. 1–104. For German interest in the New World see Eugene E. Doll, *American History as Interpreted by German Historians from 1770 to 1815* ("Transactions of the American Philosophical Society," N.S., Vol. XXXVIII, Part 5 [Philadelphia: American Philosophical Society, 1949]), pp. 423–31.

[16] Lord De-La-Warre, "The Relation of the Right Honourable the Lord De-La-Warre, Lord Governour and Captaine Generall of the Colonie, planted in Virginea," in Lyon G. Tylor (ed.), *Narratives of Early Virginia, 1606 to 1625* (New York: Charles Scribner's Sons, 1907), pp. 209–10.

dead." He told of men "being in such despaire, as they would rather starve and rot with idlnes, than be perswaded to do anything for their own reliefs." He described at length his own dealings with the Indians to renew the small supply of corn that the little colony depended upon for survival and wrote of discontent and the hangings which followed the disclosure of a mutinous plot. Although there were "occurences and accidents of noate," Smith assured the reader that all of these troubles were over and that the colonists were happy, "in good health, all . . . well contented, free from mutinies, in love one with another, and . . . in continuall peace with the Indians. . . ." They, and others to come, would now "enjoy a Country not onely exceeding pleasant for habitation, but also very profitable for commerce in generall."[17]

The Plymouth historians Edward Winslow and William Bradford, two years after the landing at Cape Cod, gave the same assurances in a number of short accounts long known as *Mourt's Relation*. The Pilgrims suffered through the severe winter of 1621, death was a daily occurrence, and they had no particular basis for hope that they would have better luck in following years; nevertheless, after alluding to these stark facts, the authors wrote with assurance that henceforth the colonists would benefit from "one of the most pleasant, most healthful and most fruitful parts of the world. . . ."[18]

The first settlers to the colonies blazed the way in an unknown land, absorbed the rigors of a primitive country, and were the first emissaries to the Indians. The savages of the new continent were both feared by and fascinating to prospective colonists in Europe. For the political theorist as well as for the curious reader, the discovery of the Indian was extremely important: here at last was a creature unspoiled by civilization, here was man in a state of nature. Catering to this curiosity, and perhaps attempting to alleviate the fears of the timorous, William Wood, in *New England's Prospect* (1634), described the more "ludicrious" of Indian customs and manners, such as their sports, their gaming, and the amount of work done by their women.[19] But for the most part early historians observed with care the nature and the habits of the Indians. As one author wrote, "Hee that sees them, may know how men lived whilest the world was under the Law of Nature."[20]

[17] John Smith, *A True Relation of such occurences and accidents of noate as hath happened in Virginia since the first planting of that colony, which is now resident in the south part thereof, till the last returne from thence* (London, 1608), p. 82. A Maryland promotion tract assured prospective settlers that "experience hath taught us, that by kind and faire usage, the Natives are not onely become peaceable, but also friendly and have upon all occasions performed as many friendly Offices to the English in Maryland." "Relation of Maryland," in Hall (ed.), *Narratives of Early Maryland*, p. 84.

[18] Edward Winslow, *A Relation or Journall of the Beginning and Proceedings of the English Plantation settled at Plimouth in New England, by certaine English Adventurers both Merchants and others* (London, 1622), p. 1. The foreword was written by George Morton, but his signature was misspelled "Mourt," hence, *Mourt's Relation*.

[19] William Wood lived in the Massachusetts Bay Colony for four years before he returned to England.

[20] Hall (ed.), *Narratives of Early Maryland*, p. 84.

Many of the accounts of the New World which dealt with the Indians suffered from a preconceived idea of the existence of a state of nature, but the only serious inaccuracies were idealizations by Theodore DeBry of John White's original sketches of the Indians in Virginia. White's sketches were realistic, but DeBry's block prints depicted the Indians as if they were citizens of early Greece. Later, John Smith reproduced DeBry's illustrations in his *Generall Historie of Virginia.* Another blind spot caused by a European preconception was a belief that monarchy was the prevailing form of government among the Indians, a concept that persisted for years.[21]

Stories of Indian cruelty and barbarism were given serious consideration by the Pilgrims before the embarkation from Leyden on the great adventure. But few stories of this sort appeared in the histories of the first settlements. Exploration parties in Virginia encountered groups of hostile Indians, and Captain John Smith was captured by Indians but gained the confidence of the powerful chief Powhatan, who freed him and assured the settlers of peace. The Plymouth colonists too had their friendly chief in Massasoit; though they lived in fairly constant feat of the Narragansetts, Winslow wrote, the Pilgrims walked "as peaceably and safely in the woods, as in the hie-ways in *England.*"[22]

In laboring to dispel the dread of Indians—a deterrent to colonization—Winslow and other historians turned the spiritual condition of the savage into an argument for immigration to America. Every English Christian had a duty, interpolated the early chronicler, to spread "true religion among the Infidels" and to win "many thousands of wandering sheepe, unto Christ's fold . . . to the everlasting renowne" of England.[23]

The Plymouth and Massachusetts Bay writers gave much emphasis to the mission to the Indians, which explains later self-conscious justifications for failure that were the histories of the Pequot War and Indian wars in the seventeenth century. The early New England historians insisted that those men might as well be dead who lived in England "for themselves alone," who sat "still with their talent in a napkin,"[24] when they could be of service both to God and to their country by becoming colonists and using every effort to convert the heathen.[25]

---

[21] A fine study of the European ideas of the Indian is a volume by Roy Harvey Pearce, *The Savage of America: A Study of the Indian and the Idea of Civilization* (Baltimore: Johns Hopkins University Press, 1953); see also Bradford Smith, *Captain John Smith, His Life and Legend* (Philadelphia: J. B. Lippincott Co., 1953), p. 258.

[22] Winslow, *Relation*, p. 6.

[23] *Ibid.*, pp. 67–68.

[24] *Ibid.*, p. 66.

[25] William Bradford, *History of Plymouth Plantation*, ed. Charles Deane ("Collections of Massachusetts Historical Society," 4th ser., III [Boston, 1856]), I, 1–11. Henceforth, references to Bradford's *History* are to this edition unless otherwise noted. Lord Baltimore insisted that saving the souls of the Indians was a "design worthy of Christians, worthy of *Angels*, worthy of *Englishmen*." "An Account of the Colony of the Lord Baron of Baltimore in Maryland, near Virginia," in Hall (ed.), *Narratives of Early Maryland*, p. 7.

The most telling point in these early histories, both implied and stated, by New Englander as well as Virginian, was that a profit could be made in the new land. That the Plymouth settlers sent off a shipload of fish and lumber for the English market during the first year of their desperate struggle for survival seemed to support the promise that "the gayne [would] give content to all."[26]

John Smith made most candid use of the profit motive in his *True Relation* and in his *Generall Historie of Virginia*. Captain Smith returned to England in 1609 after a short term as governor of the Jamestown colony. In 1614 he returned to America in charge of an expedition to explore the northern, or as Smith called it, the New England, coast. It was his last sight of America; until his death he promoted himself and the new country in unsuccessful efforts to obtain backing for another venture in colonization. In 1621 he wrote *Trials of New England*, in which he suggested a plan for another settlement in New England. He ordered several thousand copies printed and distributed to the "liveried companies" of London. One of the dedicatory letters was addressed to "The Worshipful the Master Wardens and Societies of the Cordwayners," saluting their labors in the hope that they might make use of his.[27] Smith prudently stated that he would promise no gold, but pointed out that the "warlike Hollanders" added considerably to their treasures by fishing. "Let not," he advised, "the meanesse of the word fish distaste you, for it will afford as good . . . gold as the mines of Guiana or Potassie, with Lesse hazard and charge, and more certainty and facility."[28]

In 1621 the Council of Virginia in London invited Captain Smith to write a history of the colony. "It could not," they reasoned, "but much advance the Plantacon in the popular opinion of the common subjects," and Smith's earlier pamphlet had sold well.[29] The company had to defend itself against attacks by the crown. The lottery which the company ran for the support of the colony had been prohibited by King James, and the members of the company hoped a good history might win them popular support in their fight to maintain their charter. Smith wrote a *Generall Historie of Virginia* under the auspices of the company but arranged for private backing for its publication, thus reserving the right to be critical of the company, an opportunity of which he took full advantage.[30]

For the book Smith chose to make a compilation of his previous works with some additions and some work of others. Two weeks before the book was to appear, the king revoked the charter of the Virginia Company. Nevertheless,

[26] Winslow, *Relations*, p. 61.

[27] John Smith, *New England's Trials*, ed. Charles Deane (Boston, 1873), pp. 8–9; see also Wesley Frank Craven, *The Dissolution of the Virginia Company: The Failure of a Colonial Experiment* (New York: Oxford University Press, 1932), pp. 149–50, 183–84.

[28] John Smith, *The Generall Historie of Virginia, New England, and the Summer Isles* (London, 1624), p. 219.

[29] In Bradford Smith, *Captain John Smith*, p. 253.

[30] *Ibid.*, pp. 259, 268–69.

the *Generall Historie* was published. Too late to serve the Council of Virginia, it was a proclamation of the abilities of its author as a great colonial leader, an entertaining narrative of exciting adventures among the Indians, and a moving description of a rich and rewarding land. The promise of profit was always held before the reader, for Smith was not "so simple to thinke that ever any other motive than wealth, will ever erect . . . [in America] a commonwealth, or draw company from their ease and humors at home. . . ."[31]

With the transfer of the Virginia colony from the hands of a chartered company to those of the crown, there was little incentive for further promotional literature. The pressing need for settlers, while scarcely satisfied, was recognized by periodic migrations. Certainly the crown might have encouraged the writing of the colony's history, but the early Stuarts were far too preoccupied with the struggle to preserve royal status and power to concern themselves with a hitherto not very profitable colony some two thousand miles away.

When James I cried, "I'll harry them out of the land," he announced his intention to rid England of its religious nonconformists. New England was the beneficiary. But the wealth of varied religious ideas that the newcomers brought to the Puritan shores posed new problems for the leaders of the original settlements and the upholders of religious orthodoxy in the colonies, and differences of opinions and belief became the impetus for the writing of later histories of the founding of the original colonies and the struggle to survive in the New World.

Briefly, then, the first impetus to historical writing in colonial America came of the desire to promote settlement and investment in particular colonies, to defend or explain colonial administration, and to answer the demand for information about a new world. These tracts were in no way representative of contemporary European historical writing, and therein lies a part of the significance of American historical studies. Because the authors of most of these early works offered knowledge of a strange land and of the means by which settlers could survive and prosper in a wilderness, they dealt with many subjects which the historians of Europe did not consider to be fit material for a scholarly history. Bacon and Camden and Selden wrote of kings and parliaments and such matters of importance as changing political and military policies; tracts from the New World described small companies of men and how they raised corn, caught fish, governed themselves, and made war or peace with the Indians.

When later American historians sought to re-create the past, they turned for their materials and patterns to these early promotional tracts. Europe waited for a Voltaire and the enlightenment of eighteenth-century empiricism to point the need for a social history of man and his way of life. American historians had long been cultivating this fertile field.

[31] John Smith, *Generall Historie*, p. 218. For an analysis of Smith as a historian, see Jarvis M. Morse, "John Smith and His Critics: A Chapter in Colonial Historiography," *Journal of Southern History*, I, No. 2 (May, 1935), 123–37.

2 THE PURITAN CONTRIBUTION, 1628–1702

The New England colonies, unlike the settlements to the south, suffered no hiatus in historical writing between the flurry of promotional tracts shortly after their founding and the works produced during the eighteenth century. New Englanders continued to write their history throughout the seventeenth century. This passionate self-concern, like many another eccentricity attributed to New Englanders, was an adjunct of Puritanism.[1] Although other religious sects took some solace from the past, none looked back so often or wrote so much about themselves as did the New England Puritans. Historical literature played an important role in promoting the growth of New England regionalism and supplied a theme for American history, side effects of its purpose, which was to stem the decline of the Puritan church. Historical works emphasized the unity of the past of the New England colonies, with Massachusetts men and deeds playing the dominant role.

There was much besides historical writing to encourage New England regionalism. Some of the colonies had been united for forty years in a defensive alliance, the New England Confederation. Their population was homogeneous; they had the same religion and similar governments as well as economies, and they were within a well defined area, designated by a specific name. Histories of the New England colonies made much of these elements, formalized the unity, and passed on a common heritage. This was the effect of Puritanism's constant, backward looks at a reassuring past as a bulwark against the divisive forces that threatened it with disintegration.[2]

New England Puritanism was a combination of the Calvinism of the Pilgrims who settled the Plymouth colony and the Calvinistic "federal theology" of the Puritans who followed John Winthrop to Massachusetts Bay. Both groups put forth approximately the same interpretation of their coming to the New World: God had chosen the Saints of all His people and led them out of Egypt into Canaan, or, as Thomas Morton with a show of wit characterized it, the "New English Canaan." God's purpose was to set up a model so that "the world might see a *specimen* of what shall be over all the earth in the Glorious

---

[1] To explain the great production of histories in New England compared with the paucity in other colonies by pointing to the early establishment of a printing press, a college, and schools, as does Jarvis Morse in *American Beginnings*, p. 48, is only to cite symptoms of the same cause—Puritanism. The Puritans demanded an educated clergy, and the clergy published their learned sermons in order to broadcast their exhortations and increase their influence. Thus it is not surprising that in 1639 Stephen Daye should choose to start the first printing establishment in the colonies at Cambridge.

[2] Benjamin A. Botkin (ed.), *A Treasury of New England Folk Lore* (New York: Crown Publishers, 1947), pp. xxiii–xxiv; John Adams to Abigail Adams, October 29, 1775, Charles F. Adams (ed.), *Familiar Letters of John Adams and His Wife* (New York, 1876), pp. 120–21.

Times which are expected." But the record of the past seemed to prove that no model community, however devout, had ever escaped the inevitable cycle of history; that is, a pious and virtuous beginning, rewarded by wealth, in turn followed by degeneracy and final decay. Puritan divines from John Winthrop onward insisted, and became increasingly insistent as the decline of religious piety became more and more apparent, that the founding saints of New England had made a covenant with God that would, if adhered to, exempt the Puritan community from the inexorable laws of history. The Puritan ministers, in their constant battle to win their straying flocks back to God and the letter of the covenant, and to remind them of the purpose of the settlement and the consequences of impiety, used every weapon in their arsenal, not the least of which was history.[3]

The dogmas of Separatism were the first to disintegrate. The Pilgrims brought with them a definite set of doctrines which comprised their religion. That compact little group spread out as it grew prosperous, formed separate congregations and erected new churches. William Bradford, who for years had been governor of Plymouth Plantation, feared that this diffusion would "be the ruin of New England, at least of the Churches of God there. . . ." He attempted to gain for the church the allegiance of the younger men by reminding them of their heritage, warning them that if they persisted in branching off they would "provoke the Lord's displeasure against them." Lastly, Bradford, in a series of biographical sketches, attempted to make heroes of the "old comers" who "were by the blessing of God the first beginners and in a sort the foundation of all the plantations and colonies in New England." Bradford was right; as the Pilgrim population spread, the doctrines of their church became inextricably fused with those of the Puritans.[4]

After a brief period of triumphant justification experienced with the success of the Puritan revolution in England, Puritanism itself began a long, steady decline. Puritans too used the "lessons of history— in their attempts to recall

---

[3] Based on the analysis by Perry Miller of the sermons of Puritan ministers, in *The New England Mind: The Seventeenth Century* (New York: Macmillan Co., 1939). The histories that early New Englanders wrote serve to bear out Miller's interpretation, which in turn explains much about the histories. On the other hand, Miller's theory of the rise of the "Federal theology" cannot be derived from the histories alone. Murdock, in *Literature and Theology in Colonial New England*, also deals very ably with Puritan historiography, but his explanation that early histories were written to glorify God, while true enough, is too simple an explanation to account for all of the facts that emerge from a study of those histories.

[4] Bradford, *History*, pp. 253–54. Bradford added a note to his history, saying, "Oh, that these ancient members had not died (if it had been the will of God); or that this holy care and constant faithfulness had still remained with those that survived. But, alas, that still serpent hath slyly wound himself to untwist these sacred bonds and ties. I was happy in my first times to see and enjoy the blessed fruits of that sweet communion; but it is now a part of my misery in old age to feel its decay, and with grief of heart to lament it. For the warning and admonition of others, and my own humiliation, I here make note of it." William Bradford, *Of Plymouth Plantation*, ed. George F. Willison (New York: D. Van Nostrand Co., Inc., 1948), p. 37, n. 6.

their flock straying from orthodoxy. In 1657 indications of a desire to relax the standards of the Puritan church in New England reached the synod. The synod of 1662 passed the so-called half-way covenant; a man, if baptized during his youth, could claim membership in the church without an additional regenerative religious experience, and his children could be baptized, although neither father nor child could participate in communion. The elders passed the measure in order to preserve the church, but there were others who urged that the "unregenerates" be allowed to become full communicants. The orthodox bemoaned the necessity for this relaxation of standards. They saw the sins of pride, covetousness, and profaneness increasing in "Poor New England" as church membership waned.

The histories of New England, from Edward Johnson's *History of New England* (1659) to Cotton Mather's *Magnalia Christi Americana* (1702), voiced the same theme: God carried on His work through the Puritans, His chosen people, "in despite of all opposition from His and their enemies in planting his churches in the New World.⁵

William Bradford began to write *Of Plymouth Plantation* in 1630 when the first flood of immigrants arrived. Although Bradford never completed his work, it was intended for publication as a major effort to stem the dispersion and decline of the Plymouth settlement.⁶ The people of Plymouth, encouraged by the expanding market created through the increasing flow of immigrants, spread out to cultivate more land, to start new towns. "And if this had been all," Bradford lamented, "it had been less, though too much; but the Church . . . [was] divided. . . ." Bradford saw in the success of his colony the seeds of its failure. He tried offering gifts of choice land to men who agreed to stay in Plymouth, but land was plentiful elsewhere and his inducement did little to halt the straying.

Bradford believed it was not only the promise of wealth that lured men away but that young men had lost contact with the purpose and heritage for which

⁵ Nathaniel Morton, *New England's Memoriall: or, a brief Relation of the Most Memoriable and Remarkable Passages of the Providence of God, Manifested to the Planters of New England in America; with special Reference to the first colony thereof, called New Plimouth, as also a description of divers of the most eminent Instruments deceased, both of Church and Commonwealth, improved in the first beginnings and after-progress of sundry of the respective Jurisdictions in these Parts; in reference unto sundry Exemplary Passages of their lives, and the time of their Death* (Boston, 1669), p. 84.

⁶ The source of the positive statement that Bradford did not intend to publish his history (see Bradford, *Of Plymouth Plantation*, ed. Willison, p. xxi), has eluded me. The form of the MS may have led some people to believe it was a day-to-day diary, for Bradford used the chronological form of the annalist or diarist; but the total form of the MS is that of a book, with a long introduction and careful explanatory notes, showing constant concern for the reader and posterity. Bradford inserts documents to bolster his account because "letters are considered the best part of history by some wise men. . . ." But regardless of his plans for publication, the manuscript was copied and used by almost every New England historian until it was lost sight of during the British occupation of Boston in 1775, to turn up in 1855 in the library of the Bishop of London.

their fathers had suffered. In his history of Plymouth he attempted to revivify the past. He meant no one to mistake what the Pilgrim stood for, so he made his first chapter a summary of the tenets of the Leyden Separatists. The history proved that "God . . . would have all men to behold and observe such mercies and works of His providence as these are towards His people," that is, the Pilgrims acting together under their religion.[7] Bradford demonstrated that in every adversity God was with the Pilgrims. When an exploring expedition from Plymouth ran across a small Indian war party, the Indians attacked, but a Pilgrim marksman shot their leader and the Indians ran. "Thus it pleased God," Bradford wrote, "to vanquish their enemies." Even during an epidemic, when only six or seven people were sound and death was everywhere, Bradford found the hand of God in evidence. "The Lord," the historian wrote, "so upheld these [six or seven] persons . . . [that] they were not all either with sickness or lameness," and these good people were able to aid the stricken.[8]

John Winthrop, like Bradford, kept a journal that went unpublished for many years after his death but has since become a primary source for New England historians. Winthrop called his journal *The History of New England*, although the great bulk of the work is devoted to happenings in the Massachusetts Bay Colony with only an occasional mention of other New England colonies. Later Massachusetts historians, such as Nathaniel Morton in his *New England Memorial* and William Hubbard in his manuscript history of New England, followed Winthrop's lead in usurping the name New England for Massachusetts and incorporated much of his journal in their own histories.[9]

Winthrop served for years as governor of the Massachusetts Bay Colony and was always a formidable power in that section of New England. In his

---

[7] Bradford, *History*, p. 254. The following verse is indicative of Bradford's consciousness of declining Puritanism:

A WORD TO NEW ENGLAND

O New England, thou canst not boast;
Thy former glory thou hast lost.
When Hooker, Winthrop, Cotton died,
And many precious ones beside,
And still doth languish more away.

In Bradford Smith, *Bradford of Plymouth* (Philadelphia: J. B. Lippincott Co., 1951), p. 300. Bradford's concern over the falling-away of his flock is more clearly illustrated in *A Dialogue, or the Sum of a Conference betweene some younge-men, born in New England, and sundry ancient-men, that came out of Holland and old England* (Boston, 1648).

[8] Bradford, *History*, pp. 70, 77.

[9] John Winthrop, *The History of New England from 1630 to 1649*, ed. James Savage (Boston, 1853), I, vii–ix, 356–58; Massachusetts Historical Society, *Collections*, 2d ser., IV, 200. Three volumes of Winthrop's MSS remained in the family and were lent to Morton, Hubbard, Cotton Mather, Thomas Prince, and Thomas Hutchinson. In the 1770's, Governor Jonathan Trumbull of Connecticut obtained the first two volumes, and his secretary, John Porter, edited and published them for the first time in 1790. The third volume was lost, to be discovered in the tower of the Old South Church in 1816. John Savage then compiled and edited a complete edition, which appeared, after many delays, in 1853.

journal he defended the Puritan government and its treatment of the Quakers and the Antinomians on the grounds that these sects were evil and subversive to Puritanism. Proof that God sided with the Puritans Winthrop saw demonstrated many times. In 1644, for example, the Indians massacred a number of Virginians, and Winthrop professed to see in this event God's retribution upon them for driving out "the godly ministers we had sent."[10]

The Puritans of New England did not inspire the friendship of other groups. Their church was not evangelical, although they expressed a pious intent to bring Christianity to the Indians. As a consequence of their behavior toward dissenters and heretics, the New England Puritans were often attacked. Since they used examples from history to prove themselves the favored of God, their detractors used examples from history to prove their maliciousness.

Among the enemies of Puritanism was Thomas Morton of Merrymount, who traded with the Indians. He not only reveled in sin and shocked the settlers at Plymouth and Massachusetts Bay but endangered the colonies by offering guns and liquor to the Indians. Twice the Puritans saw that he was shipped off to England, in 1628 and again in 1630. He had his revenge by writing a book in which he charged the Puritans, among other things, with charter violations, at a time (1632) when Archbishop Laud's commissioners of plantations were investigating the legality of the Bay Charter. In 1635, Morton acted as an agent for the New England Council in its suit in King's Bench to revoke the Massachusetts Bay Charter. In *New English Canaan*, Morton describes the customs of the Indians, lists the resources of the country, and recounts the history of the New England settlements. He accused the Puritans of legal discrimination against non-church members and of doing little for the Indians.[11]

In 1642, Thomas Lechford, a lawyer and resident of Massachusetts Bay but not a member of the Puritan church, wrote a critique of the government of the settlement "compared with the anciently-received and established government of England." Lechford's *Plain Dealing* did not make fun of the Puritans as did Morton's *New English Canaan*; it is serious and judicious criticism. Lechford, like Morton, accused the Puritans of doing nothing for the Indians.[12] The charge is repeated in the writings of Roger Williams, who championed the Indians in his *Key to the Language of North America* (1636).

Contemporary Puritan writers paid little attention to these criticisms when they appeared. Bradford and Winthrop, it is true, denounced Morton as a "wicked" man; and an anonymous pamphlet, *New England's First Fruits*

[10] John Winthrop, *A Journal of the Transactions and Occurrences in the Settlement of Massachusetts Bay and the other New England colonies from the year 1630 to 1644*, ed. Noah Webster (Hartford, 1790), p. 331.

[11] Thomas Morton, "New English Canaan," in *Force Tracts*, II, No. 5, 56–126.

[12] Thomas Lechford, *Plain Dealing; or Newes from New England: a short view of New England's present government, both ecclesiasticall and civil, compared with the anciently-received and established government of England* (London, 1642). For interesting sidelights on Lechford see J. Hammond Trumbull, *Note-Book Kept by Thomas Lechford* (Cambridge, Mass., 1885).

(1643), answered Lechford by recounting a number of Indian conversions and proudly detailed another accomplishment, the founding of Harvard College.

Perhaps one of the reasons for the lack of literature defending the sect was the vindication of Puritan ideals in England. A Massachusetts man, Edward Johnson, reflected the Puritan victory in *A History of New England from the English planting in the Yeere 1628 until the Yeere 1652*, published in London in 1654. Johnson saw the Puritan successes in England as an extension of the "great successe which it hath pleased the Lord to give, to this handful of his praysing Saints in New England."[13] Johnson added many homely details to the story of the New England colony. He argued that the form of government practiced at Massachusetts Bay had been proven in the wilderness as pleasing to God and therefore best for England. Johnson's chief service to history was to copy into his account some of the manuscripts of Winthrop and Bradford and to give a more intimate view of the average New England citizen than of the governing elite.

The period of success for Puritanism was brief. With the return of the Stuarts to England in 1660, New England chroniclers were put upon the defensive. The old charge of failure to Christianize the Indians stung afresh as tensions grew between New Englanders and the Indians and in 1676 exploded in the bloody and brutal King Philip's War. A flood of histories of the Indian wars in New England appeared after 1660, the like of which was not to be equaled by any other colony or group of colonies. The most striking account of the Pequot War was written twenty years later by John Mason, leader of the Connecticut men who, in 1637, massacred the Pequots at Mystic.[14] William Hubbard, Samuel Penhallow, Increase and Cotton Mather, and Daniel Gookin all wrote histories of encounters with the Indians. Only Cadwallader Colden of New York and James Adair of the Carolinas wrote of other colonies and their problems with the Indians. Colden's *History of the Five Indian Nations of Canada*, published in London in 1750, demonstrated the importance of the Iroquois to the English and pointed out the importance of New York in maintaining the friendship of the Indians in the face of the blandishments and threats of the French. James Adair's *The History of the American Indians* (1775), an account of the Indians in the South, set out to prove that they were descended

[13] Edward Johnson, *A History of New England from the English Planting in the Yeere 1628 untill the Yeere 1652: Wonder Working Providence of Sion's Savior* (London, 1652), "To the Reader," p. 93.

[14] Two earlier accounts appeared immediately after the event. Philip Vincent, a minister of the Church of England, was traveling in the country at the time and wrote a hostile description of the war, *A True Relation of the Late Battell Fought in New England* (London, 1637); John Underhill, who took part in the conflict, answered Vincent in *Newes from America* (London, 1638); both are sketchy compared to Mason's account. See also Howard Bradstreet, *The Story of the War with the Pequots, Retold* (New Haven: Published for the Connecticut Tercentenary Commission by Yale University Press, 1933), and Louis B. Mason, *The Life and Times of Major John Mason* (New York: G. P. Putnam's Sons, 1935).

from one of the lost tribes of Israel and to demonstrate the joys of life under the "plain and honest law of nature."[15]

The Puritans seized the opportunity afforded by the Indian wars to describe efforts to convert the heathen. Massacres and wars were simply evidence of savage ingratitude. The New England chronicles demonstrated that God was on the side of the Saints even when they strayed, but the tribulations visited upon them were to serve as warning of what was to come if they persisted in their sinful ways. John Mason told of surrounding the Pequot camp by night and setting fire to it with flaming arrows and killing the Indian families as they fled. It pleased God, he said, "to smite our Enemies in the hinder parts, and to give us their Land for an Inheritance."[16] William Hubbard, minister at Ipswich, wrote *A Narrative of the Troubles with the Indians in New England* (1677), in which he concluded that the English had never given the Indians cause for war but that God had doomed them to destruction because they had failed to accept Christianity. Nathaniel Saltonstall, in a short account of King Philip's War, wrote that, although God's hand lay heavily upon New England, even yet the Puritans were His chosen people—"he hath given Commission to the Sword to destroy."[17]

Increase Mather, a pillar of orthodoxy and political power in Massachusetts, found in King Philip's War of 1675 fresh support for belief in the Puritans as the chosen people. The colonists suffered many defeats before they won the war, which proved to Mather that had God not favored the New Englanders they would not have been so fortunate as to win. In his concern with the proofs of his position, Mather omitted consideration of the causes of the war and appended them in a postscript, as if an afterthought, to forestall attacks upon "the justness" of the war on the part of the colonists. The Indians, Mather asserted, "fought to disposess us of the land, which the Lord our God hath Given to us." The Puritans had certainly done their duty in attempting to convert the heathen; when they had the Indian sachem, King Philip, in their power, they offered him the Gosepl, which he disdained, and held his land in trust for his people. "And now," wrote Mather, as if indicating the events related in the

---

[15] James Adair, *History of the American Indians* (London, 1775), p. 379.

[16] John Mason, "A Brief History of the Pequot War," Massachusetts Historical Society, *Collections*, 2d ser., VIII, 151–52.

[17] N. S. [presumed to be Nathaniel Saltonstall], "The Present State of New England with Respect to the Indian War," *Narratives of the Indian Wars*, ed. Charles H. Lincoln (New York: Charles Scribner's Sons, 1913), p. 54. The very titles of other accounts reflect their themes; for example, Edward Wharton, *New England's Present Sufferings Under their Cruel Neighboring Indians* (London, 1675); Thomas Wheeler, *A Thankfull Remembrance of Gods Mercy to Several Persons at Quabaug or Brookfield* (London, 1676). Mary Rowlandson, the wife of a Lancaster minister, reflects the orthodox faith of the Puritan in the popular narrative of her captivity by the Narragansetts, *The Sovereignty and goodness of GOD, Together with the faithfulness of His Promises Displayed; Being a Narrative of the Captivity and Restauration of Mrs. Mary Rowlandson* (Cambridge, Mass., 1682).

preceding pages, "behold how they reward us."[18] Of course the people of New England were justified in the war but, more importantly, God had again demonstrated that He supported the Puritans. Without His aid they could not possibly have won.[19]

Increase Mather was at the peak of his abilities in 1692. From England he had returned to Massachusetts with a charter more restricted than the original but a personal triumph nonetheless; he had influenced the choice of a new governor as well as the appointment of councilmen; he had published more than any other minister in New England; and he was president of Harvard; yet with all his influence and with his prolific pen he could do nothing to revive the waning influence of the orthodox ministry.

His son Cotton Mather did what he could "to preserve and secure the interests of *Religion*, in the churches of that little country NEW ENGLAND." Cotton Mather's *Magnalia Christi Americana or the Ecclesiastical History of New England* (1702) recounted the by now familiar stories of Plymouth and Massachusetts Bay told by Bradford and Winthrop, Johnson, Morton, and Hubbard and brought them up to date by emphasizing the manifestations of God's intervention in the affairs of New Englanders.

Cotton Mather chronicled many strange and novel events to support the theme of the Puritans as the chosen people. Storms, harsh winters, famine, and disease were no longer unquestionable proofs; Mather claimed signs seen in the sky, odd visions, and reports of the appearance of ghost ships to support his thesis. Bradford and Winthrop felt that the survival of the first settlers, victory over the Indians, and the growing prosperity of the colony were sufficient proof of God's stewardship. These proofs had been cited so often that they seemed prosaic, incapable of startling, and weak evidence, if proof at all, of God's particular favor.[20]

Efforts to support the position of the orthodox ministry ended with Cotton Mather's *Magnalia*, but other histories of New England continued to be written.

---

[18] Increase Mather, *A Brief History of the Warr with the Indians in New England* (Boston, 1676), Postscript, p. 8 (postscript separately paginated), p. 52. Cotton Mather also wrote a history of King William's War, which he called "the sad decade," in which he concludes that the Puritans must "expect Judgements where the Gospel hath been preached; for the Quarrel of the Covenant must be Avenged." Cotton Mather, "Decennium luctuosum 1699," in Lincoln (ed.), *Narratives of the Indian Wars*, p. 293.

[19] Perry Miller, *The New England Mind from Colony to Province* (Cambridge, Mass.: Harvard University Press, 1953), p. 360. For the "chosen people" theme, see Edward Johnson's *A History of New England*, in which he declares in a note to the reader, "Behold how the Lord of Hosts hath carried it on in despight of all opposition from his and their enemies, in planting of his Churches in this New World, with the excellent frame of their government both civil and military, already established."

[20] Kenneth Murdock, *Increase Mather, the Foremost American Puritan* (Cambridge, Mass.: Harvard University Press, 1925), p. 328; Murdock, "Cotton Mather," *Dictionary of American Biography*, ed. Allen Johnson and Dumas Malone (New York: Charles Scribner's Sons, 1930), XII, 386–89; Cotton Mather, *Magnalia Christi Americana* (London, 1702), Introduction.

God was looked upon as an interested observer, events proceeded through the agency of earthly causes, and success was the reward of hard work and thrift and the blessing of a "salubrious climate." Nevertheless, for one hundred years Puritan historians had trod a path that few scholars of New England refused to follow. The theme they established early in the seventeenth century, eighteenth-century historians continued to augment with only slight variations. Nathaniel Morton wrote in 1669: "Let not the smallness of our Beginning nor weakness of Instruments, make the thing seem little . . . but on the contrary let the greater praise be rendered unto God, who hath effected great things by small means."[21] In 1747 the contentious Scotch physician, William Douglass, wrote of his adopted land in the same vein but acribed different causes. The rise of the New England colonies, he declared, "from so small a beginning in the space of 125 years, . . . to [their] present Glory," was due to the industry of the people and a favorable climate, "like England's." But the anticlerical Scot did not stray far from the path of his religious predecessors. He pointed out, with more pride than accuracy, that unlike the other colonies, "the first settlements in *New England* were upon a religious Account not Properly for Produce," a source of superiority that Increase Mather had maintained so carefully in *Brief Relation.*[22]

Early historians, in claiming that the Puritans were the new Israelites, emphasized the superiority and unity of New England as a region, an emphasis that became a habit among historians and survived its original purpose. Thomas Prince declared that his reading of Morton's *Memoriall* and other New England histories "excited in [him] a Zeal of laying hold of every Book, Pamphlet, and Paper . . . that [would] enlighten our [New England] History." Although Thomas Prince was a Congregational minister, he did not refer to Divine intercession to explain the events related in his *Annals.* He was more New Englander than orthodox minister, supporting the claims of a region rather than a religion.[23]

As the Puritans weakened in their adherence to orthodoxy, they came under the influence of Bacon, Locke, and Newton, reflected in their reading. New England ministers, in their various commemorative orations, were less and less inclined to speak of the direct intervention of God as an explanation of events. Although assuming that God saw the fall of every sparrow, they were not as certain that God's judgments would come to them in this world. New England historians now sought for and found natural explanations for their fortunes, but this was the only variation they played on the old, old theme.

21 Morton, *New England's Memoriall*, Introduction.

22 William Douglass, *A Summary View, Historical and Political, of the British Settlements in North America* (Boston, 1747–50); Increase Mather, *A Brief Relation of the State of New England from the beginning of that Plantation to this Present Year 1689* (London, 1689), pp. 3–4.

23 Thomas Prince, *A Chronological History of New England in the Form of Annals* (Boston, 1736), Introduction.

3 THE HERITAGE OF LOCALISM, 1680–1776

A new impetus appearing after 1660 sent colonial scholars up and down the Atlantic Coast to search for historical records. Charles II ascended the throne of England in May, 1660, and England again prepared to expand her colonial empire in North America. She took New York from the Dutch in 1664 and later established the colonies of the Carolinas and Pennsylvania. The Stuart kings carried on a concerted drive to consolidate and tighten royal control over the colonies, and American colonists began to fight the royal program. They used historical accounts to shout the virtues of each colony and to prove that the old order had been profitable to England. For the first time, too, historians attempted to prove the existence of historic rights; charter rights, they maintained, made new restrictions and trade regulations illegal. New England histories were written to put forth the claim that the Puritans did not come to the New World simply to establish a new church and a model commonwealth, but, since they were subject to persecution, to champion the general principle of religious liberty, a thesis that New England historians would continue to propound for two centuries and which later schools would be hard put to defend.

After the Glorious Revolution, when the Stuarts fell and the northern colonies threw off the yoke of the British governor, Sir Edmund Andros, all of the colonists looked forward to an easing of restrictions. However, their troubles were not over. In 1696 King William, in order to centralize his power over the colonial empire, established a new administrative bureau, the Board of Trade and Plantations. The board, as was true of Parliament, was susceptible to many outside pressures for preferred treatment. A struggle ensued among the colonies and interested parties in England for privileges and immunities. Each colony wanted some special dispensation: The Carolinas wanted subsidies for their industries; Virginia wanted relief from the tax on tobacco; the West Indies wanted to prohibit New England trade with the French and Dutch West Indies; and imperialists, merchants, and land speculators in England wished to see tighter control over the colonies for protection of their colonial interests against the encroachment of the French.

Until the time of the American Revolution, historical studies in America reflected the concerns of the colonists. Thus far the chief actors had written the histories or their unpublished accounts were copied by later chroniclers; but these writings were no longer sufficient to make a case for colonial preferment or to refute the claims of other colonies or those of the imperialist historians. More facts and records were necessary; hence, colonial scholars paid greater attention to the collection of historical materials and showed increased concern for accuracy. Historians used primary sources to substantiate their statements, although as yet they did not collate them, except to verify authenticity. And more often than not they used documents and letters to illustrate a point rather than to establish a fact. Nevertheless, American historians in the eighteenth century began to demonstrate a greater reliance upon the established techniques of European scholarship.[1]

The New England colonies were the first to feel the heavy hand of Charles II as their individual existence was threatened. The Puritans took up their versatile defensive weapon—historical precedent—not now to recall wayward fellows, but to uphold their government and their way of life.

In 1680, the crown launched its attacks upon the charter of the Massachusetts Bay Colony as well as upon those of other New England colonies. The general court of Massachusetts commissioned William Hubbard, a Congregational minister, to write a history of New England. Hubbard had already written and published a history of the Indian wars which supported the colonists' case against the thankless savages. The new official historian of the Bay colony soon lost what little support he had from powerful men in Massachusetts. He was a "moderate"—that is, one who refused to support the lengths to which the Mathers would go to retain the charter.[2] Hubbard was inclined to accept the naturalistic interpretations of the more worldly ministers who were beginning to make inroads upon Puritan orthodoxy. In his history he did not emphasize the thesis that New England was a protectorate of God; he chose to ignore or to explain by natural causes instances attributed by his predecessors to Providential intervention on behalf of the Puritans. True, the theme that New England and the Puritans were favored by God was to be found in Hubbard's history, but his arguments did not satisfy the General Court. Although Hubbard was paid his fee, his work was not published.[3]

Hubbard spoke to a rising generation not yet influential enough to alter the interpretation of history. But Increase Mather spoke for the standing order and gave a good indication of the sort of history it desired. In 1689, as one of his efforts to regain the Massachusetts charter, Mather wrote *A Brief Relation of the State of New England from the Beginning of That Plantation to This*

[1] Colonial historians of the eighteenth century were much more conscious of European historical scholarship than their forebears and followed more closely trends in European historical studies. Thomas Preston Peardon's *The Transition in English Historical Writing, 1760–1830* (New York: Columbia University Press, 1933) contains a good discussion of the aims and methods of the eighteenth-century rationalists in historical writing. Also see J. B. Black, *The Art of History* (London: F. S. Crofts & Co., 1926), chaps. i, ii.

[2] Perry Miller, *The New England Mind*, p. 136.

[3] William Hubbard, *General History of New England from the Discovery to MDCLXXX* (Boston, 1815). Hubbard finished his manuscript in 1682, but it was first published by the Massachusetts Historical Society in 1815. Hubbard copied large portions of his book from Morton's *Memoriall* and Winthrop's manuscript journal. For an interesting collation see James Savage's edition of Winthrop's *History;* Murdock, "William Hubbard and the Providential Interpretation of History," *Proceedings of the American Antiquarian Society,* N.S., LII (Boston, 1943), 15–37.

Present Year. The little pamphlet was written in the form of a letter to an English friend and outlined the history of New England. Mather pointed out, as did many historians who followed him, that unlike other colonists impelled by worldly interests, New Englanders came to this American "desert" for religious reasons. Mather demonstrated that under the old charter and with the active intervention of God, nothing deflected the Puritans, they subdued the Indians and prospered. But since the seizure of the charter and the "rape" of Connecticut, Rhode Island, and Plymouth, which resulted in the arbitrary and illegal deprivation of their chartered rights, New England had ceased to prosper.[4] At last, in the spring of 1689, the colonists "assert[ed] their English Liberties, Rights and Priviledges and unanimously [declared] for the Prince of Orange and the Parliament of England" by overthrowing the government of Sir Edmund Andros.[5] Thus Mather forcefully argued that under the old charter the Puritans of Massachusetts had carried on God's work and won the assistance of Divine Providence and the consequent prosperity which added to the king's revenue.

During the first half of the eighteenth century, New England continued the struggle to justify herself as an essential part of the British Empire. In 1709, Joseph Dudley, a firm supporter of central control of the colonies, accepted an appointment as governor of Massachusetts and thereafter posed a constant threat to the charters of the New England colonies. Jeremiah Dummer, a Boston silversmith and merchant who became agent of the New England colonies in London, took up the task of protecting their relatively favorable position in the empire. He used historical writings to support his argument that New England was a most essential part of the British colonial system. He reviewed the services of the northern colonies during Queen Anne's War and pointed out how useful the settlements were as outposts against French designs on the British colonies.[6]

Toward 1730, New England again took the defensive against the efforts of the British West Indies to cut off her trade with the Spanish islands. The question revolved around the relative importance to England's prosperity of the two colonies. Continuous defense of its position in the empire fed the growing self-consciousness of New England as a distinct unit. In 1728, during New England's attempts to maintain its place in the empire, Thomas Prince began his research for the meticulous work to be published in 1736 as *A Chronological History of New England*. Prince was thoroughly familiar with European historical scholarship and was one of the first American historians to follow European precedent. Upon his graduation from Harvard in 1709 and before he took his pastorate at Boston's Old South Church in 1718, he trav-

[4] Increase Mather, *Brief Relation*, pp. 3–4.

[5] *Ibid.*

[6] Herbert L. Osgood, *The American Colonies in the 18th Century* (New York: Columbia University Press, 1930), II, 140.

eled in Europe and the West Indies.[7] Prince, in his own eyes, was a chronologist in the tradition of J. J. Scaliger, the leading sixteenth-century French historian, and Archbishop Usher, the English annalist. It was not for him to interpret or to explain events, but to establish "the orderly succession of these transactions and events, as they precisely fell out in time." The basic structure of history, Prince wrote, was "too much neglected by our historians." The chronologist expressed the conviction that once he finished his task all that a "competent historian" need do to make it "proper history" would be to "fill up and beautify."[8]

Prince's chronology added the weight of ponderous scholarship, if no more, to the literature of New England regionalism. Prince believed that his fellow New Englanders should review in this "important time . . . the gradual steps that led to our present situation."[9] The subject at least was popular; at the time of publication, Prince's subscription list was crowded with names. Unfortunately for the hopeful author, the subscribers lost their enthusiasm and canceled their subscriptions as it began to be clear that the work was not to be an original history but excerpts from the works of others presented in chronological order.

Prince ceased publication after printing the forty-third number, which brought the study to the year 1633. Prince's work was never completed, it added nothing new to the New England story, and yet, because of it, he is considered an important figure in the development of American historical studies.[10] He helped to popularize the Newtonian concept of the universe, replacing with a naturalistic interpretation the providential interpretation of history.[11] He set a precedent for careful, accurate scholarship and influenced such men as Thomas Hutchinson, governor and historian of Massachusetts, Jeremy Belknap, historian of New Hampshire and founder of the Massachusetts Historical Society, Ebenezer Hazard, collector and editor of *American State Papers*, and John Pintard, founder of the New-York Historical Society. The library of books, pamphlets, and manuscripts collected by Prince while writing the *Annals* was extensive and furnished valuable material for other New England scholars before the revolution. Its partial decimation during the war stimulated the production of the "Collections of the Massachusetts Historical Society"—the "multiplication of copies" of documents.

The introduction to Prince's chronology traced the "connected line of

[7] Edward H. Dewey, "Thomas Prince," *DAB*, XV, 232–33.

[8] Prince, *Annals*, p. 44.

[9] *Ibid.*, Introduction, p. vi.

[10] William H. Whitmore, "Life and Labors of Thomas Prince," *North American Review*, XCI (October, 1860), 354–75.

[11] Prince, *Annals*, p. 44; Frederick E. Brasch, "The Newtonian Epoch in the American Colonies," *Proceedings of the American Antiquarian Society*, N.S., XLIX (October, 1939), 314–32; Chester E. Jorgenson, "The New Science in the Almanacs of Ames and Franklin," *New England Quarterly*, VIII (December, 1935), pp. 555–61.

Time" from the creation through the reigns of patriarchs and kings and the "Progress of the Reformation to the Discovery of New England," and by this emphasis placed New England as the object of all history. More particularly, Prince asserted that the settlement of New England stimulated the colonization program of both France and England. "Such a train of crosses," Prince explained, "accompanied the designs of both nations . . ." that they might have abandoned their efforts "till a pious people of England" established a settlement and by its success "opened the way for the following colonies." Prince then chronicled the success of New England.[12]

Without exception, Prince's chronology and the preceding histories of New England were concerned primarily with events which occurred in Massachusetts. "New England" was used as a synonym for Massachusetts, as when Increase Mather, having described the establishing of Harvard, boasted that "New England hath out-done all *America*."[13] Another historian titled one chapter of his history "An Apology for the Government of New England, with relation to [its] severities against the Quakers."[14] Thomas Prince announced that Massachusetts would be the concern of the "greatest share" of his work.[15] Nathaniel Morton, who professed to be writing about New England, proceeded to narrate the history of Plymouth.[16]

During a period when Massachusetts dominated the other New England colonies politically, economically, and spiritually, there seemed no reason why Massachusetts should not be given pre-eminence in historical writing. But as other New England colonies grew in strength, they challenged the dominance of Massachusetts in every field. The ties of the New England Confederation binding these colonies to Massachusetts were severed as the threat of Indian wars receded. In 1706, Governor Dudley of Massachusetts, who was charged with the control and maintenance of the militias of Rhode Island and Connecticut as well as of Massachusetts, found it impossible to assert his authority in Rhode Island. (He made no attempt to assume responsibility in Connecticut.) In the field of trade, Rhode Island was Massachusetts' chief competitor, with Providence rivaling Boston as a port.[17] Connecticut grew more independent in her trade with New York. By mid-century Governor Wentworth was making every effort to assert New Hampshire's individuality as an economic, political, and geographical entity. In theology Massachusetts'

---

[12] Prince, *Annals*, Introduction, pp. 98–99.

[13] Increase Mather, *Brief Relation*, p. 12.

[14] Daniel Neal, *The History of New England, containing an impartial account of the Civil and Ecclesiastical Affairs of the Country to the year of Our Lord, 1700, to which is added the present state of New England* (London, 1720), I, 221.

[15] Prince, *Annals*, p. v.

[16] Morton, *Memoriall*, Introduction.

[17] Everett Kimball, *The Public Life of Joseph Dudley* (New York: Longmans, Green & Co., 1911), chaps. i–iii.

influence waned as the orthodox clergy weakened. Connecticut became the center of New World orthodoxy.

The smaller colonies objected to the dominance of Massachusetts and demanded their right to be considered equal members of the New England family. To prove their claim, they sought to describe their contributions to the New England heritage. Rhode Island made the first effort to establish her position in New England's past.

In 1739, John Callender, a Baptist minister of Providence, published a history of Rhode Island. Callender wished to correct an erroneous view of long standing; to that end, he announced his intention to place the facts about the people of Rhode Island before his readers in an "impartial" narrative. His history demonstrated that the colony "was a settlement and plantation for religion and conscience sake." This was a familiar claim of Plymouth and Massachusetts Bay; indeed Callender maintained that the settlers of Rhode Island carried on that tradition. They fled, he wrote, "not from religion, order or good government, but to have liberty to worship God." The first planters came to Rhode Island "to pursue and effect the ends of their first removal into America."[18] Historical records supported Rhode Island's independence and her claim to a place of importance in New England's past; New Hampshire, Connecticut, Maine, and Vermont found similar, imposing evidence.

In 1774, Jeremy Belknap, a Congregational minister of Dover, New Hampshire, began collecting materials for a history of the colony, with the aid and blessing of Governor Thomas Wentworth. As part of New England, New Hampshire, too, had a role long obscured by her more powerful neighbor. New Hampshire colonists served valiantly in the Indian wars, and their colony was a buffer zone between the Indians and French and the people of Massachusetts. Certainly New Hampshire occupied a position in New England's economic life worthy of recognition. The mountain colony supplied the timber for Massachusetts shipbuilders and lumber and barrel staves for the West Indies trade. Jeremy Belknap asserted his patriotic regard for the colony by defending his use of local language. Outsiders might criticize it, but, he explained, "it is understood in New England." That it was the "language of the age and country" in which he wrote was justification enough.[19]

At the time Belknap was occupied with his narrative, Benjamin Trumbull was industriously collecting material for a history of Connecticut from 1630 to 1713. Published in 1797, it was a heavy-handed work setting forth Connecticut's part in the Pequot War and detailing the colony's role in the religious development of New England. Ezra Stiles, the president of

---

[18] John Callender, *An Historical Discourse on the Civil and Religious Affairs of the Colony of Rhode Island and Providence Plantations in New England, in America, from the first settlement, 1638, to the end of the first century* (Boston, 1739), p. 150.

[19] Jeremy Belknap, *History of New Hampshire* (Philadelphia, 1784–92), III, 4–7.

Yale College, also thought it time that Connecticut had an account of its past records, and he too collected manuscript materials. Stiles, an energetic, wiry little man, had too many distracting projects afoot. Although he wrote much, he published little, and, as with many of his manuscripts, he never finished his history of Connecticut. Nonetheless, he gained a reputation as an expert and was asked to supply the materials for a short history of Connecticut which became a part of the ambitious, state-by-state account of the history and geography of the United States compiled by Christoph Daniel Ebeling, professor of Greek and history at the University of Hamburg and a leading European expert on America. In the nineties, histories of Vermont and the District of Maine were published. These early histories asserted the independence of Massachusetts and laid claim to a part in New England's past in efforts to support their ambitions to a share in its future.[20]

Although in its reverence for the past and its sense of unity no other group of colonies was comparable to New England, other colonies bulwarked their claims with an appeal to history. Virginia could find much support from the past, and many new histories were written to justify its position. Upon the conclusion of Nathaniel Bacon's Rebellion, histories appeared giving "true accounts" of the opposing sides in the conflict. The governor, Sir William Berkeley, was supported by Thomas Mathew's pro-royalist history of the *Beginnings, Progress and Conclusion of Bacon's Rebellion.*[21] In 1804, Thomas Jefferson promoted the publication of a manuscript history written by one of Bacon's partisans. Robert Beverley, a contemporary of Bacon and a rich Virginia planter, presented a one-sided picture of Bacon's Rebellion. His history was written at a time when the tobacco trade continued to complain of regulation by the British government. On one of his trips to England he had the opportunity to read in manuscript John Oldmixon's ambitious, two-volume *History of the British Empire in America* (1708). Oldmixon was an imperialist; it was his major thesis that the colonies would be of greater value to England if they were more efficiently administered. Oldmixon's history was inaccurate and provided ample justification for Beverley and other colonial historians to discredit his work and his thesis.[22]

[20] Benjamin Trumbull, *A Complete History of Connecticut, Civil and Ecclesiastical, from the Emigration of its first Planters from England in 1630 to 1713* (New Haven, 1797); Roland Mather Hooker, "Benjamin Trumbull," *DAB*, XIX, 7–8; Ezra Stiles, *Extracts from the Itineraries and other Miscellanies of Ezra Stiles, 1755–1794, with a Selection from his Correspondence,* ed. F. B. Dexter (New Haven: Yale University Press, 1916), p. 518; Christoph Daniel Ebeling to Ezra Stiles, June 26, 1794, *Proceedings of the American Antiquarian Society,* N.S., XXXV (October, 1925), 281. An analysis of Ebeling's work may be found in Doll, *American History as Interpreted by German Historians,* pp. 474–93.

[21] Thomas Mathew, *The Beginning, Progress, and Conclusion of Bacon's Rebellion in Virginia in the Years 1675 and 1676* (Washington, D.C., 1835). For a thorough historiographical study of the literature of Bacon's Rebellion see Wilcomb E. Washburn, *The Governor and the Rebel* (Chapel Hill, N.C.: University of North Carolina Press, 1957), pp. 1–16.

[22] Beverley asserted that to correct Oldmixon's errors "would take a book larger than

Beverley set out to demonstrate that Virginia had been loyal to the English crown ever since James I had taken control of the colony from the hands of the incompetent Virginia Company. Furthermore, Oliver Cromwell and his "traitorous crew" had had to force the reluctant Virginians to recognize the Commonwealth; no other British colony had been so recalcitrant. It was Cromwell's Puritan reign that heaped Virginia with "arbitrary curbs" and caused most of the present dissent. Beverley's history presumed to advise the crown to do justice to its most loyal and most valuable colony.[23]

Beverley's uncritical interpretation of history exalted the power of the crown and supported the status quo in the royal colonies in spite of William III, who, in 1696, delegated the crown's authority to the Board of Trade and Plantations. Before Beverley's history could be published, it was considered behind the times; in 1722 he attempted to revise it. Instead, William Stith, the retired president of the College of William and Mary, was the first to publish a history of Virginia in the main current of English historical writing.

Stith, like Thomas Prince, received much enouragement for his project until the publication of the first volume. His tedious style alienated the support his subject gained him. Nevertheless, Stith provided plentiful documentation for what in England would be called the "Whig interpretation of history." The professor's work set forth the history of Virginia as the story of liberty, of repeated attempts to establish and maintain the ancient constitutional rights of Englishmen against the usurpation of the crown and ambitious governors. Stith believed that earlier histories of Virginia were "empty and unsatisfactory," and it was not his intention to allow the history of the colony to remain in such "confusion and uncertainty." One of the contributing

---

his own," but he would give a true picture, since Virginia had been "so misrepresented to the Common People of England." Beverley said that "some people, upon very mistaken Principles of Policy, are for loading those countries with heavy Impositions, and oppressing them with Rapacious, and Arbitrary Governours." "Milder methods," he insisted, "and the extension of the blessings of Justice, and Property to all the *English* Dominions" would result in "real advantages [to] ... England." Robert Beverley, *The History and Present State of Virginia in Four Parts* (London, 1705), Introduction, Dedication.

[23] Beverley's book, a criticism of ministerial colonial policy, was designed to give sound information as well as advice on methods of governing the colonies. In carrying out his plan, Beverley divided the book into four parts, the first three following the form of early travel accounts and promotional literature, describing discovery and settlement, geography, products of the soil, and the Indians. The last part was a description and a critical analysis of the present state of Virginia. For an example of the form that Beverley followed, see William Strachey, *The Historie of Travaile into Virginia Britannia, expressing the cosmography and commodities of the country, together with the manners and customs of the people*, ed. R. H. Major (London, 1849). Hugh Jones, a professor of natural philosophy and mathematics in the College of William and Mary, wrote *The Present State of Virginia* (1724) in an effort to arouse interest in the needs of Virginia. He termed it a "historical relation," but it contains less historical narrative than does Beverley's study, on which he based most of his historical account. The work is primarily descriptive. Hugh Jones, *The Present State of Virginia*, ed. Richard L. Morton (Chapel Hill, N.C.: University of North Carolina Press, 1956).

factors to the woeful condition of Virginia historical writing was the error of accepting Captain John Smith's biased account of the fall of the Virginia Company and his favorable report on Sir Samuel Argall's governorship of the colony. Stith thought Smith generally accurate but believed that the company's failure to reward him properly for his services had distorted his view. Stith himself went through the records of the company and found a story far more worthy, in his opinion, of Virginia's past than that related by Smith. The history that Stith wrote, as far as it went (to 1624), was of the struggle of the Virginians to maintain harmony against internal dissension fostered by a king "charmed with the unexpectedly large and rising Revenue from Tobacco." Stith described the abuses of Argall's regime and the gradual success of the struggle for self-government.[24]

Stith's history was published in 1747, near the end of Walpole's colonial policy of so-called salutary neglect. Stith's findings tended to support those who felt Walpole's policy wise, a policy for which Virginia had long fought, but in Virginia as in England there were some who felt that the colonies should be under greater centralized control.

William Douglass, in 1747 Boston's only duly licensed doctor, was one of those who called for greater control. He published two volumes of *A Summary Historical and Political View of the British Colonies in America* before his death in 1752. It was his intention to write a historical sketch of each colony, preceded by a topographical description and followed by an outline of its government and commercial prospects. Although he wished to see centralized government, he defended the colonies against England's abuses of power. Typical of the abuses Douglass deplored were the impressment of colonial seamen by the British Navy and the sending of colonial troops to fight outside the colonies. In spite of his defense of colonial rights and his New England bias, he believed the colonies should accept a government under the authority of England, a plan which was later to gain the sponsorship of Franklin and the Pennsylvania delegation to the Albany Congress of 1754 as a way of controlling western lands and Indian policy in order to thwart the ambitions of the Ohio Company of Virginia. Douglass' unfinished work is not to be taken as indication of a growing colonial nationalism, although its praise of New England added to the literary nationalism of that region.[25]

In his treatment of various colonies and his cavalier disregard for manuscript sources Douglass aroused the ire of many people. The *Summary* served as a whipping boy for historians who wrote between 1755 and 1775, a time of increasing friction between England and her colonial representatives and the American colonists. Douglass' extreme partisanship on many issues left him open to the easiest and most discrediting form of attack. He flaunted his lack

[24] William Stith, *The History of the First Discovery and Settlement of Virginia* (London, 1753), Preface, pp. 34, 330; Butterfield, *The Whig Interpretation of History.*

[25] Douglass, *Summary*, pp. 2–233, 371; George H. Weaver, "Life and Writings of William Douglass, M.D.," *Bulletin of the Society of Medical History of Chicago*, II (April, 1921), 229–59.

of respect for the use of manuscripts and gathered material to support his views from the reports of unreliable correspondents. The errors in his work were abundant, and it was an easy matter for historians to discredit this defender of the royal prerogative by pointing out his misstatements. William Smith, a prominent lawyer in New York, writing of the colony shortly after Douglass died, several times interrupts his narrative to take the "opportunity to caution the reader against the representation . . . contained in Douglass's *Summary*." And Thomas Hutchinson, Chief Justice of the Massachusetts Colony, published a history in which he took Douglass to task for the errors that he made in writing of his "Altera patria."[26]

It was not the primary aim of these provincial historians to impugn the work of Douglass but to defend their colonies in the struggle to maintain autonomy, which they had exercised for many years. Much of the constitutional debate during the two decades before the revolution dealt with the claims of historical justification. All the disputants at one time or another appealed to history. The final coup of the struggle—the Declaration of Independence—appealed to the record of the past. A "history of repeated injuries and usurpations" perpetrated by the British crown was intended to justify the revolution to a "candid world." The sober chronicles of the colonies backed the angry words of American orators.[27]

The colonial histories of the sixties and seventies supported the argument that through the grant of charters from the crown, and through debate and daily practice, the colonies had gained the exercise of certain rights. When freely enjoying these rights, the colonies prospered to Great Britain's advantage as well as their own. But when Great Britain abused those rights, the beneficial harmony existing between the colonies and the mother country was disrupted to their mutual detriment.

Thomas Hutchinson, in the first volume of a *History of the Colony of Massachusetts Bay*, upheld this colonial argument. Although later Hutchinson was to become a Tory, at the time he began his history in 1763 he was a native colonist loyal to Massachusetts Bay and supremely conscious of his position in the colony as a descendant of prominent ancestors who were present at the founding of the first settlement.[28]

Hutchinson knew the drift of British ministerial thinking toward a tightening of the imperial reins, and he did not approve. He had seen the dissension that had arisen when the general writs of assistance were issued in 1761. He himself looked forward to an age when the American colonies would form "an inde-

[26] William Smith, *History of the Late Province of New York, from its discovery to 1762*, New-York Historical Society, *Collections* (New York, 1829), IV, 35; Thomas Hutchinson, *The History of the Colony and Province of Massachusetts Bay*, ed. Lawrence Shaw Mayo (Cambridge, Mass.: Harvard University Press, 1936), pp. 178 n., 268 n., 301.

[27] Carl Becker, *Declaration of Independence* (New York: Harcourt, Brace, & Co., 1922), p. 16.

[28] Hutchinson, *Massachusetts Bay*, Preface.

pendent empire." He admitted that with the expulsion of the French from the continent and renewed influx of immigrants, the possibility of such an "empire" increased. He asserted that this knowledge among the colonists produced in them "a higher sense of grandeur and importance of the colonies." But he also saw this ambition thwarted by the Proclamation Line of 1763, a line beyond which settlement could not legally go. This, along with Grenville's measures for strict enforcement of trade regulations and collection of customs duties, multiplied the chances of discord in British colonial relations.[29]

In 1763, in this ominous atmosphere, Lieutenant Governor Thomas Hutchinson began to write the first volume of a history of the "parent of all the other colonies of New England." Hutchinson, like other New England historians, emphasized the religious basis of the Massachusetts colonies. He maintained that had it not been for the religious convictions of the Pilgrims and Puritans which led them to establish a settlement, "it was doubtful whether Britain would have had any colonies in America." Virginia, founded solely for profit, "was struggling for life." The success of Massachusetts, the historian declared, gave new hope to the English investors and banished thoughts of abandoning the Virginia venture. Hutchinson related the story of the amazing "addition of wealth and power to Great Britain, in consequence of this first emigration" of religious pioneers. It was an old and well-worn tale of the miracle in the "howling wilderness," but this member of an enlightened generation gave it new life. He did not see it as the direct work of Divine Providence but as the product of virtuous and industrious men, blessed by "the privileges of free natural-born English subjects," which had increased with the passing years. Crises had occurred when those privileges were threatened, and during the period of the Dominion of New England, Sir Edmund Andros, the colonial governor, set them aside.

At a time when the despotism of King James was increasing daily, Hutchinson wrote, "it was not likely that he should consent to any degree of liberty in the colonies." Nevertheless, Increase Mather had gone to England bearing a petition to the king, requesting that he allow a council composed of propertied men, one appointed from each parish, to pass laws for the colony, and that these laws be published. Wrote Hutchinson, "However modest these desires may appear to us, at this day, who are in possession of such ample privileges, yet they could not prevail in the reign of King James." Massachusetts then supported the Revolution of 1688, threw over the Andros administration, and declared its loyalty to William and Mary. In other words, Massachusetts had proved itself loyal to the crown and a defender of the Constitution, according to Hutchinson's ideas of law and the rights of Englishmen.[30]

Other historians came to the defense of their colonies in the face of the growing desire on the part of British ministries for more effective control of the empire. William Smith had chronicled the struggle of the New York Assembly

[29] *Ibid.*, III, 50.   [30] *Ibid.*, I, 3, 274.

for "civil liberty" against the opposition of the crown-appointed executive.[31] In 1765, Samuel Smith, a Pennsylvania printer, took it upon himself to write the history of two colonies—Pennsylvania and New Jersey. He did not publish his history of Pennsylvania, but he saw into print an account of the "progressive improvements" of "the Colony of Nova-Caesaria, or New Jersey." Smith directed his book to inhabitants of New Jersey, to unite them in the knowledge of their past. His history supported the thesis that the founders settled in New Jersey with "views of permanent stability to religious and civil freedom." By "the blessing of divine providence on their labour, frugality, and industry, [they] laid the foundation for the present improvement of territory to the Mother Country." But now, not only were the fruits of their labors to be taxed, but a "too general negligence as to particular rights of individuals" endangered the founding principles of the colony. In many parts of the province, people "justly made [this negligence] the subject of general complaint." Yet such matters "were as much secrets to most of the inhabitants, as they commonly are to strangers," a situation which the historian hoped to remedy.[32]

By the time the revolution began, each colony had recorded its own history as an independent unit of the British Empire, each had a backlog of historical literature which in its development followed a remarkably similar pattern, a pattern that would be repeated by the historians of the territories of the United States and the new states as they joined the Union. First appeared the accounts of explorers in which historic events were subordinate to descriptions of geography and the Indian population. These pamphlets and brochures were usually written at the behest of, and published by, English promoters of colonial enterprises. Next followed accounts written by the colonists themselves, emphasizing the natural attractions of their particular areas and their conquests of the wilderness, with the purpose of attracting new settlers. As the colonies grew older, historians were inspired by other problems and supported colonial rights and primacy in the British Empire. As a result of this self-conscious concern for the past, one expression of which was the writing of history, the people of each colony, at the birth of the new nation, had a deeply rooted loyalty to a political unit far older than the nation about to come into being. Jefferson illustrated this affection when throughout his life he continued to refer to Virginia as his "country" and so did John Adams when he wrote of his "overweening prejudice in favor of New England." State historians were prepared to guard this colonial heritage and maintain the individuality it implied in the face of the growing store of national chronicles which threatened to take precedence.

[31] William Smith, *History*, p. 319.

[32] Samuel Smith, *The History of the Colony of Nova-Caesaria, or New Jersey, containing an account of its first settlement, progressive improvements, the original and present constitution, and other events to the year 1721, with some particulars since; and a short view of its present state* (Burlington, N.J., 1765), Preface.

PART TWO

Problems of
National History, 1776–1815

---

4 THE REVOLUTION: NATIONAL

HISTORICAL WRITING, 1774–1800

In January, 1775, a year before the writing of the Declaration of Independence and months before the Battle of Lexington and Concord, Silas Deane of Connecticut wrote a defiant letter to Patrick Henry of Virginia. "United We stand, divided We fall is our motto," Deane declared, "and it must be—One general Congress has brought the colonies to be acquainted with each other." He hoped that time would mature this embryonic union into a "lasting Confederation." Three months later the war for colonial independence began, forming the basis for that "confederation" as well as the inspiration and theme for a new kind of history in America—national history.[1]

Many Americans realized that the colonies had to be welded into a nation, not only by the establishment of a common political system, but by the creation of a cohesive heritage. A few men turned their efforts toward the organization of a common bond. The histories they wrote subordinated the role of the individual colonies or states to the story of the nation. These summaries differed from local histories in concentrating upon events that affected in some significant way the growth of the United States. The writers were dedicated to the prospect of explaining, elucidating, or simply recording the past of the country as a whole. National histories told the story of the United States as it was reflected in the legislation and activities of the various branches of the government in the capital city. They touched upon many events that occurred in specific localities and upon persons generally associated with one place. The mention of such events and such persons was not meant to glorify or to explain the history of the area with which they were associated but to illustrate and explain the story of the nation.

Until the revolution, colonial historians concentrated their efforts upon their native colony, their "country." They saw no common themes to lure

[1] Silas Deane to Patrick Henry, January 2, 1775, *Historical Magazine*, XVII (January, 1870), 22–23.

them beyond their provincial boundaries. Of the few who did so, William Douglass was one. In 1747, he attempted to review the past of all of the English colonies; he had grown up in England and saw the colonies through English eyes. His history revealed no sense of unity among the American colonists and reflected the views of an imperialist. During and immediately after the revolution, in an effort to place the story of the United States "before the eyes of a candid world," a few American historians ignored colonial localism and jumped the borders of their states. These few men laid the foundation for and determined the course of national historical writing.

The contemporary historian bent on writing a comprehensive history of the revolution faced a major obstacle: No central body of reference materials existed anywhere in the country. The journals of Congress were secret; not until the 1820's did Congress publish its early journals and distribute its debates to colleges and libraries. There was no depository for state papers; each official kept his own correspondence, and the papers of no one man gave a full picture of the revolution. The only readily available source on the Revolutionary War was the British *Annual Register*, which included a running account of the progress of the battle. This source of information, in lieu of something better, was liberally used and copied by American historians.

A number of persons were concerned lest the American version of the war be lost for lack of material. One man, Ebenezer Hazard, decided with stubborn determination to do something about the situation. He drew a plan for the collection and publication of documents relating to the history of the colonies and the revolution.[2]

Hazard, a New York bookseller, had accepted a commission from the New York Committee of Safety to reorganize the state postal system. In 1776, the Continental Congress appointed him Surveyor General of the Post Office of the United States, and in 1782 he followed Richard Bache as Postmaster General. He kept the position until 1789 and the formation of the government under the Constitution. His services for the postal system enabled him to do much traveling, and he made good use of the opportunity to collect or copy widely scattered records. Hazard realized, as did many others during the revolutionary period, that a reasonable case for the War for Independence would depend upon evidence supplied by documents, royal charters and grants,

[2] The reverence for documents and documentary histories and collections stems from the great collections published during the Reformation in the battle between Protestants and Catholics for "control" of the past. With the rise of the science of diplomatics, authenticated documents became a source of truth beyond question. Rising monarchies called for compilations of documents to witness their claims to power over territories and peoples. In England the party in opposition to the Stuart kings used documents as weapons, and with the Whig ascendancy these documents were embodied in Thomas Rymer's tremendous twenty-volume compilation, *Foedera*, completed in 1735. In America, in 1774, Ebenezer Hazard hoped to do for the colonial Whigs what Rymer had done for the English Whigs and took *Foedera* as a model for his proposed collection of American state papers. Ebenezer Hazard to Matthew Carey, February 14, 1787, in Lea and Febiger Papers, Pennsylvania Historical Society Library.

petitions to Parliament, and legislative journals. If there was to be an American version of the revolution, historians would need these materials as well as the letters of statesmen and soldiers. So argued Hazard in 1778 when he applied for funds from Congress to support his work. Elbridge Gerry, outspoken delegate from Massachusetts, used the same argument when he made a motion that each state appoint a historian to collect and preserve "memorials" of the revolution. And John Jay, president of the second Continental Congress, wrote to John Adams that he was carefully arranging the state papers of Congress, for these would be a primary source for the historians of America.[3]

Hazard sent out a prospectus of his work to important men throughout the states in the hope of enlisting their aid.[4] He went from one state capital to another, copying papers and collecting the private papers of generals and important officials. Although in 1778 Congress had given him a thousand dollars toward the project, he did not have enough money for all that he proposed to do. He was able to publish two volumes of his *Historical Collections* in 1792 and 1794 but was unable to publish his revolutionary documents. The first volume of the *Collections* contained material relating to the settlement of the colonies and the second was devoted to the records of the New England Confederation. Hazard's project, and the continuation of his collections, was later carried out by Peter Force, a Washington printer and historian whose chief historical work became the *American Archives*.

The paucity of readily available material, the obstacle Hazard hoped to remedy, did not deter the chroniclers of the revolution. The war in America had not long been under way before the story of its rise and progress began to appear in print; and there were almost as many views about the causes and purposes of the war as there were histories. By 1800 only one American

---

3 Pierre Eugene DeSimitiere had a plan similar to Hazard's but started his collection somewhat later and never completed it. See William J. Potts, "Pierre Eugene DeSimitiere," *Pennsylvania Magazine of History and Biography*, XIII (October, 1889), 341–75; "Proposals for Printing by Subscription a Collection of State Papers, intended as materials for an History of the United States of America, 20 July, 1778," Hazard Papers, Pennsylvania Historical Society Library; Ebenezer Hazard to Ezra Stiles, August 23, 1774, in Isabel M. Calder (ed.), *Letters and Papers of Ezra Stiles, President of Yale College, 1778–1795* (New Haven: Yale University Press, 1933), p. 41. For biographical material on Hazard see W. Roy Smith, "Ebenezer Hazard," *DAB*, VIII, 469–70; also Fred Shelley, "Ebenezer Hazard: America's First Historical Editor," *William and Mary Quarterly*, 3d ser., XII (January, 1955), 44–73.

4 "Proposal to form a Collection of American State Papers: When the conduct of Individuals in a community is such as to attract public attention, others are very naturally led to many Inquiries about them; So when Civil States rise into Importance, even their earliest history becomes the object of Speculation. From a principle of Curiosity, many who have but little, or no connection with the British colonies in America, are now prying into the story of their rise and progress, while others wish for a further acquaintance with them, from better, though perhaps more interested motives. The Means of obtaining this information are not accessible by every Person, and if they were, are so scattered, that more Time would be necessary for collecting them, than would be requisite for reading them after they were collected.

"[It is proposed] to remove this obstruction from the path of science, and at the same Time to lay the Foundation of a good American History, by preserving from oblivion valuable materials for that purpose." In Calder (ed.), *Letters and Papers of Ezra Stiles*, p. 40.

interpretation of the revolution was current in the United States. All American historians agreed that the Revolutionary War was justified, that the colonies were forced to fight, and that they fought not simply for political independence but for the rights of mankind. They agreed that the Constitution, although they might differ widely in their interpretations of the document, most perfectly answered the purposes of the revolution.

This interpretation seemed to resemble that of a small faction of Whigs in Parliament, led by Edmund Burke and Charles James Fox, who had seized the opportunity offered by the revolution to discredit those in power. The so-called Whig interpretation prevailed both in England and the United States throughout most of the nineteenth century. Loyalists might have contradicted it had they had access to the evidence necessary; as it was, each understood only what had taken place in his own colony. The North ministry bowed to the Whig theories in 1778 when it offered the colonies terms that fell just short of complete independence. The terms were refused, a fact which might have proved that the colonists were determined upon independence and that nothing could have held them in the empire. But this was hardly an interpretation that British imperialists would utilize in view of their hope to maintain the rest of the empire intact.

The American revolutionaries could tolerate no other interpretation, because none would justify revolution. They insisted they were not fighting selfishly for independence, not "fighting against the name of a king, but against tyranny." Charles Thomson, a Greek scholar and the secretary of the Continental Congress, wrote a history from the sources at his command but deemed it wise to burn the manuscript because it was critical of some patriots. And throughout the nineteenth century a simplified interpretation of the causes of the Revolutionary War served the purposes of American nationalism.[5]

Some English and French accounts of the Revolutionary War entered the contest for control of the past, but few passed to the American reader without

[5] An example of the Whig interpretation may be found in the *Annual Register, 1775,* XVIII (4th ed.; London, 1783), 2. It is argued that the purpose of the so-called intolerable acts against Massachusetts was to split the colonies by closing the largest port, and that other colonial ports would happily seize Boston's trade. Thus, "besides their direct operation, these bills would eventually prove a means of dissolving that bond of union, which seemed of late too much to prevail amongst the colonies," and secure their loyalty and obedience. The bills had the opposite effect, said the Register self-righteously, "as had been too truly foretold by their opposers at home." The Declaration of Independence contains essentially the same interpretation: "The history of the present King of Great Britain is a history of repeated injuries and usurpations, all having in direct object the establishment of an absolute Tyranny over these States. To prove this, let Facts be submitted to a candid world." Henry S. Commager (ed.), *Documents of American History* (5th ed.; New York: Appleton-Century-Crofts, Inc., 1949), p. 101. For a good account of nineteenth-century interpretations of the revolution, see Sidney G. Fisher, "The Legendary and Myth-Making Process in Histories of the American Revolution," *Proceedings of the American Philosophical Society,* LI (Philadelphia, 1912), 53–75. Recent interpretations are well surveyed and criticized by Edmund S. Morgan, "The American Revolution: Revisions in Need of Revising," *William and Mary Quarterly,* 3d ser., XIV (January, 1957), 3–15.

running the gauntlet of critical attacks by American writers. No foreign interpretation gained critical acclaim during the last decades of the eighteenth century, so jealous of their history were the citizens of the United States. In 1782, James Murray, an English Unitarian, published a two-volume *Impartial History of the War in America*, but American critics did not agree with the title and quickly labeled it "defective" and a "catchpenny performance."[6] Histories by John Andrews and George Chalmers, which attempted to show that the legal position of the colonies was unfounded, evoked little criticism but that of neglect. One of the leading American historians, Jeremy Belknap, did not read Chalmers' history, published in 1780, until 1790, and only then to correct its errors.[7]

French historians, in spite of the sympathy to be expected of allies, fared no better at American hands than the British. The eloquent Abbé Raynal, who evoked John Adams' rare admiration, produced a sympathetic but not entirely accurate history.[8] The revolution's chief propagandist, Tom Paine, refused to give it his "imprimatur." Instead he published a seventy-page letter correcting the French historian's account, to "prevent even accidental errors intermixing with history, under the sanction of time and silence." He pointed out to the abbé the long series of abuses of power and colonial rights "which led on, step by step, unstudied and uncontrived on the part of America, to a revolution. . . ."[9]

Another Frenchman, the Abbé Gregoire de Mably, received discouragement even before he wrote his history of the American war. He asked John Adams to suggest sources for a "short sketch" of the Revolutionary War. Adams answered the abbé's request in several long letters but warned him that it was "too soon to undertake a complete history of that great event" and that superficial treatment would not do it justice. Adams then gave the aspiring historian a long list of sources that even a native American with time and money at his disposal might have found difficult to assimilate. As if to make sure that the abbé saw the American revolution in a favorable light, Adams suggested not only an outline divided into precise periods but an appropriate interpretation. Such an interpretation, Adams wrote, would be based upon a "general analogy in the governments and characters of thirteen states," encouraged by a wise and benevolent British colonial policy through the year

[6] James Murray, *Impartial History of the War in America* (2 vols.; London, 1781–82); William Gordon to John Adams, September 7, 1782, *Proceedings of the Massachusetts Historical Society*, LXIII (Boston, 1930), 467–68; Hazard to Jeremy Belknap, September 5, 1781, *Belknap Papers*, Part I ("Collections of the Massachusetts Historical Society," II, 5th ser. [Boston, 1877]), 108.

[7] Hazard to Belknap, December 19, 1782, *Belknap Papers*, Part I, p. 171.

[8] Guillaume Thomas François Raynal, *Revolution of America* (London, 1781); John Adams, diary entry for February 2, 1779, in *Works: with Life, Notes and Illustrations*, ed. Charles Francis Adams (Boston, 1850–56), III, 186.

[9] Thomas Paine, *Letter Addressed to the Abbé Raynal on the Affairs of North America* (Philadelphia, 1782), pp. 6–7.

1761. After that date a change in British policy, supported by ambitious ministers, provoked the revolution. The abbé wrote his "sketch" without consulting the sources to which Adams had referred him. No translation and no criticism of the abbé's work are known.[10]

Several English histories reached American readers through the barrier of criticism. The British *Annual Register* carried a running account of the revolution which American writers accepted as substantially correct. Edmund Burke and William Dodsley had established the *Register* in 1758 as a depository for Parliamentary debates, current European history, trade statistics, natural history, book reviews, and fragments of useful knowledge. American as well as British historians used it as a source-book. Many contemporaries attributed the articles on the revolution to Edmund Burke, the "friend of America," a belief which tended to mollify the criticism of American patriots.[11] The most blatantly patriotic American journal, the *Columbian*, published serially "a concise history of the late war in America," whose author admitted having copied, "without change," much of "Burke's section" of the *Annual Register* and justified his action by praising "the superior elegance of its composition." The anonymous author added "some thoughts" of his own, enough to make it an "American" history.[12]

Publishers in the United States were pleased to discover worthy of several editions a *History of North America* by an English minister, W. D. Cooper. Cooper's writings were not unknown to the American market; his histories of Greece and Rome had won popularity in the United States in the 1780's. Since he based the part of his history that covered the revolution upon the account given in the *Annual Register*, it took little editing to make Cooper's views inoffensive to patriotic readers.[13]

Nevertheless, Americans generally gave harsh treatment to foreign accounts of the revolution, and American historians turned out an abundance, thereby supplying the best defense against hostile or inaccurate interpretations. But several years were to pass before the appearance of a history of the revolution that most of the country came to accept as an authentic and accurate account of "that great event." A zealous group of early revolutionists made the first attempt to extend their control of the present into the past, to defend the war and give sanction to their cause. William Gordon, an Englishman and a Separatist minister with strong views about the rights of man, appointed himself their official historian.

[10] John Adams to Abbé de Mably, 1782, *Works*, V, 492–96.

[11] *Annual Register, or a View of the History, Politics, and Literature, for the year 1776* (London, 1777); Thomas W. Copeland, "Burke and Dodsley's *Annual Register*," *Publications of the Modern Language Association of America*, LIV (March, 1939), 223–45.

[12] *Columbian*, IV (March, 1789), 50.

[13] W. D. Cooper, *The History of North America, containing a review of the customs and manners of the original inhabitants; the first settlement of the British colonies, their rise and progress, from the earliest period to the time of their becoming united, free, and independent states* (London, 1789), p. 184.

Late in the summer of 1770, Gordon found it auspicious to leave his parish at Gravel Lane and to depart from England. He had a high opinion of his own views, which he never failed to express, and an unhappy tendency to wear out his welcome wherever he settled. There were few places in England where the minister's ebullient republican partisanship would be tolerated for long. He packed his belongings, sailed for America, and found upon his arrival that an obliging friend-by-correspondence had recommended him to the congregation at Jamaica Plain in Roxbury, Massachusetts. There he made his headquarters for his sojourn in America.[14]

In 1722, after a year on trial, Gordon won the ministry by the unanimous vote of the Roxbury congregation. He preached his own sermon of installation. Gordon pleased the Roxbury parishioners by his bearing and his persuasive manner, and they were willing to overlook the fact that he was rarely tactful and often rude.

William Gordon was a big man with a square face set off by a white wig. He had something of the dignified appearance of Washington; there ended the resemblance. Gordon talked much. He loved to give advice to people about their jobs, especially to those who held high official positions. He spoke on all subjects with a conviction that persuaded many of his superior wisdom. He was vain. He could not be put off with a rebuff, for he believed that every-one was eager for his friendship and willing to listen to his advice. In spite of these personal idiosyncrasies, he won the tolerance of the rebellious Americans by his zeal for the patriot's cause.[15]

When the position at Roxbury seemed assured, Gordon began to write for the local newspapers political tracts supporting the Popular Party. He also made the acquaintance of local politicians. By 1774 he had succeeded in making his name prominent in the region. In December, in recognition of his efforts on behalf of colonial rights, the Provincial Congress of Massachusetts asked Gordon to deliver the Thanksgiving Day sermon. The Congress followed this honor by electing him their chaplain for the following year. Gordon took full advantage of the opportunities afforded an ingenious historian by this office.[16] In 1774, during his rise to local prominence, he determined to become the Thucydides of the contest that he was certain would soon begin. The men who were guiding the revolutionary movement, such men as Samuel Adams, Tom Paine, and Patrick Henry, held much the same view as William Gordon and could be counted on to look with favor upon his project. In that

[14] William Gordon to James Bowdoin, May 18, 1770, *Proceedings of the Massachusetts Historical Society*, LXIII (Boston, 1930), 309. For biographical material on Gordon see Frank Monaghan, "William Gordon," *DAB*, VII, 426; James S. Loring, "Our First Historian of the American Revolution," *Historical Magazine*, VI (February, 1862), 41–49; *ibid.*, March, 1862, pp. 78–83.

[15] John Adams, diary entry, September 16, 1775, *Works*, II, 423–24. John Eliot referred to Gordon as "the *forth putting*, officious gentleman Dr. Gordon." Eliot to Belknap, September 11, 1780, Massachusetts Historical Society, *Collections*, 6th ser., IV, 195.

[16] William Gordon, *A Disclosure Preached Dec. 15, 1774* (Boston, 1774), pp. 17–18.

year (1774) the Provincial Congress received word that a local army officer had come into possession of a quantity of revealing letters by the former governor, Thomas Hutchinson. They commissioned Gordon to obtain the letters. Gordon immediately set out astride his "gentle bay" for Milton, Massachusetts. He worked quickly, extracting and piecing together a body of evidence to prove Hutchinson's wicked duplicity and traitorous actions as governor. The series was published together with a plea for additional letters and documents that might be scattered about the countryside.[17]

As the revolution progressed, the patriots differed in their opinions as to how the war should be conducted and the colonies governed. Gordon championed the group that opposed centralization of political power and demanded sovereignty for each colony and as much freedom as possible. The American colonies, Gordon declared, were not fighting against "the name of a king" but against "tyranny."[18] After the war the United States should "remain a collection of Republics, and not become an Empire, for then freedom will languish and die. When an individual or a congress can command at pleasure her [the country's] whole force, and make her an *offensive* power, she may be more formidable, but she will be less free."[19] Gordon was not a man to keep his views to himself. He fought a mighty paper battle against the Massachusetts constitution of 1778 and only withdrew his opposition to the constitution of 1780 when the convention added a bill of rights. While chaplain to the Continental Congress, he lobbied so vigorously for the emancipation of slaves that to save further embarrassment the Congress dismissed him before his term was up.[20]

Gordon reflected these views in his chronicle of the revolution. He sanded down the sharp edges of revolutionary propaganda, saw the document bound, and sold it as history. He devoted the first part of his work to building up the case against Parliament's claim to tax the colonies without their consent. He outlined the histories of each colony from the first charter to the year 1760 and listed the declarations, expressed or implicit, buried in charters, resolutions of assemblies, petitions, even in instructions to the governors, against taxation without consent. The revolutionary movement had its beginnings in 1761 when the general writs of assistance were issued in Massachusetts. From this period, Gordon wrote, "may be dated, the fixed, uniform, and growing opposition which was made to the ministerial plans of encroaching upon the original rights and long established customs of the colonies." He held

---

[17] General John Thomas to Colonel William Taylor, May 30, 1775, miscellaneous MSS in Boston Public Library.

[18] William Gordon, *The Separation of the Jewish Tribes, after the Death of Solomon, accounted for, and applied to the present day, in a Sermon preached before the general court on Friday, July 4, 1777* (Boston, 1777), p. 33.

[19] Gordon to John Adams, September 7, 1782, *Proceedings of the Massachusetts Historical Society*, LXIII (Boston, 1930), 469.

[20] *Independent Crisis* (Boston), March 20, April 10, 1777.

no brief for the "party of aristocracy" led by New Yorkers and supported by John Hancock. The Massachusetts constitution of 1780 went against the principles of the revolution. By giving the executive the right to veto laws it "encroached on liberty." But this version of the constitution was doomed long before Gordon published his history.[21]

By the time the minister-historian felt himself ready to write, another group of men were directing the course of the United States and preparing the country for a strong national government. Gordon grew uneasy. The eastern country, he said, was "so altered in its manners and thro' the contagions of the times the face of affairs," as well as the Congress, was so changed that "should Great Britain mend its constitution . . . life, liberty, property and character" would be safer in England than in the United States.[22] Gordon seemed to believe that he would need that assurance of safety. He wrote, "The credit of the country and of individuals who now occupy eminencies will be most horridly affected by an *impartial* history."[23] He had already inspired the distrust of influential nationalists. "Parson Gordon of Roxbury," John Adams wrote, is "not accurate nor judicious," and John Hancock, whom Gordon called "Mr. Puff," had no love for the "busy Priest."[24]

Being out of sympathy with the ideas of the men who controlled the government of the United States did not seem to hurt Gordon's subscription sales— until he incurred the wrath of the Boston printers. Everything seemed to conspire to consign his proposed history to the annals of literary infamy. Gordon had publicized his forthcoming work long and extensively and did the job so well that a New York newspaper announced in 1784 that Dr. Gordon was "now writing."[25] This, to be the first national history of the revolution written

---

[21] William Gordon, *The History of the Rise, Progress and Establishment of Independence of the United States of America* (London, 1789), I, 113, 72.

[22] Gordon to John Temple, March 15, 1786, *Proceedings of the Massachusetts Historical Society*, LXIII (Boston, 1929–31), 610.

[23] Gordon to Horatio Gates, October 16, 1782, *ibid.*, p. 475.

[24] John Adams, diary entry, September 16, 1775, *Works*, II, 423–24; for Gordon on Hancock see Gordon, *History*, II, 297.

[25] *Packet* (New York), September 2, 1784. Orin G. Libby labeled the historians of the American Revolution "plagiarists." The label, like a quarantine sticker, has warned off modern historians, and these contemporary histories gather dust in the rare-book rooms of the United States. Libby did a service in pointing out that most of the historians in the 1780's and 1790's leaned heavily upon Dodsley's *Annual Register* (see Libby's "William Gordon's History of the American Revolution," American Historical Association, *Annual Report, 1899* [New York, 1900], pp. 367–88; Libby, "Some Pseudo-Historians of the American Revolution," *Proceedings of the Wisconsin Academy of Sciences and Arts* [Madison, Wis., 1900], XIII, 419–25; Libby, "Ramsay as a Plagiarist," *American Historical Review*, VII [July, 1902], 697–703). But by emphasizing the plagiarized content, Libby frightened historians from using accounts which otherwise might have been useful to them. The fact that the *Annual Register* was used as a source of many of the histories of the period was common knowledge; if the practice was considered wrong at that time, a reader like John Adams, when comparing histories of the revolution, certainly would have pointed it out. (John Adams, *Works*, IX, *passim*.) In a laudatory review of J. Noorthouck's *Historical and Classical*

by an American citizen and already widely publicized, was a plum that each printer in Boston hoped would fall to him. It was Gordon's intention to publish his history in England. When this was learned, the printers were furious, and Boston papers were filled with "squibs . . . against a certain 'busy Priest' relative to his *British* printed, *British* history of the American Revolution. . . ."[26] Gordon's history was published three years after he left America. The old resentment flared anew when the volumes appeared. American critics labeled Gordon a traitor, "a mercenary scribbler," and called his history a product of "ill nature and revenge."[27] When someone wrote something favorable to the minister's work, the critics dismissed it as a "bookseller's trick."[28]

After disposing of Gordon's history, one writer expressed the hope that a book would be written to "do justice to the great leading characters of America." The answer to that hope was in the press. Doctor David Ramsay, a delegate to the Continental Congress, had written a history that for a long time to come would be the prototype for histories of the revolution.[29]

David Ramsay was a native of Pennsylvania and a graduate of the College of New Jersey. He took his doctoral degree in medicine at the College of Philadelphia in 1773 and began to practice in Charleston, South Carolina. Ramsay, a heavy-faced man with a dour look and a quick temper, plunged into South Carolina politics and emerged a leader of the patriot cause. When the British took Charleston, Ramsay and other Carolina leaders were made prisoners of war. Upon his release, Ramsay was sent to Philadelphia by the South

Dictionary (London, 1776), in the *Boston Magazine* of October, 1783, the reviewer says, "In a compilment of this kind, the greater part of the articles must undoubtedly be copied from preceding publications." William Gordon, in the preface to his *History*, while commenting that the English publications about the war contained many mistakes, admitted "that the *Register* and other publications have been of service to the compiler . . . who frequently quoted from them, without varying the language, except for method and conciseness." Other examples of such admissions are in John Marshall's *Life of Washington* (New York, 1804–7), I, Preface; "A Concise History of the Late War in America," *Columbian*, IV (March, 1789), 285–90; "Ramsay's History of the United States," *North American Review*, VI (March, 1818), 331–44. The fact that the *Register* was used freely by most historians of the revolution in this period need not make their works useless. All that is necessary to render them valuable sources is a careful application of the ordinary rules of historical evidence which apply to any document.

[26] *Independent Chronicle and the Universal Advertiser* (Boston), February 9, 1786.

[27] William Gordon to George Washington, February 4, 1786, *Proceedings of the Massachusetts Historical Society*, LXIII (Boston, 1930), 533 and n.

[28] *Boston Gazette and the Country Journal*, February 27, March 13, 1786. There is no doubt that William Gordon wanted to make money from his *History*. He asked all of his prominent friends, including General Washington, to circulate subscription lists. The charges that Gordon was a traitor and that his history was a product of revenge are not borne out by a reading of the text. See n. 25 for evaluation of the charge of plagiarism, one that originated with Orin G. Libby and, as far as I have been able to discover, had no counterpart during Gordon's lifetime.

[29] *Independent Chronicle* (Boston), June 18, 1789; Hazard to Belknap, July 12, 1789, Belknap to Hazard, July 18, 1789, Hazard to Belknap, July 28, 1789, *Belknap Papers*, Part II, 150, 151–52, 153; *Daily Advertiser* (New York), July 9–11, 1789.

Carolina legislature as a delegate to the Continental Congress. Ramsay joined those members of the Congress who urged a stronger form of government. He supported the Articles of Confederation and, later, actively advocated the ratification of the Constitution in South Carolina. By proposing to become a historian Ramsay took command of the past for the Federalists who, with the ratification of the Constitution, put themselves in control of the present.[30]

Ramsay not only set the pattern for later interpretations of the revolution, but his experience illustrated the change that independence wrought in American historical writing. Before the war colonial historians wrote histories of their provinces with the hope that subscribers in England as well as at home would support the work. Some, such as John Smith, Cotton Mather, and Thomas Hutchinson, were successful, but the Treaty of 1783 closed the British market to American writers, as Ramsay soon discovered.

Ramsay's *History of the American Revolution* was not his first foray into historical writing. In 1786 he had published *The History of South Carolina from a British Province to an Independent State*, a book in the tradition of local history.[31] The two-volume history appeared at a time when South Carolina was no longer one of the more prosperous of the colonies. South Carolina was slow to recover from the burdens of war, due in large part to the fact that two principal "staples," indigo and naval stores, which had been subsidized by Great Britain, could make little profit in open trade. As a result of lagging commerce, money in South Carolina was scarce and prices were high. Printing costs were such that Ramsay considered having his book printed in London; much as he hated dealing with "our late enemies," the job would be accomplished for "one half less than it would cost in this country and [would be] done twice as well."[32] At length he ordered printed at Trenton, New Jersey, an edition of 3,500 copies. He figured that he would have to sell nine hundred copies at four dollars each to pay for the printing.

Ramsay's volumes did not sell well in South Carolina, and he counted on sales in England to make up the difference between profit and loss. He packed off sixteen hundred copies to a successful bookseller in London, who announced, having first tried to censor it, that he could not sell the book:

---

[30] Robert W. Hayne, "Dr. David Ramsay," *Analectic Magazine*, VI (Philadelphia, 1815), 204–24; portrait of Ramsay facing p. 204. For other biographical material see William U. Hensel, "Dr. David Ramsay," Lancaster County (Pa.) Historical Society, *Papers*, X (Lancaster, November, 1906), 357–67; Robert L. Meriwether, "David Ramsay," *DAB*, XV, 338–39.

[31] On March 27, 1786, James Madison, president of William and Mary College, wrote Jefferson that a "Dr. Ramsay of So. Carolina had attempted a History of the late war as far as it related to that state, but I believe most of us wd. regret to have an Event so fortunate for Mankind handed down in no better a [?], yet the author has some Merit particularly that his [?] is altogether American, of wch. he makes no small boast." *William and Mary Quarterly*, 2d ser., V (April, 1925), 85; *Columbian*, I (January, 1789), 22.

[32] Robert L. Brunhouse, "David Ramsay's Publication Problems, 1784 to 1808," Bibliographical Society of America, *Papers*, XXXIX (1st Quarter, 1945), 51–67.

"It was tinctured with the imprejudice of party." No other bookseller in England would touch it. At this reception given Ramsay's work, Thomas Jefferson, minister plenipotentiary to France, was furious. He swore to sell the book himself by mail from France, and so he advertised in London newspapers. Philip Freneau damned the English censors in verse as did the *Maryland Gazette* in prose.[33]

The situation in Ramsay's case was not unique. John Adams wrote that the ban fell equally on all American productions. He cautioned the sister of James Otis, Mercy Otis Warren, who was then considering the publication of a history of the revolution, that the United States alone would have to support her work for she could expect no sales in Great Britain. From London, Adams warned that "nothing American sells here."[34]

Ramsay tried selling his history in other states, but with little success. Americans might express indignation about the treatment accorded him by the English, but they themselves did not buy his work.[35] Touchy patriots took the British treatment of Ramsay as an insult to the United States and attempted to make the affair a national concern, but the book itself evoked no lasting interest outside South Carolina because it was not a history of the revolution, but only of South Carolina's part in the revolution. John Eliot of Boston, charged with the difficult task of filling a subscription list in New England, attributed the meager sales to the high price and the narrow field of the book. In 1787, Ramsay acknowledged his failure. He was, he said, "the loser to the amount of many hundred dollars by publication."[36] He was not discouraged; he had learned by experience the lesson John Adams had sought to teach Mercy Warren. The United States must support its own historical productions, and Ramsay would give the new country a history it could support—a national history, the chronicle of all the states—the *History of the American Revolution*.

David Ramsay's second history met with an enthusiastic reception. The *Columbian* hailed it and declared that Ramsay's book was one step more in the realization of "that independence, which for some years after the termination of the late arduous conflict with Britain, existed only in name."[37] Other historians quickly followed Ramsay's lead. Jedidiah Morse included a history of the war in his geography and wrote a *History of America in Two Books*. In 1787, Noah Webster had added a history of the revolution to his *An American Selection of Readings*. Textobok histories began to appear, and one author,

[33] Brunhouse, *op. cit.*, p. 53; Philip Freneau, "On Ramsay's History," *The Miscellaneous Works of Philip Freneau* (Philadelphia, 1787), p. 84; *Maryland Gazette* (Annapolis), April 15, 1787.

[34] John Adams to Mercy Otis Warren, December 25, 1787, "Warren-Adams Letters," Massachusetts Historical Society, *Collections*, Part II, LXXIII (Boston, 1925), p. 301.

[35] John Eliot to Belknap, February 8, 1786, *Belknap Papers*, Part III, p. 309.

[36] Ramsay, in Brunhouse, *op. cit.*, p. 55.

[37] *Columbian*, IV (1790), 372–74.

Richard Snowden, wrote of the revolution in biblical style. All echoed the same theme.[38]

That theme was the nationalists' story of the past, a defense of the revolution and support of the standing order, which became the American interpretation of the revolutionary period. The nationalists' defense of the revolution did not differ greatly from the early propaganda of the war, Paine's letter to Abbé Raynal, or Gordon's history, although with the passage of time they magnified its importance to mankind. "The American cause," Morse declared, was "the cause of liberty," and the struggle for the rights of Englishmen became, upon closer inspection, a fight for the natural rights of mankind whose "legitimate freedom" did not rest upon "the almes . . . of princes."[39] Webster told the rising generation, called by John Adams the most important generation in the history of the world, that "Lexington opened the first scene of the great drama, which . . . exhibited the most illustrious characters and events, and closed with a revolution, equally glorious for the actors and important in its consequences to the human race."[40]

The conditions of America and the wise colonial policy of Great Britain had promoted the growth of "a love of liberty and a quick sense of injury" among the colonists.[41] Nevertheless, the nationalists demonstrated that the British colonials had been loyal and happy because "they shared in every privilege belonging to . . . [England's] native sons [and] but slightly felt the inconveniences of subordination" until 1764, when British colonial policy changed. The colonies objected to the "new" principle of taxation and to the mode of collection, considered "an unconstitutional and oppressive innovation." The colonists used every argument, every peaceful means, to dissuade the British ministers from their tyrannical course, until the hard-pressed Americans were convinced that they could not do otherwise—they must resort to force

---

[38] Jedidiah Morse, *The History of America in Two Books* (Philadelphia, 1790); Noah Webster, *An American Selection of Lessons in Reading and Speaking* (3d ed.; Philadelphia, 1787); Alice W. Spieseke, *The First Textbooks in American History and Their Compiler, John M'Culloch* (New York: Columbia University Press, 1938), p. 34; Richard Snowden, *The American Revolution Written in the Style of Ancient History in Two Volumes* (Philadelphia, 1793).

[39] Jedidiah Morse, *History*, p. 116.

[40] John Adams, "To the American Academy of Arts and Sciences, 23 August, 1797," *Works*, IX, 181; Webster, *American Selection*, p. 155. The point of view of the early decentralists or revolutionists like Samuel Adams, Patrick Henry, and George Bryan was represented in historical writing by the works of Thomas Paine, William Gordon, and, much later, Mercy Otis Warren. The Jeffersonian agrarians did not write history during the 1790's. Perhaps most Jeffersonians, like James T. Austin (*A Primer of True Republicanism, 1796*), were too absorbed in the present struggle for power to concern themselves with the past. Later, when the battle was won, Jefferson himself turned his attention to inspiring someone to write the history of America from a republican point of view. Austin ceased his activities as a political pamphleteer after 1800 and settled down to write a substantial, two-volume biography of Elbridge Gerry.

[41] Jedidiah Morse, *History*, p. 116.

in order to preserve their freedom. In this interpretation, certainly most of the early revolutionaries agreed with the nationalists.[42]

All the same, the nationalists had forced a constitution upon a reluctant people. Historians such as Ramsay and Webster saw that a necessary part of their task was to encourage "habits of obedience" and submission to the new government.[43] They knew that "to overset an established government unhinges many of those principles which bind individuals to each other." Not only had the United States "overset an established government" but had made the right to do so a cornerstone of the Republic.[44] The problem of the historian was to reconcile the Declaration of Independence, a revolutionary document successfully setting forth and sanctioning unsettling principles, with the hope of stability and permanence provided by the Constitution.

Ramsay, Webster, and Morse, as well as other Americans who wrote histories during the early years of the Republic, attempted to make the revolution a symbol of national unity and to demonstrate that the Constitution was the most natural and perfect embodiment of the purposes of the war. "The act of independence," Ramsay wrote, "did not hold out to the world thirteen sovereign states, but a common sovereignty of the whole of their united capacity."[45] These historians often wrote and sometimes tried to prove that the revolution was a war of all true Americans for their natural rights of life, liberty, and property, carried on not by mobs, but an an "enlightened, virtuous, substantial body of uncorrupted citizens."[46] Unity was a product of the revolution. A Continental Army and a Continental Congress, Ramsay pointed out, were the beginnings of unity. Individuals from both the army and the Congress "desseminated principles of union, . . . and a foundation was laid for the establishment of a nation. . . ."[47] Nationalist historians did not disparage or belittle the role of the early revolutionary leaders; they adopted them and failed to mention the strife of internal politics. One historian went so far as to publish in the 1790's a refutation of the claims of a British author who hinted at disunity in the American government during the Revolutionary War.

After showing that the revolution had established a great precedent for unified action and playing down any discord or neglecting it entirely, the nationalist historians moved on to write of the ratification of the Constitution. Jedidiah Morse in his history omitted the Confederation interlude, allowing

---

[42] David Ramsay, *History of the American Revolution* (Philadelphia, 1789), II, p. 316. This interpretation can also be seen in Belknap to Hazard, March 20, 1782, *Belknap Papers*, Part I, p. 121; Elhanan Winchester, *A Plain Political Catechism intended for the use of schools in the United States of America, wherein the great Principles of Liberty, and of the Federal Government, are laid down and explained, by way of question and answer, made level to the lowest capacities* (Greenfield, Mass., 1796); *History of America* (n.p., n.d., *ca.* 1798–99), in Library of Congress Juvenile Collection.

[43] Webster, *American Selection*, pp. 222–23.

[44] Ramsay, *History*, II, 323.   [45] *Ibid.*

[46] Samuel Williams, *The Natural and Civil History of Vermont* (Boston, 1795), p. 373.

[47] Ramsay, *loc. cit.*

his readers to believe that the Constitution came directly out of the revolution. Other historians acknowledged the Confederation as an amateurish experiment in government that led to disrepect abroad and chaos at home and could protect neither life, liberty, nor property, the objectives of the revolution.[48]

A concept of history current in the new nation fortified the nationalist interpretation and supplied a firm ideological basis for the Federalist form of government. The idea of historical cycles was not new to eighteenth-century Americans; it had been seen in the popular works of David Hume and in those of some of the classical historians, but only after the revolution did it become all-pervasive in American historical writings. In 1787, John Quincy Adams summarized this philosophy and applied it to the United States: "There is never a rising or meridian without a setting sun.—We it is true have happily passed the dangerous period of infancy;—we are rising into youth and manhood, with encouraging prospects. But let us remember we shall fall . . . into the decline and infirmities of old age."[49] Ministers in their sermons, politicians in their orations, authors and historians in their works, all expressed the same idea.[50]

The cyclical concept of history stemmed from a belief in a mechanical universe and the eternal sameness of human nature. Nations adhered to fixed laws, as did physical and organic bodies. Wrote Noah Webster: "Every person tolerably well versed in history, knows that nations are often compared to individuals and to vegetables, in their progress from their origin to maturity and decay." Moreover, "the resemblance is fair and just." Human nature, like basic elements in chemistry, was the common denominator. Man might differ in his capacities and faculties, but the same "passions" always actuated him. The identification of the passions included in elemental nature varied with the writer—ambition, lust, greed—any of which, if unchecked, threatened to become a destroyer of organized society. And, like a chemical element, basic human nature reacted to the same forces of history in the same way. The people of nations "in the early stages of their existence . . . are usually industrious and frugal . . . active and hardy, united and brave. Their feeble, exposed, and necessitous condition in some sort forced upon them this conduct and these habits." Although practice of virtue brings a young nation to a prosperous and flourishing maturity, its downfall begins inexorably with its success. "Prosperity inflates and debauches." The passions of "pride and avarice," "idleness and sensuality," are unloosed and bring about the ruin and destruction of the nation.[51]

---

[48] Jedidiah Morse, *History of America*, p. 148.

[49] "The Former, Present and Future Prospects of America," *Columbian*, I (January, 1787), 83–86.

[50] Stow Persons, "Progress and the Organic Cycle in Eighteenth-Century America," *American Quarterly*, VI (Summer, 1954), 147–63; Gladys Bryson, *Man and Society* (Princeton: Princeton University Press, 1945), p. 105.

[51] Webster, *op. cit.*, p. 214. For similar statements see Williams, *History of Vermont*, p. xi; *Columbian*, I (Philadelphia, December, 1787), 819–22.

This was the pattern of history which Ramsay, Webster, Morse, and other American historians at the close of the eighteenth century believed most truly represented ascertainable facts. All American colonial history pointed to the possibility of an empire. Independence was the first step, and the second was the establishment of a government which would hold in check the passions of men, "to retard, if possible, and not accelerate the progress of corruption."[52]

By 1800 the Revolutionary War no longer represented to Americans the revolt of thirteen separate colonies against imperial injustice; instead, it was the birth struggle of a new republic and a symbol of national unity. "Its records," said one writer speaking before the Massachusetts Historical Society, "ought to be sacredly preserved." The Revolutionary War was considered the noblest moment of our national glory. When the Jeffersonians came into power they would try to capture the past from the Federalists, but they would not attempt to change the national interpretation of the revolution and the Constitution. The victors of the revolution were the nationalist historians who called for the erection of a granite monument and thereon carved its story.[53]

[52] Webster, *op. cit.*, p. 215. For an analysis of Morse's thought see James King Morse, *Jedidiah Morse, A Champion of New England Orthodoxy* (New York: Columbia University Press, 1939).

[53] Belknap wrote, "Yesterday I was consulted on forming a set of inscriptions for a historical pillar, which is erecting on Beacon Hill. Some of the most striking events of the Revolution will be inscribed, beginning with the Stamp Act and ending with the *Funding Act.* These comprehend a period of 25 years. The one may be considered as the beginning, and the other as the conclusion, of the American Revolution. The pillar is to be 60 feet high; over its capital, the American eagle, which is to perform the office of a weather cock. . . . The designer is Mr. Bulfinch, a very ingenious and accomplished gentleman, and as modest as ingenious." Belknap to Hazard, September 14, 1790, *Belknap Papers*, Part II, pp. 233–34. See also Nathaniel B. Shurtleff, *Topographical and Historical Description of Boston* (Boston, 1845), pp. 174–77.

---

5 A NEW ROLE FOR LOCAL HISTORY

In the summer of 1785, two years after the Treaty of Paris ended the Revolutionary War, the *Pennsylvania Gazette* announced that American histories "are looked for with great expectation by the literati in Europe; they are anxious to behold in what manner an historian will appear in a country where the press is really free, and not under the trammels of bigotry or ministerial influence."[1] The question of what manner of history of the revolution would be produced by the United States was quickly answered. But how the history of the new nation would be written was perplexing to politicians as well as to historians.

[1] July 27, 1785, in Merrill Jensen, *The New Nation* (New York: Alfred A. Knopf, 1950), p. 94.

People could only guess what shape accounts of national history would take, and as a consequence the role of local historians was uncertain. If national history was to be written on a state-by-state basis, or even as a history of the people of the United States, then local history and the chronicling of unique local events and conditions would be an acceptable contribution to national history. If, on the other hand, national history was to be the story of the central government—its officials, laws, wars, and diplomacy—then localities would have to fight for recognition in the nation's annals, and the state historian would assume the role of the colonial historian, with the struggle for position in the British Empire becoming a struggle for primacy in the nation.

Upon examination of the number of state histories published soon after the revolution, one might easily believe that the battle between local and national history was joined. But during the formative years of the nation, local history served many masters and was the advocate of many causes. Several state histories had their origin in the pre-revolutionary period during the struggle for position in the empire, but their completion was disrupted by the revolution. This happenstance was particularly true of loyalist histories, like that written by Thomas Hutchinson, which was begun to demonstrate the historic rights and privileges Massachusetts had enjoyed in the empire and was completed as a justification of the loyalist position on independence. Some local histories served nationalist ends, since as yet the country had virtually no history. Very little time elapsed before local historians appeared as advocates of their locality for primacy in the nation's history.

The loyalist interpretation of the Revolutionary War rests primarily on state or provincial histories. Their works revealed, as did few other histories, the intense struggle for power among the colonies. At any time the losing side of a struggle has little voice in determining the accepted story of the contest, but the American loyalists faced even greater odds in gaining acceptance of their version. They represented a third party to the American struggle, with no interested group but themselves to appeal to. After the war, the greater number of loyalists became citizens of the United States, thereby "accepting" the revolution, or returned to England. Only a few determined expatriates retained their identity, and they were scarcely enough to perpetuate an interpretation of history.

The American loyalist interpretation did not appear in any treatment of the revolution as a whole. Some loyalists wrote histories of their own colony, detailing the complex political maneuvering, giving sanction to the loyalist stand against the imperial policy of Britain between 1763 and 1775, but speaking out against independence for the colony. They did not generalize, as did the national historians of England and the United States, for their positions were, they believed, explicable only in terms of the internal history of their own particular colony.

Most of these works did not appear in print until long after the death of the authors and after the American interpretation of the revolution had become fixed. Thomas Hutchinson, self-exiled to the loyalist colony in London, wrote a continuation of his history of Massachusetts Bay, published in 1828 by his son.[2] William Smith continued his history of New York while in exile, but it did not appear in print until 1829, when the New-York Historical Society reprinted his history.[3] Thomas Jones's *History of New York during the Revolutionary War* was published in 1879 by the society.[4]

A few loyalist historians published their accounts during their own lifetimes, but in the United States their efforts were either bitterly assailed or completely neglected. This was the treatment given Alexander Hewatt's *An Historical Account of the Colonies of South Carolina and Georgia*, Samuel A. Peters' *A General History of Connecticut*, and Robert Proud's *History of Pennsylvania*.[5]

Alexander Hewatt, a Scotsman and Presbyterian minister, settled in Charleston, South Carolina, to minister to the souls of Carolinians. He began his history in an effort to interest England in the commercial possibilities of the southern colonies, especially South Carolina, whose merchants were complaining bitterly of British regulation of the rice trade with the Mediterranean. The Revolutionary War interrupted Hewatt's work, and he fled to England. In 1779, in London, he published a two-volume history, from the beginnings to the outbreak of the revolution. He insisted that one cause of the revolution was a desire for power among certain groups in the colonies. In South Carolina Hewatt's history was not considered "wholly acceptable" because of his "Tory sentiments."[6]

Samuel Peters conceived his history in anger and wrote in a spirit of revenge. It was written and published in London during the course of his exile. Nevertheless, his account reflects the American loyalist—not the British—point of view, albeit in violent form. Peters, a native of Connecticut, graduated from Yale in 1757 and in 1759 took on the duties of a missionary for the Society for the Propagation of the Gospel in Foreign Parts. He ministered to the parish at Hebron, Connecticut, for fourteen years, until late in 1774 when he received two visits from the Sons of Liberty. The enthusiastic "defenders of liberty" hauled him out to the village common and forced him to recant his pro-

[2] Thomas Hutchinson, *History of the Province of Massachusetts Bay, 1749–1774* (London, 1828).

[3] William Smith, *History of New York*. Also see Maturin L. Delafield, "William Smith the Historian; Chief Justice of New York and of Canada," *Magazine of American History*, VI (June, 1881), 410–39.

[4] Thomas Jones, *History of New York during the Revolutionary War and of the leading events in the other colonies at that period*, ed. Edward F. DeLancy (New York: New-York Historical Society, 1879).

[5] Samuel A. Peters, *A General History of Connecticut from its first settlement under George Fenwick, esq. to its latest period of amity with Great Britain* (London, 1781); Robert Proud, *The History of Pennsylvania* (2 vols.; Philadelphia, 1797).

[6] Alexander Hewatt, *An Historical Account of the Rise and Progress of the Colonies of South Carolina and Georgia* (London, 1797).

British sentiments and swear he would no longer communicate with anyone in England. Late that night Peters slipped away and sailed for England, leaving behind him his wife, his children, and twenty slaves.[7]

Peters spent his time in England scribbling out his hate in a vengeful history of Connecticut. The Anglican minister was no lover of the Connecticut Puritans, and his history pointed out their "deficiency in point of right to the soil they occupied, their wanton and barbarous persecutions, illegal practices, daring usurpations, etc., etc." However violent his opinion of the Puritans, Peters did not subscribe to the British version of the causes of the revolution. Britain was to blame; the real cause of the war was the failure of England to extend her constitution to the colonies, for this failure promoted the growth of republicanism. Besides, England had given few honors or emoluments of office to native Americans and rated the colonials below the yeomanry of England. The mother country had demonstrated her view of the colonies by sending criminals to America. Peters' history only raised the patriotic ire of Connecticut men who, from John Trumbull in 1798 to William Prince in 1898, gave mention of his history only by way of refutation.[8]

American historians may have derided Peters' history, but the reading public as well as the critics ignored Robert Proud's *History of Pennsylvania*. Proud was a large, genteel English Quaker who claimed, not without warrant, that "the wind always blew in his face."[9] He arrived in America in 1759 and took a position as head of the Friend's public school in Philadelphia. He resigned in 1770 to try his skill as a merchant, but he had little talent for business; as the threat of revolution became certain, he had more and more difficulty in making a profit on the English goods consigned to him by his brother in London. When the Revolutionary War began, Proud took cover and "lived in a very private and retired way, even like a person dead amidst the confusions. . . ."[10] For a time he kept his mind occupied and his opinions to himself by accepting a Quaker commission to complete for publication a manuscript history of Pennsylvania left unfinished by the printer-historian of New Jersey, Samuel Smith.[11]

[7] Isabel M. Calder, "Samuel Andrews Peters," *DAB*, XIV, 511–12; J. H. Trumbull, *The Reverend Samuel Peters, His Defenders and Apologists* (Boston, 1877); W. F. Prince, "An Examination of Peters' 'Blue Laws'," American Historical Association, *Annual Report*, *1898* (Washington, D.C., 1899), p. 99.

[8] Peters, *History*, pp. v, 374.

[9] *Bucks County Patriot* (1826), in *Pennsylvania Magazine of History and Biography*, XXVIII (1904), 377.

[10] Robert Proud, "Autobiography," *Pennsylvania Magazine of History and Biography*, XIII (1889), 433.

[11] Robert Proud to William Proud, June 7, 1775, Proud MSS in Pennsylvania Historical Society Library; R. Proud to W. Proud, December 1, 1777, *Pennsylvania Magazine of History and Biography*, XXIV (1910), 63. For biographical material on Proud see C. W. Thomson, "Notes on the Life and Character of Robert Proud," Pennsylvania Historical Society, *Memoirs*, I (Philadelphia, 1826), 1–22; Anna Lane Lingelbach, "Robert Proud," *DAB*, XV, 247–48.

Proud's history was a long-desired defense of the Pennsylvania Quakers; it supported as well the cause of Pennsylvania loyalists. *The History of Pennsylvania* bore little resemblance to Smith's original manuscript. Eliminated were the "long and tedious disputes between some of the governors and assemblies." To be sure, Proud wrote that the sole purpose of the first planters of Pennsylvania was to restore and enjoy "those natural and civil rights and privileges, of which men . . . , by their folly and wickedness are often deprived," and he dismissed the charge that the Friends were intolerant enthusiasts, but he also attempted to demonstrate that Pennsylvanians had lost their "early state of happiness" because they had discarded the principles by which it was first obtained. It was his belief that a change had occurred from the earlier happy condition "of this country [Pennsylvania] . . . with a general cessation . . . from the former usual and useful employments among the people, who were then strangely disposed for revolution, rebellion and destruction, under the name and pretense of Liberty. . . ." According to Proud, this period of "anarchy and tyranny" was brought on by "incendiaries and usurpers."[12]

Proud completed the history in the early 1780's, but he waited until the emotions of the war had cooled before arranging for its publication. In 1798, Proud's history of Pennsylvania had an indifferent reception. Quakers, "those whom it most concerned to encourage and promote" the history, "strangely and manifestly opposed" Proud's book.[13] By the year 1807 booksellers were eager to sell the *History of Pennsylvania* for whatever buyers would offer. Such was the fate of the efforts of one American loyalist to promote the interests of the colonies and, failing in that, to correct the record of the revolution.[14]

Loyalists were not alone in having their work interrupted by the war. Jeremy Belknap put aside his history of New Hampshire to preach to the Continental Army and did not publish his first volume until 1784. The second volume included an account of the coming of the revolution. Benjamin Trumbull, a Congregational minister at North Haven, Connecticut, postponed publication of his history of Connecticut because of the revolution. After the war the Connecticut legislature commissioned him to write a history of the new nation, and he became engrossed in the task. In 1797, Trumbull published the first volume of his history of Connecticut because, he said, he owed his first allegiance to his own state. He then promised to complete a history of the United States. The second volume of Connecticut history did not appear until 1818 and did not bring the account beyond 1764. Trumbull's history, like Belknap's, was designed to give Connecticut its due in the building of the heritage of New England as well as to point out the traditional freedoms the colony had enjoyed in the British Empire before adoption of restrictive policies.[15]

---

[12] Proud, *History*, I, 6.

[13] Proud, "Autobiography," p. 438; Proud to William Brown, June 30, 1805, Proud MSS.

[14] Proud to John and Arthur Arch, March 10, 1807, Proud MSS.

[15] History, said Trumbull, "teaches human nature, politics and morals, forms the head

A number of local histories written during the early years of the nation were inspired by nationalism rather than by local pride. Judge George Minot, a staunch Federalist, began his career in historical writing with a history of Shays' Rebellion, an event given great prominence in nationalist propaganda in the campaign for a strong central government. Minot's history, little more than a Federalist tract, appeared in 1788 in time to influence the Massachusetts ratifying convention. Minot's continuation of Hutchinson's history argued the position of the conservative revolutionaries and decried the actions of mobs stirred up by such radicals as Samuel Adams.[16]

Belknap in the second volume of his history of New Hampshire, Samuel Williams in his history of Vermont, and James Sullivan in his history of the District of Maine approached local history from the nationalist point of view. America's cause was defended against European critics. Nationalist historians argued that human society tended toward freedom and that Americans, the chosen people of God and Nature, were to lead the world into freedom's path.[17] Jeremy Belknap wrote most of his third volume after the war. It was intended as a study of man in a free state—his manners, laws, and social institutions— following the example of eighteenth-century rationalists. Belknap defended the revolution and argued for a vigorous central government. Nationalists believed that the history of any state in the nation could be used effectively to illustrate the principles of the United States, because "the actions and affairs of men are subject to as regular and uniform laws, as other events; and that the same state of society will produce the same forms of government, the same manners, customs, habits and pursuits."[18]

Samuel Williams' *History of Vermont* was written to prove that the "rebellion was only the tendency of nature and society toward freedom made more

---

and heart of usefulness. . . . No history is better calculated to produce these happy effects than that of New England and Connecticut." Benjamin Trumbull, *History of Connecticut*, Introduction, p. 7.

[16] George Richards Minot, *The History of the Insurrection in Massachusetts in the Year Seventeen Hundred and Eighty-six and the Rebellion Consequent Thereon* (Boston, 1788); Minot, *Continuation of the History of the Province of Massachusetts Bay from the Year 1748* (Boston, 1798); Stewart Mitchell, "George Richards Minot," *DAB*, XIII, 31.

[17] Ralph N. Miller, "American Nationalism as a Theory of Nature," *William and Mary Quarterly*, 3d ser., XI (January, 1955), 74–95.

[18] Jeremy Belknap, *History of New Hampshire*, III (Boston, 1792), 326–34; II, Preface. Belknap believed with David Hume and other rationalists that human history was a series of experiments to achieve happiness, but that the most successful experiment was taking place in America, and that the mission of the United States was to be a model for the world. "We see man in several varieties of colour, form and habit, and we learn to consider ourselves as one great family, sent into the world to make various experiments for happiness. One of the grandest of these experiments has been made in our own part of this continent. Freedom, that noble gift of heaven, has here fixed her standard, and invited the distressed of all countries to take refuge under it." The United States was not to be an asylum but an example "to show them that they are entitled to the same rights in their native countries. . . . Like them we boasted of *English* liberty; as if Englishmen had some exclusive rights beyond any other people, on the fact of the earth." Belknap, *A Discourse, intended to commemorate the Discovery of America by Christopher Columbus* (Boston, 1792), p. 38.

active by their [the British ministers'] opposition."[19] Williams admitted the existence of agitators and mobs but said that they soon "sunk into contempt" and "the enlightened, virtuous, substantial body of uncorrupted citizens took up the business."[20]

James Sullivan wrote most of his history of Maine between cases while practicing law on the eastern circuit. His history sought to prove that "there is and always has been, something in the sentiments of the Americans, more especially of the northern part of the country, peculiarly opposed to monarchy."[21]

In 1784, Thomas Jefferson wrote a description and history of Virginia. As a supporter of nationalism, he often generalized on the basis of local facts. It was his intention to show that "America, though but a child of yesterday, has already given hopeful proofs of genius, as well of nobler kinds, which arouse the best feelings of man, which call him into action, which substantiate his freedom, and conduct him to happiness, as of the subordinate, which serve to amuse him only."[22] In 1800, Jefferson encouraged John Daly Burk to produce a complete history of Virginia which would illustrate the growth of freedom in an agrarian society.[23]

However much nationalist historians believed that the uniformity of natural laws and the laws of human nature would point up the universality of local subjects, they found that the reading public believed otherwise. English readers had taken an imperialist's interest in the colonies, but few residents of Virginia had a wish to read about New Hampshire, no matter how generally universal principles might be applied; and soon, in part for lack of an audience, the nationalist approach to local history was neglected.

Other conditions contributed to the demise of the nationalist view. The war and the first years of independence created serious economic problems for the local chronicler. He could no longer hope for an English market. He had difficulty getting his work published because publishers were looking at the national market and wished only to busy their presses with large editions of works that might appeal to the nation as a whole. He found that his prestige depended upon the size of the subject he proposed as his task. The nation laughed at him in the character of Diederich Knickerbocker, the pretended author of Washington Irving's *History of New York*. The local historian's solution to his publication problems was the formation of historical societies,

[19] Samuel Williams, *History of Vermont*, I, xi.

[20] *Ibid.*, p. 373.

[21] James Sullivan, *The History of the District of Maine* (Boston, 1795), p. 292; Thomas C. Amory, *Life of James Sullivan with selections of his writings*, II (Boston, 1859), 39.

[22] Thomas Jefferson, *Notes on Virginia in answer to 23 queries by M. DeMarbois* (Paris, 1784; new ed.; Richmond, 1853), p. 71.

[23] John Daly Burk, *The History of Virginia, from its first Settlement to the Present Day* (3 vols.; Petersburg, 1804–16). For further discussion of this work see chap. vii.

and his answer to derision was to search documents and manuscripts for "pure truth"—facts, a single one of which might "dissipate error and set us free."[24]

Most historians in the late eighteenth century and early nineteenth century discovered that publication was a problem at the best of times. The author of a book usually had to become its publisher as well; he obtained and paid for the paper, chose the type, and decided the format. He paid the printer and binder for their services and arranged for the book's distribution and sale. In order to insure against loss and to meet the immediate expenses of paper and printing, the author usually arranged to have printed a prospectus or summary of the contents of the forthcoming book. He sent his prospectus, combined with a subscription form, to friends and booksellers who were to gather the names and a small sum from those willing to order the book. As an added inducement, authors often published the names of the subscribers in each volume. In theory, an author would not publish his work if he did not gain "sufficient encouragement" from the public to defray the initial cost of printing. But writers sometimes made optimistic estimates of possible sales before their work appeared in print and proceeded with the book in spite of blank spaces on subscription lists.[25]

The inflated costs of paper and printing after the revolution was reason for caution on the part of the impecunious author. But Jeremy Belknap, the Congregational minister of Dover, New Hampshire, disregarded the warning of the half-filled subscription papers his friends returned to him in his anxiety to get his manuscript history of New Hampshire to the printer. Doctor David Ramsay, with a feeling of pride, made no attempt to obtain subscriptions and bore the entire cost of publishing his history of South Carolina in the War for Independence. Belknap, after eight years, had not sold enough copies of the first volume of his history to pay for the printing, and Ramsay conceded the loss of several hundred dollars.

After this experience, Ramsay, seeking a broader market, determined to write a history of the revolution which would cover all of the states. He thus pioneered in the writing of a national history. Ramsay and the national historians who followed him celebrated the deeds of the country, of national

[24] New Yorkers smarted under the satire of Irving, which in part inspired some to delve into and to translate the records of New Netherlands. New-York Historical Society, *Collections*, 2d ser., I (New York, 1841), Preface by George Folsum; also R. W. G. Vail, "The Society Grows Up," *New-York Historical Society Quarterly*, XXXVIII (October, 1954), 384–477; William Bentley, *True Character of the Past Generation* (Worcester, Mass., 1816).

[25] For detailed treatment of the publication problems of American historians during the late eighteenth century see Fred Shelley, "Ebenezer Hazard: America's First Historical Editor," *William and Mary Quarterly*, 3d ser., XII (January, 1955), 44–73; Robert L. Brunhouse, "David Ramsay's Publication Problems, 1784–1808," Bibliographical Society of America, *Papers*, XXXIX (1st Quarter, 1945), 51–67; John S. Bassett, *The Middle Group of American Historians* (New York: Macmillan Co., 1917), has a chapter on historians and their publishers, pp. 303–16; L. S. Mayo, "Jeremy Belknap and Ebenezer Hazard, 1782–84," *New England Quarterly*, II (April, 1929), 183–98.

heroes, and composed a "record of Americanism." Local historians continued to record the deeds of their regions, in effect to prove the importance of their state and its heroes in the nation's history.[26]

Edward Langworthy, a Georgia chronicler, was among the first of the local historians to see state prestige dependent on its national record. He wrote a "Political History of the State of Georgia, from its First Settlement, with Memoirs of the Principal Transactions which Happened therein during the late Revolution." He objected to Alexander Hewatt's treatment of Georgia in his history, and Langworthy's friends pointed out the perfunctory nature of Ramsay's treatment of Georgia in his works.[27] The *Georgia Gazette* hailed the promised history as a "well meant attempt to rescue the patriotic Exertions of our Countrymen [Georgians] from Oblivion, and the misrepresentation of some writers of American History."[28] Langworthy did not publish his book, but the task was taken on by Hugh M'Call, whose *History of Georgia* was completed in 1811.

The original thirteen states each had a share in the greatest moment in our country's history—the creation of a nation—but the western states could claim little or none of the glory associated with this historic event. The western states first made claim to a place in the nation's annals as westward expansion became of increasing importance to the prosperity of the United States. The pioneer founders of the West were in the vanguard of the expanding nation, blazing trails, fighting the Indians, clearing the wilderness, and establishing settlements. They felt they were making a significant contribution to the "manifest destiny" of the nation.

John Filson, a Kentucky land speculator and promoter, set the pattern for the writing of local history in the West. He bought up military land warrants after the revolution and lay claim to a large tract of land in the Kentucky region of Virginia. In 1784, in an effort to attract settlers to the "dark and bloody ground," Filson, a former schoolteacher, wrote a promotion tract similar to those circulated in colonial days. *The Discovery, Settlement and Present State of Kentucke*, one hundred and eighteen pages long, contained a four-page historical sketch, a description of the region, its animals, plants, and its climate, and a long appendix, "The adventures of Col. Daniel Boon, containing a narrative of the wars of Kentucke." In this sketch Daniel Boone appears not as a hatchetman for land speculators but as an advance agent of civilization in the battle against a savage wilderness. Filson's book caught the popular imagina-

[26] Ebenezer Hazard to Jeremy Belknap, March 9, 1785, *Belknap Papers*, Part I, pp. 415–17; Belknap to Hazard, August 27, 1790, *Belknap Papers*, Part II, pp. 231, 361.

[27] General James Jackson offered Langworthy his notes on Ramsay's history of South Carolina. "I have a sincere wish that you would undertake the Work. Georgia has had no Friend to step forward. . . ." Jackson to Langworthy, December 24, 1790, in L. L. MacKall, "Edward Langworthy and the First Attempt to Write a Separate History of Georgia from the Long-lost Langworthy Papers," *Georgia Historical Quarterly*, VII (March, 1923), 8.

[28] Jackson to Langworthy, March 1, 1791, *ibid.*, p. 9.

tion, and several editions were sold in the United States and England.[29] Emigrant guides and western gazetteers took up the theme, and Timothy Flint, a Congregational clergyman, gave it respectability in his compendious *Condensed Geography and History of the Western States, or the Mississippi Valley* (1828). The theme was popularized in James Hall's stories, *Legends of the West* and *Tales of the Border* (1832), and in James K. Paulding's novel *Westward Ho!* (1832), and given status in 1842 upon the establishment in Ohio of a journal called the *American Pioneer*.

Although very early some local historians assumed the role of champions of their area's history, the great surge of local historical writings came after 1815 in reaction to the rapid growth of nationalism and as a reflection of the competition between the states. Regions, states, counties, and towns developed "an individuality, a local independence . . ." which was threatened by an overweening devotion to the nation, a threat made manifest in the national histories, which followed a general pattern, detailing the founding and some events in each colony, continuing with the story of the revolution, and then jumping from one presidential administration to the next, ignoring most localities and local heroes.[30]

Earnest antiquarians sought to preserve the reputation of each locality and to see that it was not overlooked by national historians. In 1829, Thomas F. Gordon, a historian of Pennsylvania, declared that "full justice has never been done to the magnanimity and ability of Pennsylvania statesmen and warriors during the revolutionary contest." An orator before the New Jersey Historical Society told his audience that the "history of New Jersey claims not less honor or justice" than any of the other states in the annals of America, and because of its pure past New Jersey was deserving of a little higher place than most states.[31]

In order to assure their locality of its due recognition in national chronicles, self-appointed guardians of the past wrote countless histories of towns, states, and regions, watched like wary gossips for the errors or slights of others, in controversies quickly proclaimed themselves champions of the truth, and assiduously piled up documents as "materials for the future historian." To secure for his locality its deserved reputation, the historian often wrote its history himself, binding it closely to great national events, enhancing its importance,

---

[29] John Filson, *The Discovery, Settlement and Present State of Kentucke; and an Essay towards the Topography and Natural History of That Important Country* (Wilmington, Del., 1784); Reuben T. Durett, *The Life and Writings of John Filson, the First Historian of Kentucky* (Louisville, Ky., 1884); John Walton, *John Filson of Kentucke* (Lexington, Ky.: University of Kentucky Press, 1956).

[30] Hermann E. Ludewig, *The Literature of American Local History* (New York, 1846), pp. xviii–xix.

[31] Thomas F. Gordon, *The History of Pennsylvania from its discovery by Europeans to the Declaration of Independence in 1776* (Philadelphia, 1829), Preface, p. iv; Charles King, "A Discourse Delivered before the New Jersey Historical Society, May 7, 1845," *Proceedings of the New Jersey Historical Society* (Newark, N.J., 1846), I, 131.

and distinguishing it from all other regions. The American Revolution was the most important national event prior to the Civil War, and local historians celebrated without fail the great and honorable roles of Maine, Massachusetts, Delaware, and Virginia in the War of Independence.[32] Many local chroniclers would have agreed with Edward Langworthy, the prospective historian of Georgia, who, in 1791, declared that he could "no longer silently observe several respectable writers [such as Ramsay] either through misinformation or ignorance, injuring the reputation of his Country—a country though not generally known, yet of no small importance in the American Revolution."

New York City played a part in the revolution equal if not superior to that of Boston, as was made clear in William Dunlap's history of New York and Isaac Q. Leake's biography of General John Lamb, the leader of the New York Liberty Boys. But this contention was contradicted by Caleb H. Snow's history of Boston; and a reader would have been thoroughly confused if he also exposed himself to the rival claims of Philadelphia made by John F. Watson. Cities, towns, and states, no matter how large or small, laid a part of their claims to national glory upon their record in the revolution. Granite monuments sprang up in the twenties and thirties like so many asparagus stalks. If Boston could erect a monument to the Battle of Bunker Hill, New York established a monument to the Battle of Harlem Heights and South Carolina to the Battle of King's Mountain.[33]

Massachusetts and other New England states set a standard for American chroniclers. Massachusetts historians took great pains to point out that, of all the colonies, English, Spanish, and French, Plymouth and Massachusetts Bay alone were settled for "conscience' sake," and their good fortune was due to devotion to religion and religious liberty. Historians of other New England

---

[32] John F. Watson, "Annals of Philadelphia," MS Vol. I, June, 1830, in Pennsylvania Historical Society Library. The desire to immortalize one's community was illustrated by Watson when he wrote: "I have chiefly aimed to furnish *the material*, by which better, or more ambitious writers, could elaborate more formal History,—and from which as a Repository, our future Poets, Painters, and Imaginative Authors could deduce their themes for their own and their country's glory. Scanty, therefore, as these crude materials may prove,—*Fiction*, may some day lend its charms to amplify and consecrate *facts*—and 'Tales of Ancient Philadelphia' may be touched by genius and made immortal!"

[33] *Georgia Gazette* (Savannah), May 12, 1791, in L. L. MacKall, *op. cit.*, pp. 9–10; William Dunlap, *History of the New Netherlands, Province of New York, and State of New York, to 1789* (2 vols.; New York, 1839–40); Caleb Hopkins Snow, *History of Boston, the Metropolis of Massachusetts from its origin to the present period, with some account of the environs* (Boston, 1828); also see Alden Bradford, *History of Massachusetts from 1764 to 1789* (3 vols.; Boston, 1822–25); Isaac Q. Leake, *Memoir of the Life and Times of General John Lamb* (Albany, 1850); John F. Watson, *Annals of Philadelphia* (Philadelphia, 1830), p. 20. The tendency to gather all past glories to one's own state was illustrated by Charles F. Hoffman, a New Yorker, when he said that the eagle "that bears Excelsior in his beak was fledged in his own soil. He never began his soarings from Plymouth Rock. He dressed his plumage in our own lakes, and his pinions were nerved in the air of our own mountains." Charles F. Hoffman, *Address delivered before the New-York Historical Society . . . with an account of the subsequent proceedings*, in Julian P. Boyd, "State and Local Historical Societies in the United States," *American Historical Review*, XL (October, 1934), 18–19.

states maintained that their forebears were inspired by religious motives. John Callender, in a history of Rhode Island, made a special effort to show that the same principles that moved the Puritans to emigrate from England inspired the founders of Rhode Island. A historian of New Jersey insisted that the people of New Jersey were somewhat more devoted to religion than the pious New Englanders; he declared that New Jersey's "escutcheon is stained with no crime against the *aborigines*, with no persecution for conscience's sake of those who for conscience's sake had sought her shores."[34]

The New England states lay claim to superiority on the basis of their systems of education and their literary production. They pointed to the early founding of Harvard College and of Yale College, to early laws making compulsory the establishment of common schools in communities of a certain size. The realization of the importance of education was a sign of signal virtue.

During the twenties and thirties, with growing support of the public school movement, evidence of the early recognition of the importance of education was cherished as a mark of superiority, and local historians avidly copied every mention of the founding of schools in their area. Massachusetts might boast of her common school law of 1649, but a Pennsylvania historian declared that "in 1683, before our ancestors had covered themselves from the weather, a school was opened in the city of Philadelphia."[35]

Pennsylvania historians challenged, as well, New England's prominence in literature and in the early elimination of slavery. One chronicler described the movement to abolish slavery in Pennsylvania, which proved that "our forefathers were active and ardent laborers in the righteous cause of human freedom and happiness," and hoped that his essay would add esteem to Pennsylvania's "annals, character and resources, which has long been due to a state whose story in many important features is unique. . . ." Thomas L. Wharton, one of Philadelphia's richest merchants, compiled some "Notes on the Provincial Literature of Pennsylvania" for the *Memoirs* of the Historical Society. To disprove that the first settlers "decried and undervalued" human learning, Wharton wrote, "No one of the states of this Union can exhibit so early, so continued, and so successful a cultivation of letters as Pennsylvania."[36]

---

[34] For Callender see chap. i. Charles King, *op. cit.*, p. 131. Another example of New England's claims is found in a review of the Massachusetts Historical Society, *Collections*. "As there is little to blame and much to praise in these early annals, every generation will look with increased veneration to the pure virtues and inflexible constancy of our heroick forefathers, and the influence of their example may stimulate future generations to avoid degeneracy." *North American Review*, II (December, 1816), 110. Also *North American Review*, VIII (December, 1818), 72. See John Davis, "A Discourse," Massachusetts Historical Society, *Collections*, 2d ser., I (Boston, 1838), v.

[35] Thomas F. Gordon, *History of Pennsylvania*, p. 589; Richard E. Thursfield, *Henry Barnard's American Journal of Education* (Baltimore: Johns Hopkins Press, 1945), pp. 122–28.

[36] Edward Bettle, "Notices of Negro Slavery as Connected with Pennsylvania," Pennsylvania Historical Society, *Memoirs*, I (Philadelphia, 1826), 35–57; Thomas L. Wharton, "Notes on the Provincial Literature of Pennsylvania," *ibid.*, pp. 107–62.

New York historians disputed New England's claim as the cradle of the Republic and republicanism. They resented the slurs on their Dutch ancestry, such as a declaration in the *North American Review* that New York's "early history is much less interesting than that of Massachusetts or Virginia. The tameness and ignorance of its original Dutch settlers were long predominant, and being a conquered colony, those jealous feelings of liberty and early precaution for self government, which mark every step of the New England colonist were little felt or feebly attempted." On the contrary, asserted a New York historian, the heritage of the Dutch was a proud one; the Dutch had sown the seeds of republicanism in the state of New York. The historian said he was much ashamed that a talented author, Washington Irving, had felt called upon to ridicule his native state.

The first volume of the New-York Historical Society's Collections, in honor of the bicentennial of Henry Hudson's discovery of New Netherland, was devoted to documents relating to the early Dutch settlement. In 1820, the state legislature financed the translation of Dutch records, and later the society published another volume of its Collections devoted to Dutch material. George Folsom, corresponding secretary of the historical society, justified this attention to the Dutch settlers when he claimed them as "the fathers of the republic" and the "forerunners of a noble commonwealth . . . now rivaling in population and extent some of the Monarchies of the old world."[37]

Local historians set great store by the standards first established by the New England chroniclers, but they also defended the records they were collecting. One of the duties of the antiquary was to "correct vulgar errors about the past generation." The Reverend William Bentley, a Unitarian minister at Salem, Massachusetts, in an address before the American Antiquarian Society in 1816, attempted to demonstrate what might be done to restore history to its "truth and simplicity." To prove that the early Puritans were not fanatics and that austerity was not a necessary part of their religion, he cited the number of "luxury items" listed in the wills of the founding fathers. Bentley was not reluctant to woo the possessors of wealth in Massachusetts in an essay on the usefulness of the antiquary. The real movers of society had long gone without recognition in history; yet "it goes without saying," Bentley said, "how much we are indebted to the Vigilance of commerce for our present political situation. . . . It is enough if the antiquary can show us our former obligations; we trust our own prudence will accept the same guardianship, and the more you know of the true cause of our greatness, the more sure and exalted it will appear."[38]

Bentley pointed out the commission accepted by almost every town, state, and regional historian; that is, "restoring history to its truth." What history?

[37] "William Smith's History of New York," *North American Review*, II (January, 1816), 151; Dorothie Bobbé, *DeWitt Clinton* (New York: Minton, Balch & Co., 1933), p. 138; New-York Historical Society, *Collections*, 2d ser., I (New York, 1841), Preface.

[38] Bentley, *True Character*, pp. 21–26.

Certainly not the history of Plymouth as told by William Bradford or of New England as told by William Hubbard. No, Bentley was not talking of the histories written about specific areas, but of the general works which touched upon or neglected specific localities or popular ideas about the history and character of the people of particular regions. Bentley himself illustrated what he meant when he took issue with John Eliot, author of a collection of American biographies, an attempt at national history through biography. Bentley objected to Eliot's account of Roger Williams' activities while a minister in Salem and of his references to the life of William Hubbard the historian. He was writing, Bentley explained, because he feared that "the present false account [would be] left for posterity," and Eliot had so "mangled their history" that Williams and Hubbard, illustrious sons of Salem, could scarcely be recognized.[39]

Much had been accomplished since the nineties, when only a small group of men took sufficient interest in the preservation of historical materials to face the problems of publishing, including the assumption of the debts of publication. They gave as excuse for the failure of their books the "lack of taste in the age" and sought solutions to this problem. But by 1815 they had found an acceptable and, in some cases, even a popular function in defending and advocating the historical priority of their locality in the Union. They identified their regions with great national moments and supported their towns, counties, and states in the struggle for wealth, power, and prestige. As New York merchants fought to wrest trade from Boston, New York historians labored to claim some of the glory of the revolution. State histories insisted upon superiority over, or equality to, other states, and woe to the national history which failed to take cognizance of local pride.

[39] William Bentley, "Remarks on the Remarks on a History of Salem," Massachusetts Historical Society, *Collections*, VIII (Boston, 1802), 1–4; William Bentley, *Diary of William Bentley* (Salem, Mass.: The Essex Institute, 1905–14), III, 530.

6 THE RISE OF HISTORICAL SOCIETIES, 1790–1815

The historical society, the most significant development in the field of local historiography between 1790 and 1815, originated as a weapon in the battle to dominate the writing of national history. During the early years of the nation, most historians believed that the history of the United States would be made up of the histories of each state. Undoubtedly they founded their assumption upon organizational precedent set by the imperialist histories of Oldmixon and Douglass; Ramsay and Morse largely followed this form in their histories of the Revolutionary War. The states were the most significant governmental units under the Articles of Confederation, and their role, as far as contemporaries could see, had not been greatly diminished under the Constitution. The most powerful states set out to dominate the nation's historical writing, just as they sought to control its politics and economy.

Jeremy Belknap, a pioneer in the historical society movement, had become a nationalist during the revolution. After the fiasco of the first volume of his history, he moved to Boston and turned his efforts to the promotion of cultural nationalism. He favored the development of the "American language" and supported the efforts of the American Philosophical Society to stimulate the creation of a system of national education and to encourage the preservation and diffusion of the nation's heritage. This program led to the founding of an organization whose object was "to rescue the true history of this country from the ravages of time and the effects of ignorance and neglect."[1]

Belknap continued to work on his history after the move to Boston in 1788, for his friend Ebenezer Hazard, Postmaster General of the Confederation, persuaded him to believe that the appearance of the second volume might stimulate the sales of the first. During his years in Boston, Belknap befriended kindred spirits in the town. The historian of New Hampshire renewed his old friendship with the Reverend Dr. John Eliot, who had obtained William Hubbard's manuscript history of New England and was trying to get it published. He made the acquaintance of Thomas Wallcott, a book dealer, collector, "genuine antiquarian and a very friendly man." He found members of the bench very much interested in collecting or recording history. Judge Richard Minot had just published a history of Shays' Rebellion which forwarded the cause of the Constitution and was at work on a continuation of Hutchinson's *History of Massachusetts* to establish the Bay State's primacy in the nation. Judge James Winthrop had in his possession the diary of an ancestor, Governor John Winthrop, which he hoped to publish, and Judge James Sullivan was writing a history of the District of Maine. These made up the informal group of historians in Boston, the congenial milieu into which Belknap, the New Hampshire chronicler, moved.[2]

In August, 1789, a Mr. Pintard of New York called upon Belknap. Pintard was a wealthy dry goods merchant with an interest in history. After expressing his admiration for Belknap's work, the visitor suggested that they form "a society of antiquaries." Belknap was interested, but he did not act upon the suggestion, nor did Pintard. When several other men suggested similar societies, Jeremy Belknap proposed such an organization to the little group of historians in Boston. He drew a plan for a small society of historians whose objec-

---

[1] "Constitution of the Massachusetts Historical Society," Massachusetts Historical Society, *Collections*, I (Boston, 1792), 5.

[2] For biographical material on Jeremy Belknap see Elizabeth Belknap Marcou, *Life of Jeremy Belknap* (Boston, 1845); Lawrence Shaw Mayo, "Jeremy Belknap and Ebenezer Hazard, 1782–84," *New England Quarterly*, II (April, 1929), 183–98; Samuel A. Eliot, "Jeremy Belknap," *Proceedings of the Massachusetts Historical Society*, LXVI (Boston, 1942), 102–3; Mayo, "Jeremy Belknap," *DAB*, II, 147.

tive would be to collect and preserve everything that "conduces to mark the genius, delineate the manners, and trace the progress of society in the United States."[3]

The idea of a historical society was not new; when devising his plan, Belknap drew heavily upon the example set by the organization of the London Society of Antiquaries. His copy was faithful, even to the nine members necessary to make a quorum to elect new members. The Massachusetts men changed the proposed name from "the Society of Antiquaries" to "the Historical Society." The London Society, formed in 1572 and reformed many times thereafter, had grown out of the combination of a desire to support British imperialism and the old Renaissance reverence for the cultures of ancient Greece and Rome. The London Society prepared to write a history of Great Britain and her colonies and also hoped to restore "ancient methods" of historical research which might "be used afresh."

A closer spiritual kin to the Massachusetts organization was the Society of Antiquaries of Scotland, founded in 1780. This society counted among its members and officers many of the intellectual leaders of the University of Edinburgh who formed the Scottish school of moral philosophy. Although its intention was not to endanger the British Union, the Society of Antiquaries was dedicated to the resurrection of Scottish history and had no interest in preserving and recording the history of Great Britain.[4] In the course of his work, Belknap corresponded with members of the Scots' society, but the influence of other groups was limited to the organizational structure of the Massachusetts historical society.

In 1794, the Commonwealth recognized the society's services by issuing a charter, and Boston town promoters donated to its use rooms in a new civic building, the Tontine Crescent. The society in turn acknowledged its local obligations by calling itself the Massachusetts Historical Society.

As corresponding secretary of the society, Belknap pursued an aggressive policy. He did not believe in waiting around at home for historical material to fall into his lap, but in "prowling about like a wolf for the prey."[5] He traveled through the New England states collecting manuscripts and returned triumphantly, bearing the papers and letters of Jonathan Trumbull who for many years had been colonial governor of Connecticut. Belknap sent out a questionnaire to the ministers of towns throughout New England and to all corresponding members in the country, asking for information on each town, instances of unusual longevity, beneficial effects of the climate, and accounts of the deeds of unusual people. The result was that most of the town histories

[3] Hazard to Belknap, September 5, 1789, Belknap to Hazard, August 27, 1790, *Belknap Papers*, Part II, pp. 165, 231.

[4] William Smellie, "An Historical Account of the Society of the Antiquaries of Scotland," *Archaeologia Scotica; or Transactions of the Society of Antiquaries of Scotland*, I (Edinburgh, 1792), iii.

[5] Belknap to Hazard, August 21, 1795, *Belknap Papers*, Part I, pp. 356–57.

written in New England between 1792 and 1815 were published in the Collections of the Massachusetts Historical Society.[6]

Belknap early realized the value of transcripts of the debates of Congress and the papers of the federal government for a complete account of the history of the nation. He instigated a petition to Congress for "copies of all acts, journals, treaties, and other public papers printed by their order."[7] The petition failed, but Belknap continued to collect documents concerning American history and sponsored a periodical, *The American Apollo*, as the official organ of the society. Its purpose was the diffusion and preservation of its collections by "multiplying the copies." Belknap dreamed of a nationwide network of branch societies founded by corresponding members of the Massachusetts parent, which would become a clearing house for "communications" from all over the country. The Bay State example was followed in many states, but Jeremy Belknap's proposal was not realized; each new organization narrowed the bounds and challenged the dominance of the older society.

New York State would not be outdone by its northern rival, not if John Pintard had a say in it. Pintard was a civic leader with ambitions for New York. During the revolution he served for a short time as a private in Washington's army and after the war he helped to found the Tammany Society, a veterans' organization for the common soldier and a democratic antidote to the purportedly aristocratic Order of the Cincinnati. At the time he visited Belknap and suggested the foundation of a historical society, Pintard was chief sachem of the Tammany Society. Upon returning to New York he tried to effect his plan by "engrafting" upon the Tammany Society a historical museum which later would become a full-fledged "National Society of Antiquaries." The museum was a success but was soon sold by the Tammany Society, and Pintard ceased to take an active interest in it upon losing his money in some land speculation schemes. By 1804 Pintard had recovered sufficiently to resume his intention of forming a historical society. He found others to help him. Men who were promoting the growth of the state recognized the value of documenting its history. Among them was DeWitt Clinton.[8]

As early as 1797, Clinton had accepted the role of champion of New York's historical collections suggested to him by Samuel Miller. Miller was a scholarly

[6] "Introductory Address from the Historical Society to the Public," Massachusetts Historical Society, *Collections*, I (Boston, 1792), 2–4; William Jenks, "An Account of the Massachusetts Historical Society," Massachusetts Historical Society, *Collections*, 3d ser., VII (Boston, 1838), 5–25.

[7] Belknap to Hazard, December 20, 1793, *Belknap Papers*, Part II, p. 346.

[8] John Pintard to Belknap, October 11, 1790, *Belknap Papers*, Part III, pp. 469–70; Pintard to Belknap, April 6, 1791, *Proceedings of the Massachusetts Historical Society*, I (Boston, 1879), xv–xvi; "Historical Sketch of the Society," New-York Historical Society, *Collections*, 2d ser., I (New York, n.d.), 458–70. For information on John Pintard see Robert Greenhalgh Albion, "John Pintard," *DAB*, XIV, 629–30; Edwin P. Kilroe, *Saint Tammany and the Origin of the Society of Tammany or Columbian Order in the City of New York* (New York: M. B. Brown Printing & Binding Co., 1913); Morris R. Werner, *Tammany Hall* (New York: Garden City Publishing Co., 1932).

Presbyterian minister who later occupied the chair of theology at Princeton. He achieved fame with a book he did not plan to write and failed to write the local history he had intended.

As the century ended, ministers all over the country were writing and delivering "century sermons." Samuel Miller was no exception, but his approach was more ambitious than that of other ministers. In 1803, he expanded and published his century sermons, which formed a two-volume survey of the cultural achievements of Western man over a period of one hundred years and was called *A Brief Retrospect of the Eighteenth Century*. This work was not only an admirable summary of European achievements but the first attempt to summarize and evaluate the cultural progress of the United States. When Miller set to work on his century sermons, he gave up his effort to write a state history and became a national historian.

Three years before his preoccupation with the century sermons, Samuel Miller had begun to write a history of New York state. Jedidiah Morse, the "father of American geography," had complained to him of the difficulties involved in obtaining information on the history of New York. Miller told Morse of his decision to write a history but cautioned the geographer not to make his "design extensively public." Miller himself did much to publicize the project. He petitioned the legislature to allow him to search public records without paying the usual fees. DeWitt Clinton, then a member of the New York Assembly, introduced Miller's petition and obtained the permission requested. Upon informing Miller of the legislative decision, Clinton enthusiastically offered the minister assistance in "obtaining information in the important work you have in hand." Miller petitioned the legislature for various favors and kept the members informed of his progress.[9]

In 1804, when Pintard told members of the legislature his plan to found a historical society, they backed it enthusiastically. In drawing up the constitution of the New-York Historical Society, the founders copied that of the Massachusetts society. They acknowledged the older group's priority in the field and announced their desire to aid in gathering materials pertaining to American history.[10] The New York society obtained considerably more state aid than did the group in Massachusetts. As a result of the efforts of Clinton, the New York legislature awarded the society twelve thousand dollars in 1814 as its share in an omnibus appropriation for the state's cultural institutions. In 1828,

[9] Samuel Miller to Jedidiah Morse, November 27, 1797, in Samuel Miller, *Life of Samuel Miller*, p. 112.

[10] In 1814 the New-York Historical Society published the second volume of its *Collections*, timed to aid its effort to obtain state funds. The society still maintained that its purpose was national. "With the growing taste for literature and science, so rapidly advancing in the United States, it is reasonably expected that laudable curiosity will be directed towards the study of our national history and that liberal encouragement will be extended to invigorate the efforts of the Society in rescuing from oblivion documents which must constitute the materials for the use of the future historian." New-York Historical Society, *Collections*, II (New York, 1814), Preface.

the state supplied the money to send an agent to inspect the archives of Holland and England and to make transcripts of documents relating to New York.

New York's efforts to improve its cultural contributions excited the jealousy of some citizens of Massachusetts. In 1815, Josiah Quincy introduced a bill authorizing the Massachusetts legislature to underwrite the expense of a building to be used by the Bay State's learned societies. The heavy cost of the war made legislators wary of adding to that burden; and although none openly opposed the bill, most voted against it. The citizens of Massachusetts would have to take satisfaction in being "distinguished beyond the citizens of either New York or Pennsylvania, indeed of any other state, for the number and amount of their contributions to literary institutions."[11]

Pennsylvania, too, awakened by the activity of the newly-founded historical society in New York, established a historical society in Philadelphia as a branch of a national organization, the American Philosophical Society. The founders, Peter S. Du Ponceau, William Rawle, and Caspar Wistar, had decided that since they were all members of the philosophical society they would save the expense and trouble of collecting a library by organizing as a committee of the society. On March 17, 1815, the members of the American Philosophical Society voted "that a Seventh Committee be added to the six already established . . . to be designated 'the Committee of History, Moral Science, and General Literature.' " The new group quickly pared its name to the "Historical Committee" and made plans to collect a publishing fund.

The Historical Committee was a maverick among the branches of the society and enjoyed virtual autonomy, taking as its province all of the states south of Pennsylvania, since no societies then existed to preserve their history. The committee placed most of its efforts on compiling the history of Pennsylvania and neglected its broader aims; and even so the annals of the Quaker state were subordinated to the study of linguistics, the chief interest of Du Ponceau, who acted as the committee's corresponding secretary.[12]

In 1824, several members of the Historical Committee and a few wealthy Philadelphians, including Roberts Vaux, the philanthropist, came to the conclusion that the committee as presently organized was serving neither the nation nor the interests of Pennsylvania history. To restore these omissions, they founded the Pennsylvania State Historical Society and devoted themselves to "repairing the injuries which the early history of Pennsylvania . . . sustained by reason of the inattention" of their predecessors. The new society was determined to prove that "an honest, virtuous, and pious people, relinquishing their early possessions and enjoyments, laid in a wild and uncultivated coun-

[11] *North American Review*, II (March, 1816), 315–17.

[12] "Old Minutes of the Society from 1743 to 1838," *Proceedings of the American Philosophical Society*, XXII (July, 1885), Part III, 453, 456; "Minutes of the Historical and Literary Committee of the American Philosophical Society," entry for May 8, 1815, unpublished MSS in American Philosophical Society Library; Peter S. Du Ponceau to Thomas Jefferson, November 14, 1815, Historical Committee Letter Book, I, American Philosophical Society Library.

try, the foundations of a state, now eminently great, successful, and happy."[13] Like its predecessors, the society began as an attempt to control national historiography through a state organization. When other states challenged their pretensions, and when the resurgence of nationalism after 1815 threatened to subordinate all states to the nation, these societies acknowledged a measure of defeat and set about the task of championing their state's primacy in the nation.

The American Antiquarian Society was the only historical organization founded during the period which had some chance of becoming of national importance. In 1812, Isaiah Thomas, a successful printer, bookseller, and the author of a history of printing, founded the society at Worcester, Massachusetts. Thomas not only conceived the plan, wrote the bill of incorporation, and personally guided it through the state legislature, but donated his own large library to the society.[14] Although the new organization was professedly a national one, Thomas obtained the charter from the legislature of Massachusetts because he could not be sure that Congress had the power to certify acts of incorporation. The purpose of the society, according to its founder, was to "advance the arts and sciences," primarily by collecting and preserving historical materials to aid in "marking their progress," and to "assist the researches of the future historians of our country." Such an institution was needed, Thomas wrote, because "the decline as well as the rise of nations is in the course of nature . . . and in some distant period, a decline may be the state of our country," and a society of this type could preserve what otherwise might be destroyed. Even the location of its headquarters argued in favor of the American Antiquarian Society, for Worcester was well inland and thus safer from British attack than would be the port cities.[15]

In spite of its profession of being a national organization, the first volumes of its printed collections of articles and documents, the *Archaeologia Americana*, carried far more material on Massachusetts and New England than on any other part of the country. The officers of the Massachusetts Historical Society were jealous of the newcomer because it bid fair to succeed where the older society had failed but could do no more than predict that after Thomas had achieved the "honor" that he sought the antiquarians would merge with the older institution.

The American Antiquarian Society lived up to its objectives.[16] It was not restricted by a local tag, and members were elected from every part of the

---

[13] Roberts Vaux to Thomas F. Watson, September 28, 1824, in Watson MSS in Pennsylvania Historical Society Library; Pennsylvania Historical Society, *Memoirs*, I (Philadelphia, 1826), in Constitution of the society.

[14] *Archaeologia Americana*, American Antiquarian Society, *Collections*, I (Worcester, Mass., 1814), 1–9.

[15] Isaiah Thomas, *Diary of Isaiah Thomas*, ed. Benjamin Thomas Hill (Worcester, Mass.: American Antiquarian Society, 1909), I, 127, 162, 163, 164; Annie Russell Marble, *From 'Prentice to Patron* (New York: Appleton-Century-Crofts, Inc., 1935), p. 176.

[16] William Bentley, *Diary*, entries for July 26, 1814, August 10, 1815, IV, 270, 346.

country, although few outside the state attended the early meetings. "The object of the society," said its founder, "is not to reprint source works, but to collect and preserve Books of this description . . . especially those written in the country."[17] Although the American Antiquarian Society succeeded where other societies had failed, it did not inspire the writing of national histories based upon its concepts. The library of the society stands as a monument to one concept of how the nation's history should be written, state by state. To-day, the library contains the best collection of state and local histories in the country.

The historical societies of Massachusetts, New York, and Pennsylvania failed in their original objective but inspired the founding of similar societies in other states no less anxious for the future of their reputations; they had no desire to let others write—or, as was more likely, ignore—their histories. In the years after 1815, societies for the promotion of state and local history rose in rapid succession and flourished across the nation as if from scattered seeds.

[17] Isaiah Thomas to William Plumer, June 8, 1815, Plumer Papers in Library of Congress.

7 BIOGRAPHY: THE CREATION OF NATIONAL HEROES
1776–1849

In 1800 there were no comprehensive histories of the United States and no clear path for the historians of the nation to follow. Nevertheless, the nation's annals were not neglected. Biography served the nation, created national heroes, erected national symbols, inspired filial piety and patriotism, and stimulated the collection of the private papers of state and national leaders. Biography was the literary food that suited "the taste of the age" and was very nearly the exclusive medium for records of America's past. "Today's taste for biographical sketches and anecdotes," asserted one critic, "is indiscriminate."[1]

American authors took a filio-pietistic view of American subjects. The un-critical worship and near-sanctification of historic figures is to be found in the literature of most countries, but in the United States it played a far larger part in creating the national heritage and in the growth of historical studies than in the older nations of Europe. American biographers used the techniques of eulogy and of fictionalized anecdote illustrating character, and the result was legend. The reason they accepted these methods so exclusively is a significant clue to a major theme in American historiography. The United States was a new nation; but more than that, it was a new kind of nation, a model for the world and the hope for a degenerate Europe. No American of the period seemed

[1] "Patrick Henry," *North American Review*, VIII (March, 1818), 295.

to have had any doubt that the founders of the new republic, their names and deeds, would find an important place in the annals of mankind. And just as the political creation of these patriots pointed the way toward social salvation, so their lives were expected to serve as permanent examples of the personal virtues that achieved the new order. Although intelligent men rejoiced in the fact that the origins of the United States were not lost in antiquity, the existence of living memories and corroborative documents (such things did not encumber the biographers of Romulus and Remus) might have proved embarrassing to the creators of a national hagiology had it not been for the sense of piety that prevailed, inspired by a conviction of the great mission of America.

Secular biography was a relatively new art in America. Biography as a separate branch of literature was a seventeenth-century phenomenon. Plutarch in his *Lives* made no clear distinction between biography and history, and perhaps John Dryden was one of the first to state the demarcation between "History, properly so called, and Biographia, or the Lives of Particular Men." Annals, or history, Dryden declared, dealt with men in society in broad terms and was superior "in dignity" to biography in which the fortunes of a single person were all-important. In pleasure and instruction, however, biography equaled and sometimes excelled history because, Dryden reasoned, the "examples of virtue are of more vigour, when they are thus contracted into individuals," and the reader could more easily interest himself in "the fortunes of a single man than those of many, and thus a lesson in morality could be brought home with a greater degree of emphasis."[2]

In 1690 and after, the Puritan clergy of New England seized upon the medium of biography to sanctify their confreres and to present moral lessons to straying congregations. Increase and Cotton Mather made use of biography to record divine manifestations in the lives of virtuous clergymen, past and present. Cotton Mather devoted a major share of his *Magnalia Christi Americana* to an account of the lives of New England clergymen. Biographies of divines and the biographies of criminals offered a vivid contrast of virtue and vice, and these two groups were almost the sole subjects of biography in America until 1760, when the "Lives of Particular Men" taught more advanced lessons.[3]

[2] John Dryden, in John Marx Longaker, *English Biography in the Eighteenth Century* (Philadelphia: University of Pennsylvania Press, 1931), pp. 22, 23. There are earlier indications of cognizance of a difference between history and biography, but Dryden's is the first extended statement. A fuller account is to be found in D. A. Stauffer, *English Biography Before 1700* (Cambridge, Mass.: Harvard University Press, 1930).

[3] See such typical titles as Samuel Philips, *An Elegy upon the Deaths of those Excellent and Learned Divines, the Reverend Nicholas Noyes, A.M., and the Reverend George Curwin, A.M., the Pastors of the First Church of Christ in Salem* (Boston, 1717), 8 pp.; Cotton Mather, *Warnings from the Dead, or Solemn Admonitions unto all People . . . in two discourses, occasioned by a sentence of death executed on some unhappy malefactors. Together with the last confessions, made by a young woman, who dyed on June 8, 1693, one of these malefactors* (Boston in New England, 1693), 67 pp.; *The Last Speech, Confession, Birth, Parentage and Education of John Grimes, John Fagan and John Johnson, alias Johnson Cochran, who were executed at Gallows-Hill, in the City of Burlington, on Wednesday, the 28th of August, 1765, for Burglary and Felony committed in the County of Burlington* (Woodbridge, 1765), broadside; Daniel Roberts, *Some Memoirs of the Life of John Roberts* (Philadelphia, 1766), 67 pp.

With the impact of the French and Indian War, the increasing friction between Great Britain and her American colonies, and the decreasing influence of the clergy, the secular figures of military men and statesmen gained in interest. Biographical sketches of patriots and traitors, pointing out the friends and enemies of the colonies, began to appear in the almanacs published by Nathaniel Ames.[4]

In 1779, at the height of the revolution, Jeremy Belknap, busy preaching to Continental troops and writing the history of New Hampshire, suggested that his friend Ebenezer Hazard collect material for a dictionary of American biography to supplement his collection of documents pertaining to American history.[5] Hazard demurred because of the magnitude of his original project, but Belknap insisted that Hazard need simply keep an "alphabetical index" of biographical material in the documents already collected. Something of value would come of the idea, Belknap said, for there were both worthy and notorious characters in American history who "as a group would give instruction and amusement.[6]" Hazard remained adamant, and it was Belknap himself who collected biographical materials in a desultory fashion. In 1789, William Spotswood, editor of the *Columbian*, asked him for "a few guineas' worth" of material to fill some pages in the periodical. Belknap sent, among other things, a series of biographical sketches entitled "The American Plutarch." Spotswood was "elated" with the contribution; it would "interest readers on all parts of the continent." Thus encouraged, the ambitious clergyman continued to collect materials and to compile biographical sketches. In 1794, Belknap published the first volume of his *American Biography*.[7] Had Belknap lived to complete his plan, it would have been the first dictionary of American biography, somewhat on the scale of George Chalmer's British series, but he died in 1798 while the second volume was on the press. The subjects were presented in chronological order so that the author could plan, work on, and publish each volume individually. For each volume the minister was to receive three hundred dollars within a year of publication.[8]

Belknap included "Adventurers, Statesmen, Philosophers, Divines, and

---

[4] Chester N. Greenough, "New England Almanacs, 1766–1775, and the American Revolution," *Proceedings of the American Antiquarian Society*, XLV (Worcester, Mass., 1935), 288–316; "The Life and Adventures of a female Soldier, Hannah Snell," *Thomas's New England Almanac or the Massachusetts Callendar* (Worcester, Mass., 1775), unpaginated.

[5] Jeremy Belknap to Ebenezer Hazard, February 2, 1779, *Belknap Papers*, Part I, pp. 2–3.

[6] Hazard to Belknap, April 19, 1779, Belknap to Hazard, August 16, 1779, Hazard to Belknap, August 31, 1779, *Belknap Papers*, Part I, pp. 5, 7, 10–11, 20.

[7] Belknap to Hazard, January 2, 1788, Belknap Papers, Part III, p. 364; William Spotswood to Belknap, February 25, 1788, *Belknap Papers*, Part III, p. 391; Belknap, "The American Plutarch, or a Biographical Account of the Heroic and Virtuous Men who have, at any time been influential to the Foundation and Prosperity of the United States," *Columbian*, III (January, 1788), 238.

[8] Belknap to Hazard, November 20, 1793, *Belknap Papers*, Part II, p. 344.

other remarkable characters" in his roster of subjects considered worthy of biography. His sketches rarely transcended the author's avowed purpose, "a recital of the events" connecting the subject's life and actions. Belknap did little moralizing, but he took every opportunity to defend the revolution, though the first two volumes dealt only with the founders of the colonies. When writing about the Puritan migration, Belknap indignantly remarked upon the necessity impelling the emigrants to take an oath of allegiance and supremacy before leaving Great Britain. The Puritans, he wrote, had no thought of seeking independence, "nor did their successors till driven to it by Britain herself."⁹

After Belknap's death, many men tried to continue his dictionary of American biography but few attempted to imitate his factual style. John Eliot, a Congregational minister in Boston and good friend of Belknap, published in 1801 a two-volume dictionary of American biography. When Belknap was trying to interest Hazard, and others, in American biography, he suggested that Eliot might be worthy of the task if he could "attain the virtue of Celibacy."¹⁰ Whether Eliot succeeded in attaining that virtue is unknown, but he was far too concerned with an increasing number of competitors in the field to do a thorough job. Eliot rushed two volumes into print when he heard that William Allen, later president of Dartmouth College, was about to publish a collection of biographical sketches. Eliot's carelessness made him an easy mark for local historians, who jealously protested the treatment given local heroes. The Reverend William Bentley of Salem was one of Eliot's most outspoken critics. Allen's volumes came out several years later and were considered the standard reference until the publication of Jared Sparks's *Library of American Biography* series.¹¹

Belknap, Eliot, and Allen were only three among those whose early efforts were to raise the art of biography above the local level and to increase its appeal to "all parts of the Continent" by a judicious selection of figures from all sections of the country. Biographical dictionaries met with a certain success. Allen's work went through two editions, and similar collections continued to appear; but readers were not completely satisfied. Joseph Priestley, the English discoverer of "dephlogisticated air" (oxygen), who emigrated to the United States in 1794 to escape the tyranny of the younger Pitt's regime, observed that

⁹ Belknap, *American Biography: or An Historical Account of those Persons who have been distinguished in America, as Adventurers, Statesmen, Philosophers, Divines, Warriors, Authors, and Other Remarkable Characters, comprehending a recital of the events connected with their lives and actions* (Boston, 1794–98), I, 382, II, 406–7.

¹⁰ Belknap to Hazard, December 28, 1779, *Belknap Papers*, Part I, p. 26.

¹¹ John Eliot, *A Biographical Dictionary, containing a Brief Account of the First Settlers and other eminent characters among them magistrates, ministers, literary and worthy men in New England* (Boston, 1809); William Bentley, "On John Eliot's Biographical Dictionary," Massachusetts Historical Society, *Collections*, 2d ser., II (Boston, 1810), 9–10; William Allen, *An American Biographical and Historical Dictionary, containing an account of the Lives, Characters, and Writings of the most eminent Persons in North America, from its first discovery to the present time, and a summary of the history of the several colonies, and of the United States* (Cambridge, Mass., 1809).

the sketches in such compilations were far too short. "Those characters only affect the imagination, and interest the passions which we form to ourselves from the representation of a detail of actions and a course of conduct of some extent."[12]

The new republic posed something of a problem to the prospective biographer —how to select subjects whose lives, detailed at length, would maintain the interest of busy readers. In Europe no such problem existed, since the ever-popular subjects for biography were kings, noblemen, and soldiers whose careers were inextricably a part of the great events of history. In the United States, a land of citizen soldiers, of elected officials, bereft of kings and an aristocracy, the biographer found long periods when his subject played little or no part in the affairs of the nation. As yet no biographer believed that a man's private life was a topic either of interest or of sufficient importance to merit chronicling. In 1813, Judge St. George Tucker, a highly literate Virginian, wrote a letter which epitomized these problems to his friend William Wirt, who was planning a series of lives of the most eminent Virginians: "American biography, at least since the conclusion of the peace of 1783, is a subject which promises as little entertainment as any other in the literary world. Our scene of action is so perfectly domestic as to afford neither novelty nor variety."[13]

The biographer who aspired to a national market faced an additional problem. American statesmen, no matter how prominent in national affairs, were still considered primarily as citizens of the states from which they came, and their lives, until they took places on the national stage, had little to interest readers from other parts of the country. John Marshall's solution to this problem in writing his biography of Washington was to include a history of the country since the founding of the colonies as well as a history of the revolution taken from the *Annual Register*. Even this stratagem did not satisfy John Quincy Adams, who found "too much of the Virginian" in Marshall's portrait of Washington.[14]

Parson Mason Locke Weems, the jocular southern agent for Mathew Carey's Philadelphia publishing house, discovered a key and established a formula for writing biographies likely to appeal to the nation as a whole. He made national symbols of his subjects, legendary giants of republican virtue and bravery, of revolutionary figures created heroes for a hero-starved people— heroes of fact for a people accustomed to such heroes of legend as Beowulf and King Arthur. Weems put no great emphasis upon the regions from whence his subjects came and gave the fullest account of their roles in the American Revolution. He imitated the behavior books which taught such universal virtues as

[12] Joseph Priestley, *Lectures on History, and General Policy; to which is prefixed an essay on a course of Liberal Education for Civil and Active Life*, II (Philadelphia, 1803), 3.

[13] Tucker to William Wirt, April 4, 1813, in John P. Kennedy, *Memoirs of the Life of William Wirt* (Philadelphia, 1860), p. 315; *North American Review*, IV (March, 1818), 295.

[14] John Quincy Adams to William Plumer, August 16, 1809, Worthington C. Ford (ed.), *The Writings of John Q. Adams* (New York: Macmillan Co., 1914), III, 339.

honesty, bravery, and thrift by representing these qualities or the lack of them in "Miss Betsy Algood" and "Master Billy Bad Enough."[15] Weems wrote similar stories of American citizens who could be held up as shining examples of the popular virtues.

The itinerant parson was the author of several moral tracts on drunkenness. In the spring of 1799 he announced his first idealized biography. "I have nearly ready for press," Weems informed Mathew Carey, "a piece to be christened 'The Beauties of Washington,' tis artfully drawn up, enlivened with anecdotes, and in my humble opinion marvelously fitted, Ad captandum—gustum populi Americani! ! ! What say you to printing it for me and ordering a copper plate Frontispiece of that Heroe, something in this way. George Washington, Esqr. The Guardian Angel of his Country. Go thy way old George. Die when thou wilt we shall never look upon thy like again."[16] Six months later the country was in mourning and ministers were eulogizing the first President. "Washington, you know is gone!" the irrepressible parson wrote Carey. "Millions are gaping to read something about him. I am nearly primed and cocked for 'em."[17]

In the spring of 1800 booksellers were selling for twenty-five cents the eighty-two-page, rough-bound volume from Mathew Carey's press. Weems pictured Washington as a model of virtue—good republican virtue. "Dead languages, pride and pedantry, had no charms for him who always preferred sense to sound, the kernel to the shell."[18] Washington, under the parson's pen, personified the nation's titanic struggle against the tyranny of a greedy king, and everything the hero did shook the earth. Weems described the sound and action at the battle of Cowpens in this way: "As when a mammouth suddenly dashes in among a thousand buffaloes, feeding at large on the vast plains of Missouri; all at once the innumerous herd, with wildly rolling eyes and hideous bellowings, break forth into flight, while close at their heels the roaring monster follows. Earth trembles as they fly. Such was the noise in the chase of Tarleton, when the swords of Washington's cavalry pursued his troops from the famous fields of the Cowpens."[19]

[15] For an example of these behavior books see Isaiah Thomas, *The Juvenile Biographer, containing lives of little masters and misses; including a variety of good and bad characters, by a little biographer* (Worcester, Mass., 1787); Dixon Wecter, *The Hero in America* (New York: Charles Scribner's Sons, 1941), I, 1–16; Mason Locke Weems, *A History of the Life and Death, Virtues and Exploits, of General George Washington* (Philadelphia, 1800); Weems, *The Life of General Francis Marion, A Celebrated Partisan Officer, in the Revolutionary War, Against the British and Tories in South Carolina and Georgia* (Baltimore, 1809); Weems, *The Life of Benjamin Franklin; with many choice Anecdoted and Admirable Sayings of this great man, never before published by any of his biographers* (5th ed.; Baltimore, 1820).

[16] Weems to Carey, June 24, 1799, Emily Ellsworth Ford Skeel (ed.), *Mason Locke Weems, His Works and Ways* (New York: Richmond Mayo-Smith, 1929), II, 120.

[17] Weems to Carey, January 2, 1800, *ibid.*, p. 131.

[18] Weems, *Washington*, p. 71.

[19] *Ibid.*, p. 53; also quoted in Sydney G. Fisher, "The Legendary and Myth-Making Process in Histories of the American Revolution," *Proceedings of the American Philosophical Society*, LI (Philadelphia, 1912), 65.

Not many biographers attempted to imitate the parson's bombastic style, but they followed the pattern he set in writing biography. William Wirt, in an effort to win "the applause of thousands," had some success in portraying Patrick Henry as a spokesman for all of the colonies writhing under British tyranny and characterized him as the "father of the Revolution.'"[20] John Sanderson sanctified the signers of the Declaration of Independence in a nine-volume counterpart to the *Lives of the Saints*.[21] Washington Irving, with literary skill, succeeded in depicting Columbus as an American hero and a faultless example of what "human genius and laudable enterprise may accomplish."[22]

Reverence for ancestors was unflagging in early nineteenth-century America. By mid-century, filio-pietistic regard for the dead was in danger of making hypocrites of historians. Though in stuffy and stylized prefaces addressed to their readers they might make obeisance to the demands of "stern truth," without show of conscience they admitted to their intimates that they had twisted the facts somewhat to make the best showing possible. Philosophic rationalization explained in part this pious approach to history and biography, a long-standing assumption about human nature, the common denominator of mankind. Human nature contained elements both good and bad. Some men, like Hamilton and John Adams, believed that the bad elements tended to dominate the majority of men, that a social order, in the form of a nation or civilization, could last only a limited time. Greed, lust for power, and moral laxity would bring about the decay and downfall of men and nations. All history demonstrated this cycle. But Thomas Jefferson and other nineteenth-century idealists believed that under favorable circumstances good would drive out evil and that the decline of a social order did not inevitably follow its rise.

But those who accepted a cyclical theory of history and those who believed in the perfectability of man and the progress of civilization agreed that the good elements in human nature could be encouraged by education and the emulation of worthy models. Men of the past were "gifted with the same faculties, exposed to the same temptations, and impelled by the same passions as ourselves. Their virtues and their failings were our own, were those of human nature. These are to be copied and avoided, not their deeds, their character should be investigated, not their conduct; or rather their conduct should be scrutinized only as a clue to their characters."[23]

[20] William Wirt to Dabney Carr, August 20, 1815, in Kennedy, *Memoirs of Wirt*, p. 346; William Wirt, *Sketches of the Life and Character of Patrick Henry* (Philadelphia, 1818), Introduction.

[21] John Sanderson, *Biography of the Signers to the Declaration of Independence* (9 vols.; Philadelphia, 1820–27).

[22] Washington Irving, *The Life and Voyages of Christopher Columbus* (New York, 1828), I, 56.

[23] Francis C. Gray, "An Address Before the Society of Phi Beta Kapa on Thursday, the 29th of August, 1816," *North American Review*, III (September, 1816), 289. Another writer who reflected the cyclical interpretation of history believed the examples furnished in the documents published in the Collections of the Massachusetts Historical Society

Jefferson, in commenting upon the manuscript of William Wirt's biography of Patrick Henry, observed that the author omitted his subject's failings and practiced vigorously the precept *"de mortuis nil nisi bonum,"* but agreed that Wirt was "excusable in drawing the veil over them and holding up the brighter side of his character, only, to imitation.[24]

William Wirt, Parson Weems, and other filio-pietists seem to have established a definite scale of values in which moral character and local, state, or national patriotism vied for chief attention and historic truth ran a poor second. Historians of this school subordinated the facts of history to the desirable moral or patriotic lessons that might be taught. Some writers seem to have taken as their mission a determination to show the nation's best face to the world. For example, Jared Sparks, who professed himself solely concerned with the truth of history, confided to his journal on a trip through White Plains, New York, that the young men who had captured the British spy, Major André, were simply highway robbers waiting for a victim. "But," wrote the historian, "this is of little consequence in history, it is desirable for its moral and political influence that the act should receive the most favorable construction. The example will then have a value, which will operate to the benefit of posterity and exhibit human nature in a light in which it is most desirable to contemplate it."[25]

Few of Sparks's contemporaries would have disagreed with him. To them, history was a source of examples with which to implant in the minds of younger generations of Americans an established pattern of behavior, to secure desirable conformity by habit rather than by law.[26]

The United States was on trial as a political experiment, viewed skeptically from without, met with catcalls, jeers, and little encouragement, and watched

---

might serve to postpone degeneracy. "As there is little to blame and much to praise in these early annals, every generation will look with increased veneration to the pure virtues and inflexible constancy of our heroick forefathers, and the influence of their example may stimulate future generations to avoid degeneracy." *North American Review*, II (January, 1816), 110. One reviewer of Wirt's *Patrick Henry* believed that biography should "encourage by example others to overthrow the same obstacle and go on to greater heights." "Patrick Henry," *North American Review*, VIII (March, 1818), 293.

[24] Thomas Jefferson to William Wirt, November 12, 1816, in Kennedy, *Memoirs of Wirt*, p. 365; Wirt to Jefferson, October 23, 1816, *ibid.*, p. 364.

[25] Jared Sparks, entry for June 20, 1833, MSS journal, Sparks Papers in Houghton Library, Harvard University.

[26] William Holmes McGuffey, *The Eclectic First Reader* (2 vols.; Cincinnati, 1838), I, Preface; McGuffey, *McGuffey's Newly Revised First to Fifth Reader* (5 vols.; Cincinnati, 1843–44); Richard D. Mosier, *Making the American Mind* (New York: Kings Crown Press, 1947), pp. 1–56. Wirt also wished to teach lessons through biography. He wrote Jefferson in 1810 that "the times require a little discipline, which cannot be rendered so interesting in a didactic form, as if interwoven with the biography of a celebrated man. . . . Mr. Henry seems to me a good text for a discourse on rhetoric, patriotism and morals. The work might be made useful to young men who are just coming forward into life: this is the highest point of my expectation; nor do I deem the object a trifling one since on these young men the care and the safety of the republic must soon devolve." Wirt to Jefferson, January 18, 1810, in Kennedy, *Memoirs of Wirt*, p. 251.

from within with nervous anxiety in an atmosphere scarcely conducive to self-criticism. The revolution was an event to be defended and glorified, and the men who participated in it must needs be seen as heroes.[27] The Constitution and the men who made it were sacred; the document was looked upon as more than a code agreed upon by a small group of men as likely to be fallible as others. It was a Bible which carried the answer to every political exigency. The authors of such a document could not be allowed ordinary human frailties which might reflect on the perfection of its creation. Filio-pietism, a defense against criticism and a bulwark for a specific ordering of society, was inspired by the needs of early nineteenth-century Americans and fed by historians and Fourth of July orators who did as "necessary to keep alive those recollections which are part and parcel of the common patrimony of every American."[28]

Competition among local historians heightened the virtues of the fore-fathers, brightened the haloes of sanctity that floated so prominently above them, and did nothing to decrease the reverential atmosphere that swathed the nation's past. A member of the Maine Historical Society stated the aims of local biographers and historians: "Too often have instances of private toil, and sacrifice, and daring been forgotten, amid the eclat that has been bestowed upon events of a more public nature and on a larger scale. But it is due to our country and to justice to correct this neglect wherever it can be done, and to mete out to everyone, whatever may have been his rank or station, the fit measure of his country's gratitude."[29]

[27] "The Records of the American Revolution ought to be sacredly preserved. That event we justly consider as the noblest monument of our national glory. We hope, that it will not in future time reproach the degeneracy of posterity." *The Monthly Anthology*, I (October, 1804), 557. A reviewer of Wirt's biography of Patrick Henry wrote in 1818: "Above all we are pleased with tracing the progress of a great mind, struggling against the adversities of fortune and the petrifying grasp of poverty. . . . There is a sacredness in the fame of such a man." *North American Review*, VIII (March, 1818), 295. William H. Prescott wrote of his *Life* of Charles Brockden Brown, "I am very sorry to send you such sorry trash. But it was not written con amore. . . . I have praised him twice as much as I think he deserves. . . . The truth is, Brown should be worked up by someone that *feels* him. . . ." Prescott to Sparks, August 1, 1833, Sparks Papers. Benson J. Lossing wrote in respect to Lord Mahon's criticisms of Sparks's editing practices that he believed the critic to be captious and that "I, as an humble, yet profound admirer of the character of Washington—as an American desirous of having the founders of our republic appear to the world in the most favorable light, do most sincerely thank you." Lossing to Sparks, March 9, 1852, Sparks Papers.

[28] *United States Literary Gazette*, I (July 15, 1825), 92–93. Jared Sparks stated that the publication of his edition of Washington's letters was important for "diffusing more widely a knowledge of the opinions and acts of our great American hero. This latter consideration is one of great importance. . . ." Sparks to Thomas Searle, September 4, 1833, Sparks Papers.

[29] "Exertions of the O'Brien Family of Machias, Maine, in the American Revolution," Maine Historical Society, *Collections*, Documentary Series, II (Portland, Me., 1847), 45–95. A journal, in reviewing a book entitled *Female Review of Memoirs of an American Young Lady*, reported with some astonishment that the heroine had spent three years as a Continental soldier, performed the duties of every department, and "preserved her chastity inviolate." *Rural Magazine*, I (Newark, N.J., March, 1798), 113.

The "fit measure" of gratitude due a local hero, in the eyes of his partisans, seems to have been far more than that due those of other localities. It came to a point where citizens of each state and town watched carefully to see that their heroes were properly treated. In 1823, when William Sanderson was in process of publishing his multivolume biography of the signers of the Declaration of Independence, a friend wrote to William Plumer, then governor of New Hampshire, that he "hoped the editor . . . [would] give the Patriots of New Hampshire a fair and honest biography," for New Hampshire men had not had a just share of recognition for their role in the revolution.[30] Fortunately for the success of his book, Sanderson's sketches were in the accepted tradition; neither he nor any other author who expected to sell books could ignore the jealous pride of the states.[31]

The flowering of early nineteenth-century biography came with the publication, between 1833 and 1849, of Jared Sparks's huge series, *The Library of American Biography*. Sparks, a Unitarian minister and the editor-owner of the *North American Review*, had already made his reputation in biography. He published in 1828 a biography of John Ledyard, the first American to envision the commercial possibilities of the Pacific Northwest and a patriot whose dream was only then beginning to be realized in the westward expansion of the nation. Sparks had just finished editing the papers of George Washington when he noted in his journal: "I have been thinking of a project for a new publication to be entitled 'A Library of American Biography.' The purpose is to select some of the most prominent lives from the first settlement of the country down to the present time taking them at such dates that they will not interfere with each other, by running over the same events. The series will thus serve as in some degree a connected history of the country as well as to illustrate the character and acts of some of the most illustrious men of the nation." Sparks hoped to get the "most competant [*sic*] hands that can be engaged" as the authors of his series.[32] Volumes appeared from time to time, and not in any specific order of dates, as Sparks had planned. The first series of ten volumes, some containing several biographies, was so well received that a second series of fifteen volumes was published, the last volume of which appeared in 1849.

During this period, historiography, and especially historical biography, was regarded as a method of moral teaching, as a conservator of the established pattern of society, and as a product of competition between proud localities, functions of biography by no means new. Plutarch's *Lives* is largely a collection of individualized portraits of men remembered for their virtues and vices. The *Lives of the Saints* was designed as precept and example. In New England,

[30] J. B. Moore to William Plumer, August 13, 1823, Plumer Papers, in Library of Congress.

[31] Sanderson, *Biography of the Signers of the Declaration of Independence;* Timothy Flint, "On History," *Western Monthly Review,* I (1827–28), 543; Richard Hildreth, "National Literature," *American Monthly Magazine,* I (1829), 379–85.

[32] Sparks, July 28, 1832, entry in MS journal, 1832–40, Sparks Papers.

writers from William Bradford on delighted in marking the difference between black and white, good and evil, through the medium of biography, usually those of ministers and criminals. Only the application differed; history and biography were turned toward the needs of a new nation rather than toward those of a religious creed.

Histories and biographies so conceived contributed to the prevailing atmosphere of piety toward American patriots and led to the collection and preservation of the private papers of many noted leaders. Biography early dominated the historical field, attaining great popularity in the eighteenth century and continuing through the nineteenth century and into our own time. Many parents, ministers, and pedagogues felt that biography had greater instructional value than other forms of literature, as did one man who advised his son to "read no history for 5 or 6 years—if you can obtain Biographies of great men."[33] The didactic virtues added somewhat to the popularity of biography, but a consuming interest in the lives of the great and the infamous is in the nature of the majority of men and, as Jared Sparks said when he launched his *Library of American Biography*, is surely reflected in "the present reading taste."[34]

[33] Francis Walk Gilmer to Thomas Walker Gilmer, April 18, 1817, "Letters of Francis Walk Gilmer to Thomas Walker Gilmer," *Tyler's Quarterly Historical and Genealogical Magazine*, VI (1924–25), 240–41; Joseph Priestley, *Lectures on History*, II, 9.

[34] Sparks, journal entry, July 28, 1832, Sparks Papers. An excellent analysis and delightful history of biography is John A. Garraty, *The Nature of Biography* (New York: Alfred A. Knopf, 1957).

---

8 EFFORTS TO PROMOTE A REPUBLICAN VIEW OF NATIONAL HISTORY, 1800–1815

In 1800, Thomas Jefferson, the newly elected President of the United States, prepared to take control of the nation's future; to do so, he quickly discovered, he must find a way to secure control of its past. The new occupant of the White House had long been interested in American history. He held a strong faith in its social utility, although he once said that he did not believe in "history as a moral exercise" because "her lessons would be too unfrequent if confined to real life."[1] With the coming of the American Revolution he changed his mind.

In 1776, Jefferson had turned to history as well as to natural law when he

[1] Thomas Jefferson to Robert Skipwith, August 3, 1771, in Julian P. Boyd *et al.* (eds.), *The Papers of Thomas Jefferson* (Princeton, N.J.: Princeton University Press, 1950———), I, 77.

began to draft the Declaration of Independence. He wished to prove that the embattled Americans were not lawless malcontents but defenders of justice and the rights of man. In 1779 he wrote the Diffusion of Knowledge Bill for the state of Virginia, the first state to require the study of American history in the public schools. In doing so, Jefferson showed his increased respect for the didactic properties of history. He declared that the most effective way to prevent the perversion of power and the growth of tyranny was to enlighten "the people at large," insofar as this is possible, and to "give them knowledge of those facts which history exhibits, that possessed thereby of the experience of other ages they may be enabled to know ambition under all its shapes and prompt to exert their natural powers to defeat its purposes."[2]

The Republican chief was a nationalist. He urged that the states be drawn together in every possible way, that everything be done "to cultivate the idea of our being one nation. . . ."[3] Jefferson agreed, with most of the leaders who later drew up the Constitution, that the only justification for revolution was the restoration of lost liberty and lost rights; as Dr. David Ramsay put it, "to overset an established government unhinges many of those principles which bind individuals to each other."[4] To be acceptable to Jefferson, a history of the American Revolution would have to demonstrate the conservative nature and the legal justness of the American cause. Such a history would preserve the heritage of the revolution as a symbol of national unity and demonstrate that the Constitution was the most natural and perfect embodiment of the purposes of the war. It would show "that the act of independence, did not hold out to the world thirteen sovereign states, but a common sovereignty of the whole of their united capacity."[5]

Jefferson was indefatigable, as were John Adams, Dr. Benjamin Rush, and other revolutionary leaders, in promoting an American version of the history of the War for Independence. He helped to write François Soulés' *History of the American Revolution*[6] and, like Tom Paine, attacked the inaccuracies of Abbé Raynal's early history of the revolution.[7]

Soon after the Constitution had been established, Jefferson became Secretary of State. In the course of his monumental struggle with Alexander Hamilton, Jefferson realized that there existed two American interpretations of the revolution. One version, expounded by Hamilton, John Jay, and other extreme Fed-

---

[2] Jefferson, "Diffusion of Knowledge Bill," Paul L. Ford (ed.), *The Writings of Thomas Jefferson* (New York, 1892–99), II, 221.

[3] Jefferson to James Monroe, 1785, *ibid.*, IV, 52.

[4] David Ramsay, *History of the American Revolution* (Philadelphia, 1789), II, 316.

[5] *Ibid.*, p. 323.

[6] François Soulés, *Histoire des troubles de l'Amerique anglaise, écrite sur les memoires les plus authentiques* (4 vols.; Paris, 1787). See excerpts of Jefferson's correspondence with Soulés in regard to the *Histoire*, in E. Millicent Sowerby (ed.), *Catalogue of Thomas Jefferson's Library*, I (Washington, D.C.: Library of Congress, 1952), 223–24.

[7] Raynal, *Revolution of America*; Paine, *Letter to Raynal*.

eralists, maintained that the war had been fought because of specific illegal abuses perpetrated by George III and certain ambitious ministers. Temptation toward tyranny was a basic fault of human nature but could not be cited to discredit the institution of monarchy or the principle of the centralization of power. Another interpretation, that propounded by Jefferson, asserted that tyranny was the inevitable result of the concentration of power. The American Revolution began only after the failure of monarchy and its principles to further mankind's progress toward happiness.

Jefferson believed man to be a rational animal, capable of making use of education, and therefore capable of basing his decisions on an examination of fact. Men could extend their experience through the study of history, but if historians misconstrued the story of "the species," for example, by demonstrating that power rightfully descends from above, their books would have a bad effect upon the human mind and limit progress and the freedom of individuals.

Jefferson combined the English Whig interpretation of history with the French philosopher's use of history. He believed that history ought to be a record of the progress of man's mind; that progress is retarded by violations of the laws of nature and reason; and that the story of the United States was one of progressive restoration of ancient political liberties. Jefferson could agree with extreme Federalists on the causes of the American Revolution and its general history, but he could not agree upon their interpretation of the meaning of the revolution. The inalienable rights for which men fought were to be found in the Constitution, and the implementation of those rights was to be seen in the administrations of Washington, Adams, and Jefferson.[8]

When Jefferson came to the Presidency in 1801, he came as a victor in a long battle to wrest power from men whom he believed were rapidly destroying the principles of the Republic. The party struggle between the Federalists and Jefferson's Republicans was a good deal more significant than the usual battle for political power. It was, for the principals of each group, a fight to establish a single interpretation of the Constitution. This fight continued with John Adams' last-ditch effort to retain Federalist influence through control of the courts and Jefferson's vindictive measures to subdue the judicial branch of the government. During this struggle Jefferson made a concerted effort to influence the writing of American history.[9]

The rancor between President Jefferson and Vice-President Aaron Burr was set aside in preparation for the attack on the Federalist-controlled judiciary. John Cheetham, a New York publisher who hated Aaron Burr, wrote Jefferson in 1801 that a history of the Adams administration had been written at the in-

---

[8] For an excellent analysis of Jefferson's adaptation of the Whig interpretation of history see H. Trevor Colburn, "Thomas Jefferson's Use of the Past," *William and Mary Quarterly*, 3d ser., XV (January, 1958), 56–70.

[9] Adrienne Koch, *The Philosophy of Thomas Jefferson* (New York: Columbia University Press, 1943), 124–25.

stigation of a group of Republicans. It was the first Jefferson had heard of the project, and he grew more interested when Cheetham informed him that certain New York Republicans were trying to suppress the book. The book appeared in 1802, in part as a result of Jefferson's influence.[10] John Wood, the author of this controversial work, was a writer of some experience. He had come to the United States from England in 1797. He was filled with an idealistic love of liberty but had no knowledge of politics in the United States. In June, 1801, Wood contracted with the New York printing firm of Barlas and Ward to write a history of the Adams administration, to be finished by the end of August. Wood found that a good history would take him several years to write, but Barlas, an ardent Republican, insisted upon the original deadline. Wood hastily completed the book, using as sources only the Philadelphia *Aurora*, the most violent and vitriolic of the anti-Federalist papers, some personal letters from William Duane, editor of the *Aurora*, and James Callendar's annual summary of political events, the *National Register*. Aaron Burr read the book in manuscript. He found many errors but was most concerned about the aspersions cast upon the character of George Washington, a politically dangerous move. It would have been especially so for the ambitious Vice-President, who was not beyond using the Federalists if he could. Burr agreed to buy from Barlas and Ward the plates and the first edition, only to discover that Barlas, contrary to their agreement, had distributed some copies to friends, including Burr's implacable enemy, James Cheetham. The damage was done; to buy the remaining copies would be a waste of money. Barlas demanded the money promised him. "If Mr. Barlas looked to him for money," Burr scribbled angrily, "he might look."[11] Meanwhile, Jefferson had urged that the book be issued.[12]

In 1802, with the backing of the President and a few judicious changes in the references to Washington, the book appeared. Wood transformed Washington into a leading Jeffersonian and concentrated his fire on John Adams. He argued that under the administration of "the illustrious Washington" America had enjoyed advantages that resulted from the "prudent policy of a virtuous magistrate" because "his interests and passion were the same as those of the people . . . ," whereas under the administration of that "Monarchical President," John Adams, "tyranny and corruption . . . disfigured" national life.[13]

It was not enough, Jefferson realized, to give the people a knowledge of history; it must be history "republicanized." A faulty interpretation or a deliberate misrepresentation could do much to undermine the free principles of the

[10] James Cheetham to Jefferson, December 29, 1801, Sowerby, *Jefferson's Library*, I, 247–49.

[11] John Wood, *A Correct Statement of the Various Sources from which the History of the Administration of John Adams was compiled, and the Motives for its suppression by Col. Burr, with some observations on a narrative by a citizen of New York* (New York, 1802), pp. 5–6.

[12] Jefferson to Cheetham, November 14, 1801, Ford (ed.), *Writings of Jefferson*, VIII, 72.

[13] John Wood, *The History of the Administration of John Adams, Esq., Late President of the United States* (New York, 1802), p. 2.

American Constitution. For a time the President was satisfied to create an atmosphere favorable to the kind of historiography that condemned tyranny and glorified the spirit of democracy. He wrote testimonials for authors who displayed republican sentiments and dedicated their work to liberty.

In 1805, Mercy Otis Warren, then a peppery lady of seventy-seven, felt that at last her history, much of which had been written during the revolution, would meet a favorable reception. Mrs. Warren had been an outspoken partisan of the revolutionary movement. She, along with her brother, James Otis, had opposed any form of government that showed the least indication of being or becoming authoritarian. She had been a strong proponent of the Bill of Rights. The heroes of her history were the first agitators of the revolutionary movement, and she was free with her criticism of those who hesitated in their allegiance or who were not entirely committed to the cause of liberty. Even her friend John Adams suffered the bite of her pen for his monarchical views, a criticism which caused her the loss of the former President's friendship and ten years of acrimonious correspondence. Jefferson may have smiled when he read Mercy Warren's opinion of Alexander Hamilton, a "foreign adventurer" with crackbrained financial schemes. Jefferson received her volumes happily and sent Mrs. Warren a letter of praise for her efforts.[14]

For years Jefferson had encouraged William Wirt in his long-term project, a biography of Patrick Henry. Wirt was an ambitious lawyer of Virginia who had proved himself a man of "reputation, talents and correct views" as far as Jefferson was concerned.[15] In 1800, Wirt defended James Callendar, one of the Republican editors imprisoned under the Alien and Sedition Acts, and he put on a dramatic performance as a government lawyer at the trial of Aaron Burr. Here, Jefferson hoped, was a man who would tell the Republican story in the biography of a popular revolutionary hero, but Wirt disappointed him. In 1817, after seemingly endless correspondence and stoppings and startings, Wirt produced a biography that both Republicans and Federalists labeled a "panegyric." Jefferson, who had read and criticized the manuscript, observed that Wirt had failed to explain the reasons for Patrick Henry's defection to the Federalists, which could be found in his faults.[16] Wirt replied that he thought himself "excusable in drawing the veil over [Henry's faults] and holding up the brighter side of his character, only, to imitation." But Jefferson would have none of it. Wirt had glossed over Henry's last years, but what Jefferson had hoped for was an explanation or condemnation of his defection.

Jefferson was not satisfied that the story of American history was being told,

[14] Mercy Warren, *History of the Rise, Progress, and Termination of the American Revolution* (Boston, 1805), I, 25, 46, 137, III, 133–34; Maude MacDonald Hutcheson, "Mercy Warren, 1728–1814," *William and Mary Quarterly*, 3d ser., X (July, 1953), 397.

[15] Jefferson to Wirt, January 10, 1808, *The Writings of Thomas Jefferson*, ed. Andrew A. Liscomb and Albert Ellery Bergh (Washington, D.C.: The Thomas Jefferson Memorial Association of the U.S., 1903), XI, 423.

[16] Weems, *Washington*, p. 71.

nor was he satisfied with his passive role in encouraging such a history. At this time he learned that John Marshall was writing a biography of Washington. For all the years of Washington's presidency and after, as long as Alexander Hamilton's influence held sway and Hamilton opposed Jefferson, Washington's popularity was a Federalist possession. But with the election of Jefferson, writers began to win the Washington legend for the Republican party. John Wood had made him a "man of the people," and in his popular biography the wily Parson Weems had separated Washington from all former political ties by a long discourse upon the first President's hatred for the "unutterable curses of Faction and Party" and, by implication, labeled him "a pure Republican."[17] Weems wrote Jefferson in 1809 that he had not visualized Washington "as a Common Hero for military ambition meanwhile to idolize and imitate—nor an Aristocrat, like *others* had, to mislead and enslave, but a pure Republican whom all our youth should know that they may imitate his Virtues and thereby immortalize 'the last Republic' now on earth. . . ."[18]

The Federalists had sought to find someone to do a biography of Washington. Bushrod Washington was "very much solicited . . . to prepare for publication a history of his life" and was able to interest John Marshall in writing the work with his assistance.[19] John Marshall, although adept in expression of rich and concise judicial opinions, was not an experienced biographer. But he had debts to meet, and a popular biography of Washington would be very profitable. Having made up his mind to write it, Marshall convinced himself that he could make his fortune.

Marshall felt that as a background to the life of Washington he must write a history of the colonies. His account of the founding of the colonies filled one volume and the biography of Washington occupied four more, much to the disgust of the publishers, who had looked forward to a mass sale and a nice profit on one volume. Weems, who was circulating subscription lists for the book— he never allowed politics to interfere with business—advised the publishers that some people were "very fearful" that the biography would be "prostituted to party purposes. . . . For Heaven's Sake," Parson Weems urged the publishers, "drop now and then a cautionary hint to John Marshall Esq. Your all is at stake with respect to this work. If it be done in a generally acceptable manner you will make your fortune. Otherwise the work will fall an Abortion from the

---

[17] Weems to Jefferson, February 1, 1809, in Sowerby, *Jefferson's Library*, I, 249.

[18] Bushrod Washington to Rufus King, June 12, 1800, in Charles R. King (ed.), *Life and Correspondence of Rufus King* (New York, 1894–1900), III, 255.

[19] Weems to C. P. Wayne, December 10, 1802, in A. J. Beveridge, *Life of John Marshall* (Boston: Houghton Mifflin Co., 1916–19), III, 232. In another letter to Wayne, Weems advises the publisher that "patriotic orations—gazetteer Puffs—Washingtonian anecdotes, sentimental moral military and wonderful—All shd. be tried." Weems to Wayne, December 22, 1802, *ibid.*, p. 233. For an analysis of Marshall's sources for his history see William A. Foran, "John Marshall as a Historian," *American Historical Review*, XLI (1937–38), 51–64.

press."[20] No one made a fortune, but the publishers sold some eight thousand copies of the set.

The last volume of Marshall's life of Washington angered Jefferson and stirred him to action. Jefferson had little quarrel with the earlier volumes; when Marshall was not copying earlier histories and the English *Annual Register*, he used them as references. But for the last volume Marshall drew upon his own experience. The fifth volume covered the years after 1789, the years in which Jefferson's and Marshall's partisanship went different ways. Marshall attempted to stamp the Republicans as lawless rabble, the instigators of Shays' Rebellion and the Whiskey Rebellion. The disorganizing influence of the Republicans was seen as an obstacle to the smooth running of the government under the Constitution.[21] If a reader were to form his opinion of the Republicans on Marshall's volume alone, "He would suppose the republican party ('who,' said Jefferson, 'were in truth endeavoring to keep the government within the line of the Constitution, and prevent its being monarchical in practice') were a mere set of grumblers and disorganizers, satisfied with no government, without fixed principles. . . ."[22] Jefferson was determined to correct this view.

The President and his Secretary of State, James Madison, agreed that Joel Barlow, the poet, patriot, and diplomat, should write an "impartial" history of the period as an antidote to Marshall's work. During the revolution, Barlow had been a classmate of Noah Webster at Yale; unlike Webster, a staunch Federalist, he became an enthusiastic Republican. Soon after his graduation, Barlow wrote a long poem, "The Vision of Columbus," which, considerably lengthened, was published in 1802 as *The Columbiad*, the first epic poem of the new nation. In the eyes of Jefferson, Barlow was qualified to step into the shoes of Philip Freneau as poet and publicist of the Republican party.[23]

Jefferson informed Joel Barlow that "Mr. Madison and myself have cut out a piece of work for you, which is to write the history of the United States, from the close of the war downwards. We are rich ourselves in materials, and can open all the public archives to you; but your residence here is essential, because a great deal of the knowledge of things is not on paper, but only within ourselves, for verbal communications. John Marshall is writing the life of General Washington from his papers. It is intended to come out just in time to influence

[20] John Marshall, *Life of George Washington* (Philadelphia, 1804–7), V, 33–34, 85–87, 731–32. It has been suggested that the success of Marshall's *Life* may have been hindered by Jefferson's use of his official position to prohibit mailing privileges. This is an interesting idea but no evidence yet uncovered substantiates it. Certainly the postmasters did not circulate subscription lists as they had done for Jeremy Belknap's *History of New Hampshire*.

[21] Jefferson, "Notes on the Fifth Volume of Marshall's Life of Washington," Ford (ed.), *Writings of Jefferson*, X, 262.

[22] *Ibid.*, p. 321. T. A. Zunder, *Early Days of Joel Barlow* (New Haven: Yale University Press, 1934), 311; Charles B. Todd, *Life and Letters of Joel Barlow, LL.D.* (New York, 1886), p. 243.

[23] Jefferson to Barlow, May 3, 1802, Liscomb and Bergh (eds.), *Writings of Jefferson*, pp. 321–22.

the next presidential election. It is written, therefore, principally with a view to electioneering purposes. But it will consequently be out in time to aid you with information, as well as to point out the perversions of truth necessary to be rectified."[24]

When both the President and the Secretary of State urged him to write a history of the United States, Barlow consented. The most important portion of his history (to his thinking, and to that of Jefferson and Madison), the last years of Washington, was to be written first. Barlow, consul to Algiers and, later, minister to France, was a dilettante, and year after year he failed to begin his history.[25]

In 1807, William Plumer, senator from New Hampshire, visited President Jefferson to announce that he had decided to write a history of the United States. William Plumer was a convinced Federalist and had been one of that small group of New Englanders who, in 1802, had plotted secession in protest against the proposed purchase of New Orleans. Jefferson concealed his displeasure and offered what aid he could give the prospective historian. Now he had all the more reason to urge Barlow on, and he offered him the notes and comments he had made on Marshall's fifth volume.[26]

John Quincy Adams encouraged Plumer's project but suggested he "adopt Hume's mode: that is, begin the last part first."[27] It was an opportunity, Adams felt, to smooth over an old political error which Plumer and other New England Federalists had made in protesting the Louisiana Purchase and an opportunity to avoid a similar mistake threatened by objections to the embargo of 1807. Adams wrote Plumer that "the moral of your history will be the indissoluable union of the North American Continent, to counteract the tendency of these partial and foolish combinations." Adams said he knew of nothing "so likely to have a decisive influence as historical works, honestly and judiciously executed."[28]

[24] Madison to Barlow, June 16, 1809, Gaillard Hunt (ed.), *Writings of James Madison* (New York: G. P. Putnam's Sons, 1900–10), VIII, 283. Barlow wrote to Mercy Warren informing her of his intention to write a history of the United States, to be divided into three periods: colonial, revolution, and the first twenty years of the Constitution. He intended, he said, to start "wrong end foremost." He explained, "I look upon the last period as the most important of the three in every political and moral point of view. The object of history is instruction. The history of our country is the history of liberty; its two former periods may teach men how to acquire liberty, the last should teach them how to preserve it. Now in the present state of things with us it is much more important to know how to preserve liberty than how to acquire it. For in my opinion the loss of liberty in this country is not an impossible event." Barlow to Mercy Warren, December 29, 1810, Warren MSS in Massachusetts Historical Society Library.

[25] William Plumer, February 4, 1807, entry in MSS "Register of Opinions," Plumer MSS, Library of Congress.

[26] *Ibid.*, February 9, 1807.

[27] John Quincy Adams to Plumer, August 16, 1809, Worthington C. Ford (ed.), *The Writings of John Q. Adams* (New York: Macmillan Co., 1914), III, 339.

[28] Jefferson to Barlow, April 16, 1811, in Sowerby, *Jefferson's Library*, I, 242–43.

Neither Barlow nor Plumer finished his work. In 1811, Joel Barlow accepted a mission to Napoleon, then in Russia. Jefferson wished him well, but not without misgivings. "What is to become of our Post-revolutionary history?" he chided the poet.[29] Barlow died in a village near Cracow, his history still unborn, and William Plumer laid aside his manuscript to attend to his political career.[30]

Jefferson, failing in his efforts to get others to apply "the antidote of truth to the misrepresentations of Marshall," decided to write a history himself. In 1818 the retired President assembled his notes and memoranda. By way of preface, Jefferson wrote ruefully that, had Washington written a history from the materials assembled by his biographer, "it would have been a conspicuous monument to the integrity of his mind, the soundness of judgment, and its powers of discernment between truth and falsehood, principles and pretensions."[31] Jefferson's manuscript remained unpublished at his death.

Jefferson did not limit his efforts to an explanation of the Republican view of American history. He hoped that William Baxter's revision and abridgment of Hume's *History of England* would become popular in the United States. In 1770, Jefferson had been a great admirer of Hume's work, but after the American Revolution he looked upon it as insidious and dangerous, at least to a republic. "This single book," he declared, "has done more to sap the free principles of the English constitution than the largest standing army of which their patriots have been so jealous." In 1807, Jefferson declared that "it was unfortunate that he [Hume] first took up the history of the Stuarts, became their apologist and advocated all their enormities." Hume selected and arranged his materials to support the thesis that "the free principles of the English government . . . were usurpations on the legitimate and salutary rights of the crown. . . ."[32] The change in Jefferson's views came about not only because of his

[29] Plumer's unfinished manuscript history of the United States is among the Plumer MSS in Library of Congress.

[30] Jefferson's "Notes on Marshall's Life of Washington," *ibid.* Jefferson wrote to Judge William Johnson, "Let me, then, implore you, dear Sir, to finish your history of parties, leaving the time of publication to the state of things you may deem proper, but taking especial care that we do not lose it altogether. We have been too careless of our future reputation, while our Tories will omit nothing to place us in the wrong. Besides the five-volumed libel which represents us as struggling for office, and not at all to prevent our government from being administered into a monarchy, the life of Hamilton is in the hands of a man who, to the bitterness of the priest, adds the rancor of the fiercest federalism. Mr. Adams' papers, too, and his biography, will descend of course to his son, whose pen, you know, is pointed, and his prejudices not in our favor. . . . On our part we are depending on truth to make itself known, while history is taking a contrary set which may become too inveterate for correction." Jefferson to Johnson, March 4, 1823, Liscomb and Bergh (eds.), *Writings of Jefferson*, XV, 419–20. The fight was continued after Jefferson's death, taken up by William Sullivan in *Familiar Letters on Public Characters and Public Events from the Peace of 1783 to the Peace of 1815* (Boston, 1834), p. vii.

[31] For Jefferson's pre-revolutionary views of history see Jefferson to Skipwith, July 17, 1771, in Boyd *et al.* (eds.), *Papers of Jefferson*, I, 77–78.

[32] Jefferson to John Norvell, June 14, 1807, Ford (ed.), *Writings of Jefferson*, X, 415; Jefferson to John Adams, January 11, 1817, *ibid.*, XII, 46.

recognition of Hume's sympathetic treatment of the Stuarts, but because he had formed his own view of the nature of the development of civilization. Hume, in his history, had expressed a cyclical theory of the growth and decay of civilizations, thus justifying a comparative study. Hume's opinion was shared by other philosophers and, in America, by such staunch Federalist leaders as Alexander Hamilton and John Adams during the latter part of the eighteenth century. Jefferson promoted an American edition of Baxter's abridgment, which was unpopular in England because of its democratic overtones, because he thought it excellently suited to the needs of the United States.[33]

Jefferson believed that written history should free men from the past. England's history rightly read would show in what manner the natural rights of men had been subverted by the events of history and encrusted by tradition, and how Englishmen had progressively pried loose the "dead hand" of tradition in an effort to restore their natural state of freedom. Therefore, Hume's sin and that of Marshall and the Federalists was not so much in mistaking the facts as perverting the use of history, forging a chain to bind the present generation to the mistaken traditions of the past, failing to show how one remains free by recognizing and avoiding the possibility of future chains forged in the same manner. Jefferson looked upon Baxter's abridgment as an antidote to Hume and an urgent necessity to preserve the future of democracy. Though he took every opportunity to point out to American publishers the need for an American edition of Baxter's history, Jefferson was unable to find one to assume the task.[34]

In an attempt to aid Louis Girardin, one of his French refugee friends, Jefferson suggested that he translate a history of the American Revolution by the Italian republican, Carlos Botta. Botta had had only secondary sources and often copied Marshall's work; but, nonetheless, Botta "transfused into his narration his own holy enthusiasm for liberty, of which his icy original had not one spark."[35] Before Girardin had fairly begun his work, George A. Otis completed and published in 1820 a translation of Botta's history. Girardin abandoned his project and, with a compatriot, Nicholas G. Dufief, completed Beverley Tucker's history of Virginia. This latter work pleased Jefferson, for it exemplified on a local level the view of history he had attempted to promote on a national level.[36]

Thomas Jefferson's efforts to reinterpret the history of the United States were a failure, but he continued to fight the Federalist interpretation of Ameri-

[33] Denniston and Cheetham to Jefferson, January 30, 1802, in Sowerby, *Jefferson's Library*, I, 248.

[34] Jefferson to Louis Girardin, December 26, 1818, *ibid.*, I, 251.

[35] Edith Philips, *Louis Hue Girardin and Nicholas Gouin Dufief and Their Relations with Thomas Jefferson* (Baltimore: Johns Hopkins University Press, 1926), p. 33.

[36] Even after his death, and the acceptance by the Democrats of Federalist principles, Jefferson was considered a threat to orderly society. William Sullivan, an ex-Federalist, published a history in 1834 to offset "the dangerous principles which the publication of Jefferson's Memoirs and Writings tend to perpetuate." Sullivan, *Familiar Letters*, Preface, p. vii.

can history until his death. After 1815, Jefferson's voice was lost in the re-surgence of patriotic nationalism. The political program of the Republican party altered and took on the hue of the old Federalist party.

By 1857, Lord Macaulay, observing American affairs and recognizing that the country was becoming ever more democratic, more Jeffersonian, and conse-quently less in harmony with the ideals of Washington, found it exceedingly "strange that while this process has been going on, Washington should have been exalted into a god, and Jefferson degraded into a demon."[37]

Jefferson's reputation has been rescued in recent years, but the observation of England's noted historian describes a condition that existed throughout the remainder of the nineteenth century and seems a contradiction of the old saying, "The victor writes the history." This contradiction, however, is superficial. Jefferson's primary goal in securing the presidency was to halt the trend toward centralization of power in the Federal government. This trend, he charged, was a product of Federalist rule, of their anti-democratic principles, supported by their interpretation of history, and would subvert individual freedom, ending in some form of tyranny. He proposed to put the nation back on its original course, establishing the principle of the diffusion of power as a permanent part of national policy, based upon his interpretation of history. This was the es-sence of the "Revolution of 1800," but Jefferson and his party sacrificed its principles to the expediencies of governing the nation and maintaining them-selves in office. Jefferson, in this regard, was not the victor but the vanquished.

[37] Thomas B. Macaulay to Henry Stephens Randall, January 18, 1857, in *The Corre-spondence between Henry Stephens Randall and Hugh Blair Grigsby, 1856–1861*, Frank J. and Frank W. Klingberg (eds.), (Berkeley and Los Angeles: University of California Press, 1952), p. 185 n.

PART THREE

Nationalism versus Localism, 1815–60

---

9 TEACHING PATRIOTISM: EMPHASIS
ON POPULAR HISTORY, 1815–50

When the news of the victory at New Orleans and the treaty at Ghent spread through the land, bonfires were lit in celebration, jubilant citizens paraded on Main Street, and toasts were drunk to the "Second War for Independence." Unnoticed in the uproar of rejoicing in Washington, D.C., were the petitioners to Congress from the Hartford Convention, representatives of local sovereignty and national disunity, who thought it best to steal quietly home. The war which they opposed had ended and public enthusiasm for the nation in its success would not welcome the suggestion that the power of the federal government be decreased.

All the same, the New Englanders who had opposed the war agreed with William Ellery Channing that something would have to be done about the "literary delinquency of America" if the country were to realize its independence.[1] Benjamin Elliott, a friend of Hezekiah Niles, the Baltimore publisher of Niles' Weekly Register, pointed out that "events of the late war have imparted a glow of national feeling for everything republican." He advised Niles to publish something on American history; far too many American histories had been written by Europeans or by Americans who accepted Europe's views. "If such men are to select our political lessons, I need not tell you what must be the opinions of the rising generation, nor of their certain degradation."[2]

The desire to see the United States acquire an "American character" inspired a resurgence of interest in the education of the rising generation. Writers, teachers, and politicians urged that American history be given a place in the school curriculum. To meet the demand, New England authors turned to the writing of textbooks, and an increasing number of public schools and libraries carried these national histories to every state.

The New England emphasis stemmed in part from a Boston Congregational minister, Abiel Holmes, from whose work many early textbook writers drew

[1] William Ellery Channing, "Reflections on the Literary Delinquency of America," North American Review, II (November, 1815), 33–43.

[2] Benjamin Elliott to Hezekiah Niles, November 23, 1816, in Hezekiah Niles, Principles and Acts of the Revolution in America (Baltimore, 1822), Preface.

their material. Holmes had sought to bridge the gap between local historians and national historians and between the eighteenth and nineteenth centuries. In his *American Annals* he surveyed the history of all of the colonies from their beginnings to the close of the eighteenth century. Holmes utilized the works of New England historians, and his book tended to prove that the foundation of the nation lay in New England. He was jealous of his region's history and carefully corrected "mistakes and misrepresentations" about it. Of the southern states, in spite of his seven years as a minister in Georgia, he found little or nothing to praise.[3] Virginia was settled for crassly economic purposes, unlike New England, whose settlers were motivated by the "natural and pious desire of perpetuating a church. . . ."[4] Holmes had no ordinary sympathy for rebellion against the established order, although he approved of the Puritan Revolution and the War for Independence. He considered Nathaniel Bacon to be a "bold, seditious, and eloquent young man" and the "author of calamities." Daniel Shays he found anything but a hero.[5] Even so, Holmes was a pioneer, a local historian who ventured to map the poorly blazed wilderness of national history, and for many years his two volumes were looked to for guidance.

From 1815 until 1830, textbook writers and biographers dominated the field of national history, and for the most part they took Holmes's *American Annals* as their authority. David Ramsay or Jonathan Trumbull might have attained the same position with their histories but neither finished his work. A maniac shot Ramsay and his unfinished history of the United States was put together in haphazard fashion by a friend with more love for Ramsay than knowledge of history. Whether by merit or default, Holmes's *American Annals* stood for almost twenty years as the standard reference work for writers of American history. [6]

Prior to 1820, American schools, including the academies, taught little but Greek and Roman history. Some general histories, such as Alexander Tytler's *Universal History*, revised for the American market, found their way into the schools. John McCulloch's *History of the United States*, Morse's geographies, and Webster's readers were for many years among the few volumes from which an American pupil might learn something of the history of his country.[7] In the decade of the twenties, textbook writers become so prolific that a new magazine, the *United States Literary Gazette*, established in 1824, devoted its

[3] Abiel Holmes, *American Annals* (Cambridge, Mass., 1805), I, 197.

[4] *Ibid.*, II, 472–73.

[5] *Ibid.*, I, 436–37.

[6] *United States Literary Gazette*, I (April, 1824), 1; William Grimshaw, *History of the United States* (Philadelphia, 1824), Preface.

[7] Alexander J. Inglis, *The Rise of the High School in Massachusetts* (New York: Columbia University Press, 1911), pp. 6–7.

book reviews almost exclusively to American textbooks, as did the *American Journal of Education*, established in 1826, and other journals for teachers.[8]

The flood of textbooks was stimulated, at least in part, by intellectual leaders who were intrigued by the opportunity to test fresh ideas in the building of a new society and seized upon education in its various forms as the means of sustaining the benefits achieved during the revolution. Many of the advances in educational theory were inspired by the American Philosophical Society, which offered prizes for the best of them. Unfortunately, the majority of these plans remained untried; the opportunities for change were far less than thought; patterns of everyday life in America were little altered by the War for Independence.

During the twenties, immigrants crowded the coastal towns. Advanced views of education brought from Europe challenged American educators, who took them up enthusiastically. Men like Walter R. Johnson of Pennsylvania, Thomas H. Gallaudet of Connecticut, and James G. Carter of Massachusetts stormed the legislatures with bills and petitions for better and more extensive school systems.

State pride and competition between the states, ever present in those years and always a motivating force in social improvement, played roles in furthering new developments in public education. For example, the New York Free School Society, established early in the twenties, helped New York State surpass the famed (but run-down) school system in Massachusetts and was one of the goads utilized by Horace Mann to achieve educational reforms in the Bay State.[9]

The new interest in education, the rising enrolment in schools, and the erection of new schools created a vast and relatively untapped market for American authors. And it was the current increase in interest in educational theory that cleared the way for the teaching of American history.

A writer in those years could scarcely mention education without invoking the name of Johann Heinrich Pestalozzi, the Swiss disciple of Rousseau. Pestalozzi learned the value of a concrete approach to education, and his method was to teach from the particular to the general, from the familiar to the unfamiliar, and from the tangible to the abstract. As one writer for the *American Journal of Education* declared, the day had passed when a teacher could make Tytler's *Universal History* a child's introduction to history; the child should be taught the history of his own country before that of the rest of the world. Many writers carried this logic to the extreme. One complained that pedagogical error was not yet overcome: "The order of nature, the order of the mind,

---

[8] James G. Carter, "The Schools of Massachusetts in 1824," *Old South Leaflets*, No. 135 (Boston: Directors of the Old Southwork, 1903), p. 24; *United States Literary Gazette*, II (February, 1825), 322.

[9] Allen O. Hansen, *Liberalism and Education in the Eighteenth Century* (New York: Macmillan Co., 1926), p. 84; Louise H. Tharp, *Until Victory* (Boston: Little, Brown & Co., 1953), pp. 29–31; Merle E. Curti, *Social Ideas of American Educators* (New York: Charles Scribner's Sons, 1935), pp. 101–38.

is still inverted; our youth are taught first the history of the United States; and afterwards they pick up, if they think proper, a few disjointed facts in the history of their own particular state." The proponents of local history argued that if children were taught early the history of their own town and their own state it "might interweave itself with the texture of their earliest thoughts and feelings, and lead to a sound and deep felt attachment to the scenes and society of their native regions." True patriotism would thus be promoted, for, according to this argument, patriotism is an expansion of the sentiments with which "the virtuous ever regard the place of their birth and education."[10]

Some authors of history texts bowed to the prevailing theory and produced histories of individual towns, and others treated each state individually, but as many general histories of the United States were written as before. The educational theories of Pestalozzi served both nationalism and the writers of textbooks by giving good cause for the addition of the history of the United States to the curriculum of every school.

Certain other conditions encouraged the production of history books. One organization offered a substantial prize for the best text in American history. At a meeting in 1820, the American Academy of Language and Belles Lettres resolved to offer a prize of four hundred dollars and a gold medal worth fifty dollars to the author who submitted within two years of that date the best history of the United States designed for schools. The premium was sufficient to inspire at least four contestants; Salma Hale's popular text, *A History of the United States from their first Settlement as Colonies, to the Close of the War with Great Britain in 1815*, was the winning entry.[11]

Another incentive for the production of histories of the United States was the adoption of state laws requiring the teaching of American history. British travelers and British reviews often commented on America's slavish acceptance of European cultural standards. American intellectuals, intent upon establishing an independent culture, insisted "most strenuously on the propriety of introducing the history of . . . [our] country, in every proper shape and form, into . . . [the] public schools."[12] In March, 1827, the Massachusetts legislature passed a law to provide for the instruction of youth. Public high schools were established and an education commission was chosen, of which Horace Mann served as secretary. The first section of the Massachusetts law referred in the broadest terms to general curriculum content but specifically required the teaching of the history of the United States. Vermont followed suit in the same

[10] *American Journal of Education*, I (1826), 53; Samuel Knapp, *Lectures on American Literature with remarks on some passages of American History* (New York, 1829), p. 287.

[11] Salma Hale, *A History of the United States from their first Settlement as Colonies, to the Close of the War with Great Britain in 1815* (New York, 1822), Preface; Plumer, January 18, 1822, entry in MSS diary, Plumer Papers.

[12] Knapp, *Lectures*, p. 287.

year, and before 1860 New Hampshire, Rhode Island, and Virginia put the same requirement into law.[13]

The history texts produced to meet the ensuing demand preached the conservative virtues of Puritanism and proclaimed the true heritage of the United States a bequest of the settlers of New England. The sources on which these texts were based, Holmes's *American Annals* and the Collections of the Massachusetts Historical Society, were written or edited by New Englanders, and the texts found their most certain market in the New England schools. In 1824, Charles A. Goodrich, a Massachusetts minister and a brother of Samuel G. Goodrich, a publisher and the author of the "Peter Parley" books, wrote for schools a history of the United States that went through many editions. Like other textbook writers, Goodrich had an "overweening prejudice for New England." In writing about the colonies, he declared that "in Virginia the free and licentious manners of society produce a government unsteady and capricious. This government reacts upon their manners, and aids rather than checks their licentiousness. In New England the severe puritanical manners of the people produce a rigid, energetick [*sic*] government."[14]

Textbook histories taught young readers their duties as citizens and their obligations as patriots, obedience to law, and acceptance of the existing social system; they were designed "to restrain some of the common vices . . ." of the country.[15] Bacon's Rebellion, Shays' Rebellion, the New Hampshire riots, and the Whiskey Rebellion were held up to view as examples of a lawless rabble attempting to seize control for its own benefit or as examples of the dangers of weak government.[16] In his history, Noah Webster took occasion to warn his readers that "all secret attempts, by associations or otherwise, to give one set of men or one party advantages over another, are mean, dishonorable and immoral." Webster placed special emphasis on the rights of property, drawing the moral that "in regard to property, you are to pay punctually all your just debts."[17]

Textbooks written by New Englanders, in which New England played the leading role and New England virtues set the standard for patriotism, spread wherever the history of the United States was taught. Throughout the decades of the twenties and most of the thirties, these books were very nearly the sole source of information on American history. The New England bias, the "senti-

[13] "An Act to Provide for the Instruction of Youth," approved March 10, 1827, *Acts and Resolves passed by the General Court in the year 1827* (Boston, 1828); *Boston Courier*, March 4, 1827.

[14] Charles A. Goodrich, *A History of the United States* (Boston, 1823), p. 61.

[15] Noah Webster, *History of the United States to which is prefixed a brief historical account of our English Ancestors, from the dispersion at Babel, to their migration to America and of the conquest of South America, by the Spaniards* (New Haven, 1832), p. 1.

[16] Grimshaw, *History*, pp. 198–99; Hale, *History*, pp. 24, 219; Goodrich, *History*, pp. 24, 72, 226–27.

[17] Webster, *History*, pp. 300, 305.

ment of having discovered and applied the seminal principles of the Revolution," spread from the general histories of the region to the textbooks, to the centennial and Fourth of July orations, and was taken up by the newspapers.[18] By 1845, a writer for a national magazine could say without question of serious dispute that "New England opinions and enterprise are so interwoven with the social agencies of the whole country and so constantly eulogized on public occasions, that they may be justly deemed the active and prominent element of American life."[19] But while Salma Hale, Samuel Goodrich in the guise of "Peter Parley," Charles A. Goodrich, Emma Willard, John Frost, Jesse Olney, and Marcius Willson were teaching Americanism in school texts and "with strenuous industry" seeing that the books circulated throughout the country, another group of writers prepared to appeal to the national pride of older citizens.

Cheap labor, the steam press, inexpensive paper and, in 1842, electrotyping, made it possible to turn out low-cost books in large editions. Book publishers, with the means for mass production, sought to satisfy a market occasioned by the rising tide of literacy. They pirated the novels of Dickens and Thackeray, catered to the rage for self-improvement in such series as Harper and Brothers' "Family Library," which contained well over a hundred titles, and recognized that the subjects of history might be considered inspirational or cautionary moral tales, as indicated by the enormous interest in Sparks's edition of the Washington papers, Irving's *Columbus*, and Prescott's *Ferdinand and Isabella*.[20] If relatively heavy works could find a market, then history, illustrated and intended for a wider audience, might sell many books. Publishers sought and found men with facile pens to apply the formula of Parson Weems and appeal to those "who cannot spare the time or the expense of reading or procuring a full and complete history."[21]

Popular historians, Joel T. Headley, John Warner Barber, Jacob and John Abbott, like Benson John Lossing, a leader in their midst, prepared to make history "accessible to our whole population, . . . to scatter the seeds of knowledge broadcast amid those in the humbler walks of society because adventitious

---

[18] Job R. Tyson, *Discourse Delivered before the Historical Society of Pennsylvania on the Colonial History of the Eastern and some of the Southern States* (Philadelphia, 1842), p. 8.

[19] *United States Magazine and Democratic Review*, XVI (1845), 79. For an analysis of nationalism in American textbooks before 1860 see Ruth Miller, "Nationalism in Elementary School books used in the United States from 1776 to 1865"; Columbia University Ph.D. thesis, 1952, on University Microfilms. For a contemporary analysis of some of the history textbooks see Marcius Willson, "A Critical Review of American Common School Histories," *Biblical Repository and Classical Review*, 3d ser., I (July, 1845), 517–39. For an analysis of the sources drawn upon by the authors of school histories see Alfred Goldberg, "School Histories of the Middle Period," Eric F. Goldman (ed.), *Historiography and Urbanization* (Baltimore: Johns Hopkins University Press, 1941), pp. 171–88.

[20] Bassett, *The Middle Group of Historians*, pp. 309–15.

[21] John Warner Barber, *Interesting Events in the History of the United States, being a selection of the most important and interesting events which have transpired since the discovery of this country to the present time* (New Haven, 1828), Preface. Another edition of this book, titled *Incidents in American History* (New York, 1847), appeared nineteen years later.

circumstances deny them access to the full granary of information, where the wealthy are filled; for these humble ones . . . are not less powerful than others at the ballot box where the Nation decides who its rulers shall be."[22]

Lossing and other popular historians who attracted many readers in the years after 1830 were writing for publishers who produced "cheap and compact" books and depended upon mass sales for their profits. Books of a purely local or sectional nature could not attract the desirable mass sales as surely as could works of national appeal. Publishers like Harper and Brothers, J. B. Lippincott and Company, and Baker and Scribner increasingly turned to writers who could appeal to the nation; though they continued to publish local and sectional histories, more and more they did so at the author's risk.[23]

Most historical popularizers did not bother to consult original source material but like textbook writers assembled their accounts from the works of others. John Warner Barber, author and illustrator of one of the earliest illustrated histories of the United States, acknowledged that he had taken most of his paragraphs "from Holmes' *Annals* and other works."[24] In 1847, Lossing published a history of the American Revolution he had written in less than eight months and frankly admitted that "we freely appropriated to our use the fruits of the labors of others."[25]

There were some few exceptions. Lossing, for instance, did original research for some of his books. He was an artist, his first trade had been engraving in wood, and it was as an illustrator that he engaged in research. As he was riding from Stamford to Greenwich, Connecticut, in 1848, he noticed a rude rock stairway partly concealed by the brush on a hill. He asked about the spot and learned that it was the place where in 1779 General Israel Putnam escaped Tryon's dragoons. Lossing sketched the stairway and that evening conceived the idea of a *Pictorial Field Book of the Revolution* (1852). He planned to sketch historic sites and relics of revolutionary battles in the hope that "a record of the pilgrimage, interwoven with that of the facts of past history, would attract the attention, and win to the perusal of the chroniclers of our Revolution many who could not be otherwise decoyed into the apparently arid and flowerless domains of mere history."[26] Lossing produced a lively, two-volume, illustrated account of his journey about the battlefields and included descriptions of the

---

[22] Benson John Lossing, *Biographical Sketches of the Signers of the Declaration of Independence* (New York, 1854), p. iv. For a more extended treatment of Lossing see David D. Van Tassel, "Benson J. Lossing; Pen and Pencil Historian," *American Quarterly*, VI (Spring, 1954), 32–44.

[23] Lossing to Lyman C. Draper, May 1, 1855, Draper correspondence, Wisconsin State Historical Society library.

[24] Barber, *Interesting Events*, Preface, p. ii.

[25] Benson J. Lossing, *1776* (New York, 1847), Preface.

[26] Lossing, *The Pictorial Field Book of the Revolution* (2d ed.; New York, 1885), I, 3; James C. Derby, *Fifty Years among Authors, Books and Publishers* (New York, 1884), p. 687; Alexander Davidson, Jr., "How Benson J. Lossing Wrote his Field Books of the Revolution, the War of 1812, and the Civil War," Bibliographical Society of America, *Papers*, XXII (1937), 58.

battles based upon interviews with local historians and old residents and upon manuscripts that he collected.

To appeal to the whole country was difficult at a time when the sectional controversy between North and South was spreading. The Mexican War and the martial spirit that quickly possessed American citizens suggested a solution. Books akin to Charles J. Peterson's *Military Heroes of the War of 1812* and *Military Heroes of the War with Mexico* came from the presses of New York, Philadelphia, and Cincinnati. Some critics complained that American histories placed entirely too much emphasis upon wars, battles, and military leaders, and that the true stuff of history was the progress of society. But the martial theme was too popular to be abandoned. It offered the opportunity to dodge controversial topics by describing at length the "British atrocities" of the burning of Newark and Washington during the War of 1812, and the heroism of Americans in the revolution.[27]

Some popular historians such as Jacob and John S. C. Abbott, who later dealt with American history, at first avoided controversial material and chose romantic and exciting subjects from European history. Others wrote on *Washington and His Generals* and *The Pictorial History of the American Revolution*.[28] One author, Jesse Ames Spencer, was careful to state that he had given arguments on every side of all the great issues, such as "federalists and democrats, internal improvements, the United States Bank, Missouri Compromise and the Slavery question," thus demonstrating his impartiality. Spencer went on to make clear that only where the United States was concerned was he truly biased. "By birth and education an American," he declared, "I claim to be alive to everything which affects the honor, the good name, the glory of my country." The major theme in Spencer's book, as in most of the national histories written during the three decades before the Civil War, was that in unity alone lies a nation's strength, supported by the virtues of courage, patriotism, and democracy.

Textbook writers and popularizers eulogized revolutionary heroes, the signers of the Declaration of Independence, and the fathers of the Constitution. They advocated a flamboyant patriotism which declared independence of all things European and declared that kings and rulers, who held power by "grace of bayonets and gunpowder," were of little significance when compared to the President of the United States, "the chosen servant of a mighty and free nation."[29] But if kings gave way before the nationalism of these authors, so did the heroes of local history. State historians, who before 1815 attempted to keep in public memory regional pride and a sense of place, found much of their work passed over in the assembly of national annals and feared that loss of concern for states' rights might follow lack of concern for separate identity.

[27] Charles J. Peterson, *The Military Heroes of the War of 1812, with a Narrative of the War* (Philadelphia, 1848); Peterson, *Military Heroes of the War with Mexico* (Philadelphia, 1848); Robert Sears, *The Pictorial History of the American Revolution* (New York, 1846), pp. 159, 167.

[28] Joel Tyler Headley, *Washington and His Generals* (New York, 1847); Henry B. Dawson, *The Battles of the United States on Land and Sea* (New York, 1859); Sears, *Pictorial History*.

[29] Lossing, "Arlington House," *Harper's*, VII (September, 1853), 434.

10 HISTORICAL SOCIETIES: BASTIONS OF LOCALISM
1815-60

Local historians in the first quarter of the nineteenth century, no less patriotic than textbook writers and popularizers, displayed the same pride of country and the same belief in the boundless future of the United States. As yet, no real conflict existed between love of one's town and state and love of one's country. The nationalism that inspired the author of "The Star-Spangled Banner," and an overwhelming number of Fourth of July orators before the Civil War, made few demands on local loyalty. A choice between home-ties and duty to the nation-state would not be forced until the Civil War made the choice an issue. Meanwhile, what local historians sought and failed to find in histories of the United States was a just share of national glory. Schools and publishers were joined to promote a national history; interested folk of state, town, and county gathered to organize historical societies or worked alone to preserve, protect, and disseminate their local heritage.

Historical societies supplied the meeting place for local historians who shared a wish to commemorate the honor and glory of the past. At times they argued the relative worth and importance to the history of the state of their various communities or counties, as when, in 1794, a historian of Duxborough, Massachusetts, attempted to establish priority of settlement over neighboring Scituate, although Duxborough received its charter "eight months after Scituate." And, indeed, such community pride led to the founding of county and town historical societies. It was the duty of a town society, the president of one society declared, to "preserve the good name of [their] forefathers" and to protect the reputation of the town's founders "from all injurious representations . . . with the broad shield of truth."[1]

Historical societies rose in rapid succession all over the country. Massachusetts, New York, and Pennsylvania, the foremost contenders for first place among the states in trade, literature, education, and a leading role in the annals of America's past, pointed the way for other states no less anxious for the future of their reputations.[2] In New England, historical societies in Maine, Rhode Island, Connecticut, New Hampshire, and Vermont challenged the position of the Massachusetts Historical Society as guardian of all New England history. The Maine Historical Society, founded in 1820, the first year of Maine's statehood, led the way in objecting to the dominion of the Massachusetts society over New England's past. The new organization asserted its prerogative to cherish Maine's past by republishing the "Brief Narration of Sir

[1] "A Topographical Description of Duxborough, in the County of Plymouth," *Massachusetts Historical Society, Collections,* II (Boston, 1794), 8; *Proceedings of the Essex Institute,* I (Salem, Mass., 1856), 256.

[2] For a general account of American historical societies see Leslie W. Dunlap, *American Historical Societies, 1790–1860* (Madison, Wis.: Cantwell Printing Co., 1944).

Ferdinando Gorges" and the "Voyage" of Christopher Levett, which the Massachusetts society had published in its Collections. It was deemed "peculiarly proper that a narrative written by the founder of . . . [their] state . . . should be preserved in the transactions of a society which professed to search out and perpetuate the early attempts to colonize and cultivate . . . [their] soil."³

In 1823, some young New Hampshire men thought it "expedient" to form a historical society in their state. The occasion was the two hundredth anniversary of the settlement in New Hampshire. There were no famous names among the founders of the society, but the support of older, more prominent men in the state was solicited. The corresponding secretary, *pro tem.*, wrote to the former governor William Plumer, who, since announcing in 1807 his intention to write a history of the United States, had been engaged in collecting Americana, that the society's "usefulness and respectability" depended upon men like the governor. Another member of the society wrote proudly to Plumer, "though we may not be able to vie with our neighbors in magnificency, we *may* emulate their usefulness, and preserve *among ourselves* the Memorials and relics of the past. . . ." In the first volume of its Collections, the society laid firm claim to Jeremy Belknap, the founder of the Massachusetts Historical Society and historian of New Hampshire, by publishing part of his correspondence with Governor John Wentworth concerning the colonial history of the state.⁴

In the years before 1825 and 1830, historical societies sprang up in the territories as in the older states. Tennessee, Ohio, Illinois, Indiana, and Michigan proclaimed the frontiers tamed and advertised the foundation of that epitome of culture, the historical society. No monuments, no broken arches, "no place is found," an orator proudly assured members of the Michigan Historical Society, "in all our borders where the traveller can meditate upon the instability of human power, amid the evidence of its existence and decay . . . our country is yet fresh and green." Yet historians had the wreck of Indian civilization to ponder, an opportunity of which they took full advantage. They produced myriads of learned articles on Indian mounds, Indian languages, and Indian manners, with the ultimate question always in mind: "Who first peopled America?" The societies encouraged the preservation of the memoirs of first settlers and "pioneer reminiscences."⁵

In their first years almost all of the frontier historical societies suffered from a lack of popular support; neither their production nor their membership was large. But more important than their efforts was the fact of their existence. Like the schools, churches, and branches of the Masonic lodge, historical societies

³ Maine Historical Society, *Collections*, II (Portland, 1847), Preface.

⁴ "Sketch of the Formation of the New Hampshire Historical Society," New Hampshire Historical Society, *Collections*, I (Concord, 1824); John Kelly to William Plumer, 1824, in Plumer Papers, Library of Congress.

⁵ Lewis Cass, "Discourse," *Historical and Scientific Sketches of Michigan* (Detroit, 1834), pp. 5–6.

served as evidence to their own citizens as well as to prospective residents that "civilization" had reached Ohio, Illinois, and Michigan. The establishment of historical societies in the western territories was part of an unconscious effort to achieve cultural equality with the older states commensurate with the political equality assured them in the Constitution. The desire to take pride in its history stimulated the urge to write a definitive account, and the frontier historical society unanimously expressed as an eventual goal the writing of the history of its state.[6]

In the thirties, the southern states, led by Virginia, suddenly entered the lists with the establishment of five new historical societies. Southern intellectuals had flayed the South for its careless disregard for the records of the past and excused the South because its sons had been too busy making history to gather or to write it. A book agent predicted in 1826 that "there will be no such thing as bookmaking in Virginia for a century to come. People here prefer talking to reading."[7] In spite of general indifference to native literary and intellectual efforts, a small group of men organized societies in most of the southern states before the Civil War.[8]

The Virginia Historical and Philosophical Society began in 1831 with the election of Chief Justice John Marshall as its president. St. George Tucker, the eminent jurist who prepared an annotated edition of *Blackstone's Commentaries*, said that the purpose of the organization was "to pluck up drowning honor by the locks, without other regard than the participation with our great co-rivals [Massachusetts and Pennsylvania] in all the dignities of science."[9]

North Carolina followed hard on the heels of Virginia with a historical society founded by Governor David L. Swain. The son of a Massachusetts migrant, Swain had become a patriotic North Carolinian interested in raising his state by its cultural bootstraps and established the state's first historical society, chartered while he was governor in 1833. Interest lagged, but, undaunted, Swain, as president of the state university, founded in 1844 the Historical Society of the University of North Carolina, which lived as long as he did.[10]

Judge Henry Adams Bullard, with James D. B. DeBow, the publisher-editor of *DeBow's Review*, promoters of the Port of New Orleans and the South,

[6] For a more extended discussion of the use of cultural institutions to promote settlement in a territory see David D. Van Tassel, "William Rudolph Smith; A Cultural Capitalist," *Wisconsin Magazine of History*, XXXVI (Summer, 1953), 241–44, 276–80.

[7] Jared Sparks, "Journal of a Southern Tour," entry for March 29, 1826, in Herbert Baxter Adams, *Life and Writings of Jared Sparks* (Boston, 1893), I, 417.

[8] A valuable survey of southern historical activity is E. Merton Coulter, "What the South Has Done about Its History," *Journal of Southern History*, II (February, 1936), 3–28.

[9] St. George Tucker, "Address to the Virginia Historical Society," *Southern Literary Messenger*, I (1836), 259; Virginia Historical and Philosophical Society, *Collections*, I (Richmond, 1833), 12.

[10] J. G. de Roulhac Hamilton, "The Preservation of North Carolina History," *North Carolina Historical Review*, IV (January, 1927), 6–7; *First Report of the Historical Society of the University of North Carolina, June 4, 1845* (Hillsborough, N.C., 1845), p. 3.

helped to found the Louisiana Historical Society in 1835 and to rejuvenate it eleven years later.[11] In Arkansas, in 1837, Edward Cross, a citizen of Little Rock and a member of the state legislature, sponsored the charter of the Antiquarian and Natural History Society of the State of Arkansas.[12] In 1838, Taliaferro P. Shaffner, a Louisville lawyer, helped to found Kentucky's historical society. The young lawyer offered his services as corresponding secretary and space in his office in which to stack the books and manuscripts of its growing library. Not long after, Shaffner asserted, perhaps ruefully, "I have been the society now for several years."[13] In 1839, the state of Georgia announced a historical society founded in Savannah by a "Boston boy" and famed collector of autographs, I. K. Tefft, and by Dr. William Bacon Stevens, later commissioned by the society to write "a complete history of Georgia."[14]

During the two decades before the war the story was repeated in five other southern states. A few men, active in promoting the future of their state, were interested in establishing its prestige in the Union and its unqualified respectability.[15] A historical society was one such agency for "internal improvement." In 1842, James G. M. Ramsey, an East Tennessee doctor and banker engaged in promoting a railroad to connect Knoxville with Charleston, noted that he had come upon still "further Tennessee-material moral and intellectual."[16] Among Ramsey's agencies for the promotion of the welfare of Knoxville and vicinity was the East Tennessee Historical and Antiquarian Society which he had helped to organize during the city's semicentennial celebrations. In 1849, Nashville, in competition with Knoxville, founded the Tennessee Historical Society, which failed to survive.[17]

By 1860, Alabama, South Carolina, Florida, and Mississippi had established historical societies, but most of these societies, like that at Nashville, "had a hasty accouchement, breathed once after it got into its nurse's lap, gave a convulsive gasp to let its aunts and its cousins know that it had vitality enough to squeal, gave a wild stare upon its seniors, and suddenly swooned away."[18]

[11] J. D. B. DeBow, "An Account of the Louisiana Historical Society," B. F. French (ed.), *Historical Collections of Louisiana* (Philadelphia, 1850), II, 3–8.

[12] Myra Vaughan, "The First Historical Society of Arkansas," Arkansas Historical Association, *Publications*, II (Fayetteville, 1908), 346–55.

[13] Shaffner to Lyman C. Draper, February 20, 1847, in William F. Hesseltine, *Pioneer's Mission: The Story of Lyman Copeland Draper* (Madison, Wis.: State Historical Society of Wisconsin, 1954), p. 68; Edward Jarvis, "Some Account of the Kentucky Historical Society," *American Quarterly Register*, XV (August, 1842), 77.

[14] William Harden, "The Georgia Historical Society," *Georgia Historical Quarterly*, I (March, 1917), 3–12; "I. K. Tefft," *Virginia Historical Register*, II (1849), 176.

[15] Archibald D. Murphey to General Joseph Graham, July 20, 1821, in William Henry Hoyt (ed.), *The Papers of Archibald D. Murphey* (Raleigh, N.C.: North Carolina Historical Society, 1914), I, 211.

[16] J. G. M. Ramsey, *Dr. J. G. M. Ramsey, Autobiography and Letters*, ed. William B. Hesseltine (Nashville: Tennessee Historical Society, 1954), p. 46.

[17] *Ibid.*, p. 50; Dunlap, *Historical Societies*, pp. 209–11.

[18] Ramsey, *op. cit.*, p. 63.

The dissolution of historical societies was common in the South and the West, though the causes differed. Both regions were sparsely populated, and their towns were often no more than crossroads or river confluences and market places. There were few citizens with either the time or the inclination for activities that did not directly relate to the material prosperity of the town and the family business or farm. In the South, the men most likely to support the activities of historical societies were unable to contribute more than their time and access to their private libraries; they had no capital with which to endow the struggling societies. Long before his death, Thomas Jefferson sold his library to Congress to pay his debts. Governor David L. Swain, the mainstay of the Historical Society of the University of North Carolina, bequeathed nothing to the organization; his widow sold a large part of his library, which contained most of the society's collection.[19] In the same period, historical societies in the North were beginning to build endowments by tapping their "many capitalists."[20]

Western historical societies were beset by all the problems faced by the societies in the South as well as the problem of a transient population. In a single decade between 1830 and 1850, many western towns had a complete change of population. Such conditions did not lend themselves to the long life of cultural organizations.[21]

One solution to the problem was to gain the support of a relatively stable public or private institution; alone with any promise of permanency in the volatile West was the government of each state. Many societies, including that of Massachusetts, had obtained state aid on occasion, but none expected or required continuing government support. Wisconsin, with the smile of fortune, and the rigorous politicking of Lyman C. Draper, led the way. A society had been organized in 1846, but it soon dissolved. It was reorganized in 1849 and again failed to receive support, but struggled on until 1854, when Lyman C. Draper, a native of western New York and a long-time collector of material on western pioneers and the border wars, moved to Wisconsin on the promise of a job as secretary of the historical society. Upon arrival he found that the job paid no salary and the society was all but disbanded. With the help of a college friend, Judge Charles Larrabee, who had called him to Wisconsin, and Gov-

[19] Many valuable historical collections were sold after the Civil War. Southern material went North and West because the South lacked funds to keep it. For instance, Robert A. Brock, long-time secretary of the Virginia Historical Society, built a large collection of southern Americana which was sold after his death. It is now in the Henry Huntington Library in San Marino, California.

[20] We [the Pennsylvania Historical Society] are now going on swimmingly. Our rich members contribute to the expense of our Publications—But we have numerous Capitalists, and you have but few." Peter S. DuPonceau to Peter Force, March 7, 1837, Force Papers, Library of Congress.

[21] An extended account of the development of learned societies in Kansas is James Malin's "Notes on the Writing of General Histories of Kansas," *Kansas Historical Quarterly*, XXI (Autumn, 1954), 184–223; (Winter, 1954), 264–87; (Spring, 1955), 331–78; (Summer, 1955), 407–44; (Winter, 1955), 598–643.

ernor Leonard J. Farwell, Draper obtained a new charter and an appropriation from the legislature to cover his salary and to allow for a book purchasing fund. Thereafter, by electing honorary and corresponding members from all over the United States, by soliciting the contribution of volumes on science, agriculture, and geography for the library, and by trading the society's publications and state-printed documents, he demonstrated how a historical society could serve its home state. The Wisconsin Historical Society became, as many similar organizations hoped to become, a means of advertising the state and its potentialities.[22]

The founding of historical societies seemed to have grown to be a national pastime by 1860. In the decades between 1790 and 1820, only four historical societies were established; in the decade between 1820 and 1830, ten societies were founded; between 1830 and 1840, twelve societies were announced; and in the period 1840 to 1860 forty historical societies were organized. A young lawyer, George Templeton Strong, viewing the rapid multiplication of societies dedicated to Clio, the Muse of history, and the sudden, popular devotion she occasioned, said the phenomenon proved that Americans craved "a history, instinctively"; they had "no *record* of Americanism" and felt its lack.[23] There was a parallel development of an ardent nationalism as the government of the United States shook its fist at France, Mexico, and England and declared manifest its destiny to rule from ocean to ocean.

The announced objectives of historical societies suggest the concept of history "craved" by Americans of the early nineteenth century. Although these societies were bastions of localism, they shared a cultural tradition. Almost all expressed a desire to collect government documents and manuscripts, church and school records, town and county records, Indian treaties, and "antiquities, geological and mineralogical specimens, geographical maps and information." They proposed, in short, "to gather every fact that [would] illustrate the manner of life, the style of living, the habits of thought, the motives of action—of every kind and class of people" in the state to which they devoted their attention. The whole range of human knowledge and endeavor, reflecting the eighteenth-century idea of a learned society, first represented in the United States by Benjamin Franklin's American Philosophical Society, was to be their field of inquiry. The Massachusetts Historical Society proposed only a slight shift

---

[22] Wisconsin, like most of the western states, had a history of exploration, Indian trade, wars, and settlement that long predated statehood, but could claim little or no share in the great national moments of the Federal Union. As if to compensate for this lack, establish the individuality of the states, and make explicit unique features acquired by the Union when these regions became states, local historical and pioneer societies concentrated, almost to the neglect of all else, on the "golden age" of the pioneer period and territorial days. Thus most western historical societies are strong in materials on early periods, weak on more recent records as states. Hesseltine, *Pioneer's Mission*, pp. 121–43; Van Tassel, "William Rudolph Smith," p. 278.

[23] For historical societies established between 1792 and 1860 see Appendix; G. T. Strong, *Diary*, ed. Allan Nevins and M. H. Thomas (New York: Macmillan Co., 1952), II, 196–97.

away from the aims of Franklin's society, which sought to further all human knowledge; Belknap's organization would collect and preserve such evidence as served to advance understanding of Massachusetts and the United States. Most of the historical societies which followed took the Massachusetts society as a model; the Pennsylvania Historical Society itself at one time had been a part of the American Philosophical Society; and some organizations made their objectives explicit by calling themselves historical and philosophical societies.[24]

Somewhat later, data pertaining to anthropology, archeology, geography, and economics—the bulk of the material contained in the publications and collections of the state societies, and especially of the western states—would be classified in fields of specialization outside the immediate jurisdiction of history, but meanwhile a comprehensive view of pertinent records was peculiarly suited to the needs of the states, cities, towns, and counties, permitting, under the guise of scholarly respectability, the gathering and dissemination of the very facts about climate, geography, mineral resources, agriculture, schools, and churches most likely to attract settlers and new capital. Lyman C. Draper, in a preface to one of the volumes of the Wisconsin Collections, wrote that it was intended to show "the wonderful advance the great North-West in general, and Wisconsin in particular, are making in all the elements of greatness and prosperity."[25] The volume contained sketches of towns, a description of two rivers, and a pride-filled account of the number of libraries then in the state.[26]

Many of the state historical societies made a humble and patriotic proposal to help in gathering and publishing material which would form the basis for a comprehensive history of the United States. But, far from co-operating to assemble the materials for such an undertaking, they were soon competing for the glory of building that foundation from materials in the archives of their own state.[27]

One way in which historical societies measured their success was to point not to the quality but to the quantity of documents they had put into print. The Massachusetts Historical Society continually assessed its contribution by counting the number of volumes of Collections produced. Other societies seem to have accepted the standard set by Massachusetts; they urged their members to make frequent contributions, however small or trivial. A single document or

[24] See chap. vi.

[25] Wisconsin Historical Society, *Collections*, III (Madison, 1857), Preface; Hesseltine, *op. cit.*, pp. 149-51.

[26] Hesseltine, "Lyman Copeland Draper, 1815-91," *Wisconsin Magazine of History* XXXV (Spring, 1952), 163-76.

[27] Ebenezer Hazard, *Historical Collections*, I (Philadelphia, 1792), Preface (2d pub.; 1794); "Circular Letter of the Historical Society," Massachusetts Historical Society, *Collections*, II (Boston, 1793), 1-2. These local societies, as a general rule, were not interested in national history. Although the Massachusetts Historical Society did profess such an interest, in 1839 it rejected a proposition to support a history of the United States. See Increase Tarbox (ed.), *Diary of Reverend Thomas Robbins* (Boston, 1886-87); Massachusetts Historical Society, *Proceedings*, II (Boston, 1880), 132-34.

manuscript might appear insignificant, but in the aggregate they formed the stuff from which history was distilled.²⁸

There was little organization of these collections of documents; indeed, in many volumes the number of speeches and addresses rivaled the number of documents and manuscripts reprinted. Nonetheless, the societies based claim to recognition upon collections of this type. Sometimes a society made an effort to organize its material in some meaningful form. In 1809, the bicentennial of Henry Hudson's sail up the river to the site of Albany, the New-York Historical Society issued a volume of Collections centered upon Hudson's journal of the voyage. The Pennsylvania Society issued a similar volume in celebration of William Penn. But these were the exceptions. As one of the editors of the New-York Historical Society wrote, and as illustrated by other volumes of collections, the organization of documents in chronological order or upon a specific subject was not considered essential "or even important in a compilation professing to furnish *materials* for historical composition. . . ."²⁹

In spite of the mixed motives for establishing historical societies and the conglomerate nature of their publications, these organizations did much to further the development of historical studies in the United States. Their comprehensive view of history, a legacy of the eighteenth century, helped to make manifest the democratic history demanded by many contemporaries—the story of the common people. Details of everyday life, the private papers of countless citizens, the accounts of businessmen, lawyers, and pioneer settlers, resulted in the growth of a healthy skepticism toward the accurateness and validity of "official history" contained in government documents and publications and the works produced by "official historians" and the writers of textbooks. Out of the haphazard materials gathered by state historical societies would come Justin Winsor's monument to critical scholarship, John B. McMasters' social history of the American people, innumerable monographs on American institutions, and the hypothesis proposed by Frederick Jackson Turner concerning the significance of the frontier in the development of the nation.³⁰

²⁸ For examples of the measuring of accomplishment by quantity of publication see Jonathan P. Cushing, "First Annual Address to the Virginia Historical Society," Virginia Historical and Philosophical Society, *Collections*, I (Richmond, 1833), 12. Peter DuPonceau to Peter Force, March 7, 1837, speaks of the Pennsylvania Historical Society as having "produced only six half volumes" in twelve years. Force Papers, Library of Congress. *Southern Literary Messenger*, I (February, 1835), 259. The practice of actively urging members to participate in building a society's collections seems to have been primarily a nineteenth-century phenomenon. Most modern societies, perhaps for lack of space, wait for the occasional donation. A few societies have energetic collectors on the staff or hire field workers, but all could benefit from the early practice of enlisting the aid of members as an obligation of membership. A recent survey and analysis of the development and present activities of historical agencies, based in part on replies to an extensive questionnaire, is David D. Van Tassel and James A. Tinsley, "Historical Organizations as Aids to History," *In Support of Clio; Essays in Memory of Herbert A. Kellar*, ed. William B. Hesseltine and Donald R. McNeil (Madison, Wis.: State Historical Society of Wisconsin, 1958), pp. 127–52.

²⁹ New-York Historical Society, *Collections*, II (New York, 1814), Preface; Pennsylvania Historical Society, *Memoirs*, I (Philadelphia, 1826), *passim*; New-York Historical Society, *Collections*, I (New York, 1811), vi.

³⁰ Hesseltine, "Draper," shows Turner's specific debt to Draper.

11 DOCUMANIA: A NATIONAL OBSESSION, LOCALLY INSPIRED, 1815–50

The central activity of American historical societies was the collection, preservation, and publication of "materials for history." To historians of the eighteenth and early nineteenth century, these materials were solely government documents, treaties, laws, legislative journals, and official correspondence. There were sources in plenty for the period after 1776, but those states whose histories extended from colonial times were less well documented. When historians sought to tell the history of the first colonies in the long struggle for liberty, they discovered that the most revealing sources were in England, France, and Spain.

In the twenties, local historians and historical societies, continuing their ceaseless effort to collect documents that would complete the record of the past and restore "history to its truth," stung national pride with the revelation that England and other nations controlled many manuscripts and records pertinent to American colonial history. Local efforts to obtain source materials stimulated national efforts to collect, publish, and distribute government documents. The value placed on manuscripts and documents encouraged autograph-collecting and an interest in genealogy in the thirties and forties, which further stimulated the publication of documents. What began as an urge to collect local memorabilia became a national obsession—documania.

Following the Peace of Ghent, the free-for-all among the states for economic superiority animated the scramble for documents. North Carolina was a case in point. Many states were seeking federal aid for internal improvements, as was North Carolina. New York had begun construction of the Erie Canal; Pennsylvania was working out its transportation system; and by the end of the decade Massachusetts was dreaming of a Boston-to-Albany railroad. Archibald DeBow Murphey was North Carolina's champion of internal improvements. Murphey resembled DeWitt Clinton of New York, who promoted his state in every way he could. Like Clinton, Murphey combined the roles of politician, advocate of internal improvements, and historian in order to advance the prosperity and prestige of his state. In 1820, Murphey proposed a vast canal system for North Carolina. Federal funds would be needed, and thus far North Carolina had received little federal bounty, merely "two miserable lighthouses." Murphey declared, "We have been considered the outcasts of the Union, whose virtues and intelligence gave claim to the high honors of the Government. . . ." He berated his fellow citizens by claiming that this condition was due to the "supineness and apathy of the state in its want of pride and character."¹

Murphey, the North Carolina promotor, had an answer to local indifference. He proposed a history of North Carolina, a work which, if well executed, would "add very much to our standing in the Union, and make our state respectable in our own eyes." Character was as important to a state as it was to an individual, but no state established a character until its history was written and its people recognized the truth of the portrait. "To visit a people who have no history," Murphey claimed, "is like going into a wilderness where there are no roads to direct a traveller. The people have nothing to which they can look back; the wisdom and acts of their forefathers are forgotten; the experience of one generation is lost to the succeeding one; and the consequence is, that people have little attachment to their state, their policy has no system, and their legislature no decided character."²

Murphey set about with diligence to remedy this fatal lack. He wrote prominent men, urging them to search out documents and manuscripts. He sent out questionnaires to those who had played significant roles in the state's history and asked for their memoirs. The accumulation amassed was far beyond his expectation and the expense of handling it was far beyond his pocketbook. From the state legislature he obtained an agreement to finance a part of the project. In 1826, Edward Everett, the congressman from Massachusetts and chairman of the House library committee, suggested that Murphey might find material relating to North Carolina in the Plantation Office in London. Murphey thanked his illustrious correspondent; he had already obtained a list of materials in London and hoped to receive from the North Carolina legislature the funds to have the documents transcribed. But Murphey's history of North Carolina was never written; he became far too involved in gathering materials. His collection of documents eventually became the foundation of the library of the North Carolina Historical Society.³

In 1826, the raid upon foreign archives began. The year 1826 was the semicentennial of the proclamation of the Declaration of Independence (and the year in which Thomas Jefferson and John Adams died). John Pintard of New York was collecting material for a chronology of 1776, "to revive attention to the events of that disastrous year and therebye call up if possible the gratitude our country owes to the soldiers of the Revolution."⁴ (Congress was wrangling

---

¹ "The New York Canals," *North American Review*, XIV (January, 1822), 230–51; Archibald D. Murphey to General Joseph Graham, July 20, 1821, Hoyt (ed.), *Papers of Murphey*, I, 211; II, 176.

² *Ibid.*, II, 207.

³ Herbert B. Adams, *The Life and Writings of Jared Sparks*, I, 242, 444; Edward Everett to Archibald D. Murphey, December 4, 1826, Hoyt (ed.), *Papers of Murphey*, I, 346.

⁴ John Pintard to Eliza Noel Pintard Davidson, August 14, 1826, Dorothy C. Barck (ed.), *Letters from John Pintard to His Daughter Eliza Noel Pintard Davidson, 1816–1833* (4 vols.; New York: New-York Historical Society, 1937–40), II, 292.

over the question of whether pensions should be paid to the survivors of the war.)

American historians, who bore witness to and supported the spirit of nationalism which, since 1815, had been growing in the United States, were aware that a similar spirit had swept over England, France, and Prussia. England had organized a record commission in 1800 to systematize public documents, and by the 1820's the commission had begun to publish some of the older material. A French commission, under Napoleon, made a long report on what realms of European history had been explored and what they proposed be next, a report that was thoroughly reviewed in the *American Monthly Register*. After Napoleon's downfall, the French historians founded a new historical society and corresponded with the secretaries of American historical societies. In 1821, Heinrich Friedrich Karl, Baron vom und zum Stein sponsored a new historical society to interest his countrymen in their past, and in 1823 he appointed Georg Pertz, the historian, to edit documents relating to the Carolingian period. In 1826, Pertz published the first volume of *Monumenta Germaniae historica*, which immediately became a model for published source material.[5]

International competition in the preservation and publication of documents, competition between the states in the publication of historical source material, and a growing interest in works concerning state and local history brought to the fore the problem of procuring and publishing materials for a history of the United States.

An unusual request made by Joseph Y. Bevan, historiographer of the state of Georgia, attracted public attention to the difficulties faced by American historians.[6] In 1824, Bevan obtained an appointment "to collate, arrange and publish all papers relating to the original settlement or political history of Georgia." Bevan was not long at his researches before he discovered large gaps in the early state records; they could be filled only by reference to the files of the Board of Trade and Plantations in London. Bevan wrote to his good friend, Colonel George Tattenal, a Georgia congressman, asking if the government could help him to obtain information about material in the State Paper Office in London relating to the history of Georgia. Congressman Tattenal passed on the request to the Secretary of State, John Quincy Adams, who set diplomatic machinery in motion. (At this time the administration was paying

---

[5] Nicholas Harris Nicolas, *Observations on the State of Historical Literature* (London, 1830), p. 189; *Literary Magazine and American Register*, I (October, 1803), 1–21.

[6] Jared Sparks, "Materials for American History," *North American Review*, XXIII (October, 1826), 276. Jefferson, who was sifting and arranging his correspondence, continued to urge the collection of documents. In 1823 he said, "It is the duty of every good citizen to use all the opportunities which occur to him, for preserving documents relating to the history of our country." Jefferson to Hugh P. Taylor, October 4, 1823, Liscomb and Bergh (eds.), *Writings of Jefferson*, XV, 473; "Von Ranke's Princes and Nations," *North American Review*, XXXI (October, 1830), 291–308. Judge Law, in an address before the Georgia Historical Society, expressed jealousy of other nations, especially England, which published documents relating to American history. Georgia Historical Society, *Collections*, I (Savannah, 1840), 6.

unusually close attention to the wishes of Georgia's representatives to avoid the precipitation of a crisis, for Georgia was threatening to take matters into its own hands if the federal government did not remove the Creek Indians from rich cotton lands within the state.) Bevan's request reached Richard Rush, United States minister to the Court of St. James, without delay.

George Canning, the British Foreign Secretary, was no friend of the United States, but he had recently attempted an Anglo-American alliance. Although balked by the announcement of the Monroe Doctrine in 1823, Canning continued overtures of friendship in an effort to prevent the United States from taking possession of Cuba. In 1825, as one more indication of England's cordiality, Canning forwarded a complete list of the correspondence and other papers relating to Georgia to be found in His Majesty's State Paper Office and gave permission for any "respectable person" designated by Rush to transcribe the material. Rush notified the new Secretary of State, Henry Clay, who passed on the information to Colonel Tattenal.

Bevan was not able to take advantage of the offer at once. He had acted on his own initiative in making the original request and had neither the money nor the authority to have the records copied. The following year when the legislature convened, approval was granted for the project. Governor George M. Troup sent a special message requesting that Bevan be appointed Georgia's agent to transcribe the British documents.[7]

Meanwhile, "the subject [had] excited considerable interest in different parts of the country." Legislators and governors, who had spent long hours planning commemorative celebrations and composing semicentennial orations, were prepared to support measures for the preservation of state and national historical material. DeWitt Clinton, the governor of New York, in his annual message to the state legislature in 1826, urged that provisions be made to obtain from British archives copies of documents relating to American history. Jared Sparks, the editor and publisher of the *North American Review*, after a trip through the South to examine state archives, announced to his readers that nothing approaching a complete history of America would be written until the documents pertaining to American colonies were exhumed from their sepulchers in the various departmental archives in London.[8]

In the same year, Congress showed signs of interest in procuring materials concerning American history. During the summer of 1826, most of the members of the Thirteenth Congress had been busy delivering anniversary orations. Among them was Edward Everett, the representative from Massachusetts,

---

[7] "Report of the House Committee on the Library," February 24, 1827, *Report 91*, 19th Congress, 2d session, Part I; George M. Troup, "Address to Georgia Legislature, November 2, 1824," *Journal of the House of Representatives of the State of Georgia for the year 1824* (Milledgeville, Ga., 1825), p. 24.

[8] Joseph Y. Bevan's statement to the governor of Georgia on his progress as state historiographer, in a letter by George M. Troup to the Georgia Senate, November 13, 1826, *Journal of the Senate of the State of Georgia for the year 1826* (Milledgeville, Ga., 1827), pp. 45–46.

who returned to Congress fired with patriotic zeal. In his capacity as chairman of the House Committee on the Congressional Library, Everett asked that England's apparently generous offer be considered; Congress itself might appropriate funds for the transcription of all material relating to the colonial history of America. Privately, Everett asked the opinion of Abiel Holmes, author of *American Annals*, corresponding secretary of the American Antiquarian Society, and a member of the Massachusetts Historical Society. He received a long reply from Holmes, a memorial from the Massachusetts Historical Society, and favorable resolutions from the American Antiquarian Society and the Rhode Island legislature. All urged Congress to adopt measures to have the documents copied. Everett's committee offered such a resolution, only to have it tabled by the House.[9]

The headlong rush to British archives, a fresh source of documents, had been initiated by the state of Georgia and Everett's congressional committee. Now began the unending pilgrimage of American scholars to British museums, libraries, and universities. Both North Carolina and South Carolina appointed agents to transcribe records relative to their history; the South Carolina agent, Henry Granger, stayed in London for three years. Jared Sparks spent five months in London in 1830 studying manuscripts in British archives. By the mid-thirties, George Bancroft, the historian, had copyists at work in the State Paper Office. In 1838, William Stone, owner of the *New York Commercial Advertiser* and author of several biographies of Iroquois chiefs as well as *Border Wars of the Revolution*, organized the New York Historical Agency which sent abroad John Romeyn Brodhead, the historian, to transcribe colonial documents in foreign archives. The state of Georgia fell behind with the death of Bevan, the historiographer, but in 1837 the governor appointed a new agent, a minister, Charles W. Howard, who after two years in London brought back twenty-two folio volumes of transcripts. These closely written volumes became the nucleus of the library of the Georgia Historical Society.[10]

While local groups were making their forays upon European archives, printers in Washington, D.C., planned a great national project for which they asked the support of Congress. Since 1822, when young Hezekiah Niles published a compilation of documents, *Principles and Acts of the Revolution in America*, Peter Force, a Washington printer, had been collecting material for a similar volume. Force enlarged his plans after the appearance of the House library committee report in 1827. He knew that Joseph Gales and William W. Seaton, his competitors and publishers of the *Register of Debates in Congress*, had obtained a contract from Congress to print a compilation of *American State Papers*. Force, encouraged by the success of others, made a determined effort to gain federal support for his project. He formed a partnership with Matthew

---

[9] "Report of the House Committee on the Library," p. 6; Jared Sparks to Henry W. Dwight, January 5, 1829, Sparks Papers, Harvard Library.

[10] Alexander C. Flick, "William Leete Stone," *DAB*, XVIII, 90–91; Georgia Historical Society, *Collections*, I (Savannah, 1840), viii.

St. Clair Clarke, clerk of the House of Representatives, and prepared a memorial to Congress, asking that he be named to print all material relative to the American Revolution, from 1763 to its conclusion, and to the establishment of the Constitution in 1789, including pertinent papers in state and foreign archives.[11]

Others had asked for a similar contract, but Force had a great deal to offer. By 1831 when he sent his memorial to Congress, he had been collecting material for nine years; the year before he had dropped all other work in order to devote full time to the project, gambling everything upon the willingness of Congress to support his plan. Jared Sparks was one of those who asked for the same commission. Gulian C. Verplanck, chairman of the House library committee, received a number of offers. Sparks said he was prepared to assume the task as soon as he had finished editing the *Diplomatic Correspondence of the Revolution*.

Force, an astute lobbyist, scheduled his memorial to Congress shortly after the appearance of the 1831 edition of the *National Calendar*, a compilation of miscellaneous information and important events of the year, of which he was editor. Force included in the volume a prospectus of his work and as many documents as he could find on the Stamp Act Congress of 1765 to illustrate how little was known of so important an event. Force was granted the contract and over a period of twenty years published nine heavy volumes of *American Archives*.

It was Franklin Pearce's Secretary of State, William L. Marcy, who called a halt to what had become a major drain on the national treasury.[12] In the years that Peter Force pursued this major project, document collections became increasingly popular. John Warner Barber sold ten thousand copies of *Historical Collections of New York*, an imposing sale at a time when the average edition printed by such successful publishers as Ticknor and Fields was between one and two thousand copies.

---

[11] Signs of early interest in collecting documents for the history of the United States may be seen in the letter from Benjamin Elliott to Hezekiah Niles, November 23, 1816, which inspired Niles to publish his *Principles and Acts of the Revolution in America* (Baltimore, 1822). Elliott wrote, "The present is a most propitious period. The feelings and sentiments of '76 were never so prevalent as at present." In Niles, *Principles*, Preface. Matthew St. Clair Clarke to Edward Everett, January 26, 1832; Peter Force to Clarke, February 1, 1832, in Force Papers, Library of Congress. Force, *Report made to the Hon. John Forsyth, Secretary of State of the U.S. on the subject of the Documentary History of the U.S. now publishing under an Act of Congress by M. St. Clair Clarke, and Peter Force* (Washington, D.C., 1834), p. 8.

[12] Sparks to Gulian C. Verplanck, December 23, 1831. Sparks offered to buy Force's contract with the government in 1833. Sparks to Force, December 10, 1833; Force to Verplanck, November 12, 1831; all in Force Papers. For more biographical material on Force see Frederick R. Goff, "Peter Force," Bibliographical Society of America, *Papers*, XLIV (1st Quarter, 1950), 1–16; Ainsworth R. Spofford, "The Life and Labors of Peter Force, Mayor of Washington," Columbia Historical Society, *Records*, II (Washington, D.C., 1899), 219–35; Bassett, *The Middle Group of American Historians*, pp. 233–302; Newman F. McGirr, "The Activities of Peter Force," Columbia Historical Society, *Records*, XLII (Washington, D.C., 1942), 35–82.

A phenomenon new to republican America developed in the twenties and thirties and added to the popularity of published documents; a rapidly growing number of people in the old towns along the Atlantic sea coast devoted considerable time to the cult of genealogy. Members of the declining merchant class, who had long held unchallenged status, began an avid search for ancestral roots. A new group, grown wealthy with the rise of manufacturing, made bids for political power and social status. One of the stratagems used by the old merchant class to maintain their social position was the establishment of a breastwork of long-dead ancestors to meet the challenging foe. This was the time when Judge John Lowell, whose family had made its money privateering during the American Revolution, traced his ancestry to discover a family coat of arms. When the researcher discovered a relatively valid escutcheon, the old judge had it painted on the sides of his carriage for all to see. In 1829, a New Hampshire printer, John Farmer, found that there had "begun a curiosity among many of the present generation to trace back their progenitors in an uninterrupted series to those who first landed on the bleak and unhospitable shore of New England."[13]

In the thirties and forties genealogy engaged the time and energies of New Englanders, who were reacting to the influx of Irish and German immigrants, a stimulus that at the same time encouraged other forms of "native American" exclusiveness. The genealogists sought public documents of all kinds, especially church records, ships' passenger lists, lists of town fathers, muster rolls, and other proofs of lineage and a place among the early settlers. For years the compilers of historical collections were alone among those who in any way met the needs of the seekers after ancestors. By 1845, the year in which the Native American party was formed, the study of family pedigrees had a sufficient number of devout adherents to support a journal dedicated to their needs —*The New England Historical and Genealogical Register.*[14]

John Warner Barber and Henry Howe achieved fame and fortune as the result of the demand for "documentary histories." In 1828, Barber, an engraver and printer of New Haven, Connecticut, published a small book of illustrated anecdotes called *Interesting Events in the History of the United States.* It went through several editions, and its success encouraged Barber to search for other historical subjects which he could treat in a like manner. He conceived the idea of writing a history of Connecticut.[15] Barber set out in his one-horse shay over the dirt roads of Connecticut to visit every town. He sought out local anti-

[13] Ferris Greenslet, *The Lowells and Their Seven Worlds* (Boston: Houghton Mifflin Co., 1946), p. 4; John Farmer, *A Genealogical Register of the First Settlers of New England* (Lancaster, Mass., 1829), Preface.

[14] For a history of the New England Historic Genealogical Society see William Carroll Hill, *A Century of Genealogical Progress* (Boston: The New England Historic Genealogical Society, 1945).

[15] For the influence of Pestalozzi see *American Journal of Education,* I (Hartford, Conn. 1826), 53 and *passim.* Barber, *Interesting Events.*

quarians and old people, collecting favorite local stories and traditions and interesting documents relating to the history of the area. Barber carried with him a sketchbook and brought back rude drawings from which wood cuts of historic spots could be made. After months of work, Barber produced an illustrated volume called *Historical Collections of Connecticut* in which he mentioned the names of the first settlers and founders and anecdotes about every town and hamlet in the state. The volume was extremely popular in Connecticut; Barber's future partner, Henry Howe, insisted that "never had any book been published on any state that so fed the fires of patriotism as did that [history] of the people of Connecticut."

Barber took in Howe as a partner in 1840, and the two began to produce similar collections for other states, with Howe traveling about to collect the necessary material. In a five-year period the team produced collections for New York, New Jersey, and Virginia. John C. Calhoun asked them to do a similar volume on South Carolina, but the partnership was dissolved in 1845 before work could begin on a new project. Alone, Howe produced a volume on Ohio which sold over eighteen thousand copies, a success that encouraged him to spend the rest of his life preparing similar historical compilations.[16]

By 1850 most of the states had some published collections of documents. Since 1828, Congress had furnished to historical societies and other depositories copies of federal statutes, congressional debates, and government publications. In 1852, Samuel Hazard, the son of Ebenezer Hazard, began to publish the *Pennsylvania Archives*. He announced that the project would be the Quaker State's major contribution to history. At the same time, New York, Massachusetts, New Jersey, Maryland, Virginia, and other members of the Union had begun the publication of their colonial and revolutionary histories. Many Americans believed, as did Thomas Jefferson, that it was a duty of citizenship to take every opportunity to preserve documents relating to the history of the United States. State documentary and manuscript sources were held essential to historical writing in nineteenth-century America, but surely the political structure of the United States, which led to competition between the states, did much to stimulate the preservation of the sources of our nation's history.

[16] Ralph C. Smith, "John Warner Barber," *DAB*, I, 589; Joseph P. Smith, "Henry Howe, the Historian," Ohio Archaeological and Historical Society, *Publications*, IV (Columbus, 1900), 312, 313, 317, 327. Howe and Barber dissolved their partnership in 1845 but continued to produce single books together, such as *Our Whole Country* (New Haven, 1860) and *The Loyal West* (New Haven, 1867). A recent account of the publication of documents and the development of public archives is G. Philip Bauer's "Public Archives in the United States," Hesseltine and McNeil (eds.), *In Support of Clio*, pp. 49–76.

12 RISE OF THE ROMANTIC NATIONALISTS, 1830-60

The patriotic clamor for a national literature, a national history, and a national character was satisfied in the 1830's by the glowing rhetoric of the romantic nationalists, cosmopolitan champions of the democratic faith. The works of Jared Sparks, Washington Irving, George Bancroft, William H. Prescott, John L. Motley, and Francis Parkman had their being in the historical ferment of the years following the Peace of Ghent. All were conscious of a mission to spread the light of the gospel of freedom and the hope of mankind to a benighted world. The message was embodied in the history of the United States, its rise and progress. Sparks and Irving told it in the form of carefully edited papers and artfully written biographies of American heroes. Bancroft expanded the theme of the chosen people, from the exclusive concept of the Puritans of New England, to include the whole country, wove it into the fabric of national history, and translated the democratic faith into the language of German romanticism. Prescott and Motley infused the American theme into European subjects. Parkman illustrated the superiority of the Anglo-Saxon race in the struggle for the "great American forest" and succeeded in blending the influences of the romantic movement with the main current of American historiography.

Romantic thought in Europe, as expounded by Rousseau in France and Herder in Germany, contained three ideas that were particularly attractive to Americans. Rousseau replaced Voltaire's enlightened despot with an enlightened people as the foundation upon which to base his utopia. Nothing, Rousseau said, was to run counter to the "general will" of the people, who at different times would have goals either more or less enlightened. In Germany, the gen-will became the "spirit" or "idea" of the nation which gave it its unique character and governed the course of its development. Inherent in the first idea is the second, the belief that the "general will" or governing idea always exists and that every age displays some facet of it. Hence, every age is worthy of study. European historians were to be noted for the romantic zeal with which they explained the Middle Ages, scorned by eighteenth-century rationalists as a time of barbarism. Romance-minded historians were also marked by their reverence for manuscripts and documents, relics and artifacts of a past era. This reverence frequently degenerated into the antiquarian's love of the ancient for its own sake. The contents of the early museums or "cabinets" of nineteenth-century American historical societies bore witness to a tendency to cherish indiscriminately any and all reminders of times past.

A third tenet significant in romantic thought was a belief that the history of the human race was a series of events, each developing out of the one before and all combining to illustrate the progressive education of the human mind. Each stage of civilization marked a phase in the development of man. The welter of ideas current among Americans of the early nineteenth century shows the heterogeneous and eclectic nature of much that was written and in part explains the immediate success and as quick demise of the work of a small group of romantic national historians.[1]

The concept of history which evolved from the disparate elements of eighteenth-century rationalism and nineteenth-century American filio-pietism and European romanticism was in opposition to the divisive tendencies of historical activity in the United States. As the nation began splitting at its sectional seams, as local historians fought over which locality was to be considered the trunk of the family tree, some few historians drew closer in agreement on the need for a national history and the functions which that history should perform. In the two decades after 1830, the Jeffersonian belief in progress was the rock on which they planned to build. Jefferson and those of his turn of mind had put their faith in the trend of civilization toward continual betterment. The course toward a freer individual was not a goal but a concomitant of the acceleration of civilization on its ascendant path. Jeffersonian philosophy substituted an educated elite for Voltaire's enlightened despot, and laid emphasis upon the individual and upon small social and governmental units, both as operators in and subjects of history. It gave sanction to the filio-pietistic biography which considered a man's life not simply as it was but for what it could teach.

American biographers believed that a great man, by definition, was one who had found a formula for the control of human nature, that common denominator of all Homo sapiens. The formula, once understood, could be used by others in like situations, indeed needs must be used if humankind was to progress. The philosophy of history which grew from this belief was described by one author as "the science of human nature as shown in a full, correct and philosophical account of the experiments which have been tried upon humanity ever since its first existence."[2]

Soon the bare bones of an individualistic philosophy of history acquired flesh. The core of Jeffersonian philosophy, faith in progress, remained; the atomistic approach was changed to a collective one. The American historian in 1840 studied the fortunes of the mass of men, their "opinions, characters, impulses, hopes, fears, arts, industry, in the field, in the workshop." It was not enough to follow the actions of a few leaders; such a study could not succeed in explaining the history of a democratic nation. Each nation with a legitimate right to be called a nation was known "by permanent distinctive traits of moral and intellectual character." A study of its history would "reveal and

---

[1] For a full discussion of certain European ideas of history see R. G. Collingwood, *The Idea of History* (New York: Oxford University Press, 1956), pp. 86–104; Peardon, *The Transition in English Historical Writing, passim.*

[2] "The Philosophy of History," *North American Review*, XXXIX (July, 1834), 36. Francis Gray, "An Address before the Society of Phi Beta Kappa on Thursday, the 29th of August, 1816," *North American Review*, III (September, 1816), 289.

display that character, the knowledge of which was necessary in determining the appropriate frame and action of its government."[3]

Most of the young historians in the decades from 1830 to 1860 either implied or propounded this philosophy of history, the assumptions that progress is inevitable, that an underlying plan or set of laws governs the affairs of men and nations, and that nations are not simply political units but mystical entities with an individual character and spirit.[4]

Each historian had his own idea as to the nature of progress, but all agreed that, in general, it was the continual betterment of human society. John W. Monette, an Alabama physician and self-styled historian of the Mississippi Valley, believed that all existence formed one great chain of being, each link of which, each living thing, was created for its own happiness but depended upon all others for fulfilment. The progress of the American West resulted from the "benign influences of a republican form of government, which in turn depended upon other factors in history for its existence."[5]

In the winter of 1853, the theologian William G. T. Shedd delivered a series of lectures at Andover, Massachusetts, on the philosophy of history, in which he said that "unceasing motion, from a given point, through several stadia to a final terminus, is a characteristic belonging as inseparably to a historic process as to that of any evolution whatsoever." Shedd believed, as did most of his contemporaries, that history was a "progressive expansion," an evolution from a primitive to an ever more civilized, complex society.[6]

American historians in mid-century regarded progress as a self-evident fact, but if proof were required, a cursory glance at the pages of history would establish its presence; only the underlying laws which governed human affairs within this all-encompassing principle of progress were sometimes difficult to ascertain. An essay in the *New American Cyclopaedia* defined the science of history as a search for those "laws of human events, the ideal formula which rules all forms of human effort and attainment, the principles whose development creates nations and civilizations, the forces and the direction of forces

[3] George Perkins Marsh, *The American Historical School* (Troy, N.Y., 1847), p. 10.

[4] Rufus Choate, *The Works of Rufus Choate with a Memoir of his Life*, ed. Samuel Gilman Brown (Boston, 1862), p. 323. One writer declared, "It is not our own history only, but that of the whole human race, which is to be written in accordance with the principles here unfolded and established. . . . It would be the nucleus of a distinct national literature. It would at once give us an original national character. The successful completion of such an universal history, would place us on equal terms [with other free states]." "Philosophy of History," *North American Review*, XXXIX (July, 1834), 54. See also Ralph Waldo Emerson, "History," *Essays* (New York: Modern Library, Inc., 1944), p. 6.

[5] John W. Monette, *History of the discovery and settlement of the Valley of the Mississippi* (New York, 1846), I, Preface; Monette, "The Limited Nature of Human Research," *Southwestern Journal*, I (December 15, 1837), 5–8.

[6] William G. T. Shedd, *Philosophy of History* (Boston, 1853), p. 10; Thomas W. Gilmer, "An Address on the Value of History Before the Virginia Historical and Philosophical Society," *Southern Literary Messenger*, III (February, 1837), 97.

which move the world to its destiny."[7] Assuming that such laws existed and
were discoverable, the student of the past would be able, eventually, to dispel
the "mists and vapors of unfinished history."[8]

Of necessity, most American historians took on faith the idea of progress
and the existence of an underlying pattern of laws which gave order to the
chaos of history. Their immediate and primary concern was an inquiry into
the nature of the Republic. That the nation had a character, a "spirit" and
"idea," they did not question, but what were the elements of this character,
what was the "idea" of the United States? A study of American history would
answer these questions and would serve to clarify and crystallize that character; it would "be the nucleus of a distinct national literature."[9]

To discover national character, the historian must study not only the leaders,
for an examination would give an "inadequate conception . . . of the times, the
country and the people to which it relates." To do his job properly, the historical scholar must explain the "condition and character of the great body of
people . . . , the origin, state, and progress of opinions, and . . . the spirit of
the age."[10] In order to accomplish this task, he would have to become familiar
with the everyday life of the people; he must concern himself with the acts
of statesmen, the exploits of soldiers, the "wages paid to carpenters, and the
style of living in Fifth Avenue."[11] History was less and less the story of a few
great men and more the collective biography of a people; men regarded not
as individual entities but as social beings, significant only for their relation-
ships with other men.

A history that set forth the nation's character in bold and clear terms would
be both a monument to the country and to the historian who conceived it.
Such a history would be the basis for a single national literature, which, de-
claimed Rufus Choate in a speech during the nullification crisis, "would be a
common property of all states. . . . The exclusiveness of state pride, the narrow selfishness of a mere local policy, and the small jealousies of vulgar minds,
would be merged in an expanded, comprehensive constitutional sentiment of

[7] George Ripley, "History," *New American Cyclopaedia, A Popular Dictionary of General Knowledge*, ed. George Ripley and Charles Dana (New York, 1859–60), IX, 208.

[8] William Parker Foulke, *The Right Use of History, Annual Address to the Historical Society of Pennsylvania* (Philadelphia, 1856), p. 43.

[9] "Philosophy of History," *North American Review*, p. 37. Theodore Parker to Francis Parkman, December 22, 1851. Parker asserts, "It always enriches a special history to drop into it universal laws or any general rules of conduct which distinguish one nation from an-other. The facts of history cannot all be told . . . ; the historian must choose such as, to him, most clearly set forth the Idea of the Nation—or the man—he describes." In Mason Wade, *Francis Parkman, Heroic Historian* (New York: Viking Press, Inc., 1942), p. 312. Robert Davidson, *The Study of History, an Address Delivered at the Anniversary of the Freehold Young Ladies' Seminary* (Freehold, N.J., 1853), p. 19.

[10] March, *The American Historical School*, p. 29.

[11] "Editor's Table," *Harper's New Monthly Magazine*, X (May, 1855), 835.

old family fraternal regard. It would reassemble, as it were, the people of America in one vast congregation."[12]

Although most historians of the period agreed with the philosophy of history then current, certain of them offered variations on the theme in their works. Southern historians like William Gilmore Simms and Charles E. A. Gayarré emphasized the romantic nature of historical progress, presenting it as the "source of those vigorous shoots of thought and imagination, which make a nation proud of its sons, . . . and which save her from becoming a by-word and reproach to other nations."[13] Northern historians were apt to express a rational approach. Bancroft, for instance, believed that by the study of history, laws that men arrive at by reason or intuition "can be tested . . . by experience, and inductions will be the more sure, the larger the experience from which they are drawn."[14]

Basic agreement on the importance of national history, which might have been expected to result in harmony, instead served as the grounds for dispute among historians. Historical society charters, addresses, and orations proclaimed the importance of national history; state laws requiring that United States history be taught in the schools, efforts to encourage the study of American history in colleges, legislation proposing that the government obtain pertinent documents from foreign archives, only emphasized the increasing importance granted a national history in the public mind. State and local historians increased their efforts to secure for their state or town dominance, or at least an important role, in the story of the nation. The same phenomenon took place in politics; as the federal government increased in power, state representatives doubled their efforts to gain influence. Oblivion was the consequence of indifference, and there followed the galling experience of seeing more energetic states garner the greater share of national glory and claim leading roles in the nation's past.

The southern and western states were last to awaken to the importance of sharing in the ethos of national history by proclaiming the varied contributions of their regions. In the decade between 1820 and 1830, ten historical societies were founded in the New England states and the old northwest, largely settled by New Englanders. During the following ten years, twelve others were founded, all but one in southern and southwestern states. Between 1830 and 1840, the *Southern Literary Messenger* was established and William Gilmore Simms began to write "Border Romances," a series of ardently southern novels; in the West, James Hall founded the *Western Monthly Magazine* and William Holmes McGuffey began to write the readers which made

---

[12] Choate, *Works*, p. 344.

[13] William Gilmore Simms, *Views and Reviews in American Literature, History and Fiction* (New York, 1845), p. 9.

[14] George Bancroft, *The Office of the People in Art, Government and Religion* (Boston, 1835); Russell Nye, *George Bancroft* (New York: Alfred A. Knopf, 1949), p. 101.

his name a byword, including "Western Books for Western People." Hitherto inarticulate states found voices; interest in local history was one manifestation of a newly aroused self-consciousness.[15]

The consequence of the increased interest in regional history in the South and West was a corresponding show of resentful and defensive bitterness against the New England states, the only section which maintained a steady flow of histories, local, regional, and national. Few literary men in the South boasted of the literary pre-eminence of their region; nonetheless, they reacted violently when New Englanders claimed first place in historical writing and in the creation of a national literature. An article in the *Southern Review* expressed in strong terms the opinion that "what-ever be the wonders that Cotton Mather and his heroical successors have affected, we not only think that the English literature is good enough for us at present, but may be for a century."[16] In the eyes of southerners loyal to their region, such reasoning was a shocking negation of southern pretensions to a share in the intellectual and cultural leadership of the nation. These southern patriots found a champion in the *Southern Literary Messenger*, which began its first volume in 1835 by castigating the southern literati for being content with the laurels earned by politicians and allowing New England to lay claim to intellectual leadership.[17]

In the year the *Southern Literary Messenger* began publication, George Bancroft, former headmaster of the Roundhill School in Northampton, Massachusetts, launched the first volume of a *History of the United States*. Bancroft's predecessors as national historiographer, Holmes, Trumbull, Ramsay, and Pitkin, received little notice, but Bancroft did not escape some criticism for his attempt to record the story of the nation "from the discovery of the American continent." His first volume received widespread reviews, but there were some who did not accept his work as the authentic story of the early colonial period of America.[18]

Bancroft assumed the viewpoint and the pattern set by New England historians who came before him, as epitomized by Abiel Holmes's *Annals*, a book that Bancroft greatly admired.[19] In Bancroft's account, the colonies early displayed the spirit of liberty and independence, and this spirit became the unifying principle, the "idea," of the young nation, for to Bancroft the colonial period represented the youth of the nation. "The maturity of the nation," he

[15] William H. Venable, *Beginnings of Literary Culture in the Ohio Valley* (Cincinnati, 1891), pp. 147–60; R. Carlyle Buley, *The Old Northwest, Pioneer Period, 1815–1840* (Indianapolis: Indiana Historical Society, 1950), II, 550–56.

[16] "Knapp's Lectures on American Literature," *Southern Review*, VII (August, 1831), 438.

[17] *Southern Literary Messenger*, I (January, 1835), 1.

[18] George Bancroft, *History of the United States from the Discovery of the American Continent* (Boston, 1834), I, vii; see also IX (1866), 5; "Bancroft's A History of the United States," *Southern Literary Messenger*, I (June, 1835), 587.

[19] George Bancroft, "Review of Force's Documentary History of the American Revolution," *North American Review*, XLVI (April, 1838), 481.

wrote, "is but a continuation of its youth. The spirit of the colonies demanded freedom from the beginning."[20]

Bancroft accomplished the even more difficult feat of bringing the state of Virginia within his scheme. Bancroft was so proud of this accomplishment that he made special mention of it in the preface to the first volume of his history. He could not "regret the labor which . . . enabled me to present, under a somewhat new aspect, the early lover of liberty in Virginia; the causes and nature of its loyalty; its commercial freedom; the colonial policy of Cromwell; the independent spirit of Maryland; the early institutions of Rhode Island; and the stern independence of the New England Puritans."[21]

In the name of Virginia, the new *Southern Literary Messenger* disagreed. Virginians had opposed the usurpations of Cromwell before they took refuge "where the spirit of loyalty was strongest," in the Old Dominion. "What is the meaning," asked the reviewer, "of this strange attempt to pervert the truth of history and to represent Virginia as being as far gone in devotion to the parliament as Massachusetts herself? Why does it come to us sweetened with the language of panegyric, from those who love us not, and who habitually scoff at and deride us? Is it intended to dispose us to acquiesce in the new notion 'that the people of the colonies, all together, formed one body politic before the Revolution'?" As if pointing a warning finger at Bancroft's work as a case in point, the critic admonished his southern readers, "let them [our northern neighbors] write our books, and they become our masters."[22]

But the South was not the only region which shouted objections at New England's version of national history in general and Bancroft's work in particular. As the historian's volumes followed one after the other in slow and steady procession from the press to the patient and aging reader, criticism mounted—criticism motivated not so much by professional disagreement upon the interpretation of certain incidents, the selection of facts, or the style, but by sectional jealousy undisguised.

In 1842, Job R. Tyson, a Philadelphia lawyer who had a deep, if unproductive, interest in Pennsylvania history, rose before a meeting of the Pennsylvania Historical Society and declared that the "integrity of truth" demanded a new history of colonial settlements. Tyson pointed out that as soon as the colonies declared their independence each tended to magnify its role in gaining independence; but was this not a minor fault compared to the "higher pretensions" of New England? "The historians of the New England states contend, that to them belongs the exclusive honour of having *originated* the free principles which followed our independence, as a political society, by sowing the seeds which gave them birth."[23]

[20] Bancroft, *History of the United States*, I, vi.

[21] *Ibid.*, I, viii; IX, 5.

[22] "Bancroft's *A History*," *Southern Literary Messenger*, p. 591.

[23] Tyson, *Discourse Delivered Before the Historical Society of Pennsylvania*, p. 6; "Bancroft's History," *American Quarterly Review*, XVI (September, 1834), 206.

The general public received Bancroft's history with all but unanimous applause. Because he expressed ideas that had become common currency, and because of his own prodigious efforts at documentation, Bancroft was hailed as America's foremost historian.[24] Only the local historians objected to Bancroft's history; on the other hand, they joined the public in praising the writings of Francis Parkman. Parkman, like Bancroft, was a romantic nationalist, but whereas Bancroft's works provoked hostile irritation, Parkman's history was applauded and became subject to imitation.[25]

Bancroft began his study of history at the University of Göttingen, one of the centers of the romantic movement in Europe. Upon his return from Europe, with another graduate of the German university, Joseph Green Cogswell, Bancroft put European ideas of education into practice at the Roundhill School in Boston. Bancroft translated some of the works of Arnold Hermann Ludwig Heeren, his professor of history at Göttingen, and in 1834, still strongly influenced by German romanticism, he began writing a history of the United States.

He drew little of his concept of history from native historical tradition apart from his reliance on Puritan historians, whose thought he made the cornerstone of democracy, expanding the Puritan theme of a chosen people to include the entire nation. His interpretation of American history was full blown before he set pen to paper. Bancroft was to write about the "spirit" of America, which from the beginnings demanded freedom, and how that spirit triumphed. His volumes contained many generalities about the American people and the colonists, and he personified the "general will" in accounts of specific colonies and of particular heroes, such as Roger Williams, George Fox, and William Penn. Bancroft collected, read and collated more manuscript sources than had any other general historian, and his history was reasonably accurate, but he made one irreparable error.

Bancroft, the student and translator of Heeren's pioneering works on ancient and modern states, could not have been expected to avoid a view of history that made his interpretation unpalatable to southern critics, local and state historians, and all "true patriots." They complained that Bancroft submerged the individuality, the uniqueness, of each colony into a unanimously shared common goal and common spirit—an inevitable consequence of his thesis and the philosophy of history from which it stemmed. Local historians, who shared the chauvinism and the filiopietism of the early nationalists and fought to give their locality its full portion of national glory, agreed that the historian should study the thought, actions, and lives of the people; but, unlike Bancroft, they interpreted this to mean a study of particular people, local pioneers, politicians,

[24] M. A. DeWolfe Howe, *The Life and Letters of George Bancroft* (New York: Charles Scribners' Sons, 1908), II, 105–7; Watt Stewart, "George Bancroft," *Marcus W. Jernegan Essays in American Historiography*, ed. William T. Hutchinson (Chicago: University of Chicago Press, 1937), pp. 12–13.

[25] Joe Patterson Smith, "Francis Parkman," Hutchinson (ed.), *Jernegan Essays*, p. 59; Mason Wade (ed.), *The Journals of Francis Parkman* (New York: Harper & Bros., 1947), I, ix.

soldiers, and intellectual leaders. Throughout his life, Bancroft engaged in word battles with local and family historians who, on the basis of their particular knowledge, took exception to his right to the title, "the historian of the United States."[26]

Francis Parkman suffered no such disesteem, though he wrote on a scale very nearly as broad as Bancroft's, and romanticism dominated his view of American history. Parkman began his foray into the past some eight years after the publication of the first volume of Bancroft's history. His romanticism, finding no object in the milieu of Boston in the 1830's, was fired by the novels of James Fenimore Cooper which increased his enthusiasm for the Indians, "the American forest," and "Old French War."[27] He had begun to dig into the history of the French and Indian War before 1843 when he made his first trip to Europe. Although Parkman was to become the historian of the struggle for empire in America, his original conception was not so grand; in inspiration and method he differed little from the best of the local historians.[28] As a young man Parkman wanted only to write the history of an American war, a war in which his ancestors had participated in a region he knew well. The greater theme emerged as he worked on his materials. At the same time that Lyman C. Draper was building his great collection of western and southern Americana, interviewing early settlers, gathering old manuscripts, and dreaming of the history he hoped to write of the wars of the western border during and after the revolution, Parkman sought relics of the "Old French War" as he tramped the forests and sketched the ruins of French forts.

Parkman's romanticism was tempered by experience; his historical method grew out of his purpose and his contacts with local historians. In 1846–47, he traveled to the West and lived among Indians scarcely touched by civilization, and this contact changed his conception of the Indian as a "noble savage" in an unspoiled state. The impact of reality turned him from any thought of emulating his youthful idol, James Fenimore Cooper.[29]

Perhaps from his contact with rules of law, Parkman gained a greater respect for the use and testing of evidence than his illustrious predecessors displayed. In 1844, Parkman attended the Dane Law School at Harvard, an experience he regretted. But he took this opportunity to audit the lectures of Judge Simon Greenleaf, who two years before had published the classic *Treatise on the Law of Evidence*, and became aware of the principles that would become a part of the scholarly apparatus of American historians to this day.[30]

[26] Howe, *Life of Bancroft*, I, 239; II, 107–11; David D. Van Tassel, "Henry Barton Dawson: A Nineteenth Century Revisionist," *William and Mary Quarterly*, 3d ser., XIII (July, 1956), 336–37.

[27] Wade, *Journals of Parkman*, I, xi.

[28] Hesseltine, *Pioneer's Mission*, pp. 39–46.

[29] Francis Parkman, "The Works of James Fenimore Cooper," *North American Review*, LXXIV (January, 1852), 151–53.

[30] Wade, *Journals of Parkman*, I, 283–95.

Parkman's brush with the rules of law may or may not have altered the development of his historical method, but certainly his purpose in studying history tempered his romantic nationalism with realism and a disciplined fidelity to facts. He aimed to re-create the past—"the truth of history"—and to "imbue himself with the life and spirit of the time" so that he might describe events as "a sharer or a spectator of the action." Such an aim made him kin to the rising group of critical historians who, for the most part, were local scholars. He carried on an extensive correspondence and familiarized himself with their works.[31]

Parkman's style and his choice of subjects put him among the ranks of such literary historians as Bancroft, Prescott, and Motley.[32] His scope made him a national historian and his love of the dramatic event and the heroic individual suggested his underlying romanticism. His intimate knowledge of the writings of others, primary sources, legend and lore, and all aspects of the geography of the localities he wrote about put him at one with local historians.

The romantic nationalists continued to write throughout the Civil War and until 1890, adding volumes to their epic of America, but their place in the main stream of American historiography remains the three decades before America's war for national unification. Bancroft drank deep of the fountain of German romantic nationalism and imbued his history with a national spirit that acknowledged no state boundaries. His sense of nationalism, which carried over into the Reconstruction era, was justified by the results of the Civil War, but later historians rejected his leadership in history. Francis Parkman continued to write from 1850 to 1890, at once influencing and escaping unscathed from the critical spirit rising in American historiography.[33]

[31] *Ibid.*, I, 322–29.

[32] Because of the subject matter of their histories, Prescott and Motley are not discussed here.

[33] Historians who have dealt with Parkman have disagreed widely as to where he belongs in the development of American historical studies. Clarence W. Alvord had no doubt that his place was among the literary historians, but John Spencer Bassett refused to deal with Parkman as one of the "middle group" of American historians because Parkman was "obviously a misplaced scientific historian." Others have placed him in a no man's land between the two groups. Otis A. Pease, the latest scholar to deal with Parkman's work, convincingly absolves him from any large debt to the early romantic nationalists—Bancroft, Prescott, Motley—and from debt to Carlyle and Macaulay, but leaves him a genius standing alone. Pease hints but does not state that there may be other debtors, hitherto unrecognized, in the shaded background of the Parkman portrait. Otis A. Pease, *Parkman's History* (New Haven: Yale University Press, 1953), pp. 79–86.

13 LOCAL HISTORIANS AND THE GROWTH OF THE CRITICAL SPIRIT, 1850–60

While Irving, Bancroft, and Parkman gathered public acclaim as national historians, while Peter Force and the local historical societies collected and published documents to preserve the record of colonial times, while Jared Sparks and his collaborators produced in rapid-fire sequence a number of volumes in the *American Biography* series, a younger generation of local historians, appearing in the late 1840's, viewed the work of their elders with a skeptical eye. These men sought to infuse a new spirit into the study of the history of their localities; they took a closer look at often-repeated stories and burrowed into accumulated documents to verify and correct older histories. They devoted themselves to the exposure of "historical jackdaws" and to the "reestablishment of long obscured truths." This unsung group, flourishing in the valley between the giant peaks of the romantic and the professional historians, not only raised the general standard of scholarship but also improved current methods of collecting, evaluating, and editing documents.[1]

The reasons why these men shunned the practices of their filio-pietistic elders were almost as numerous as the men who gave allegiance to this new critical spirit. Some, like Timothy Flint, a Presbyterian minister and the editor of the *Western Monthly Review*, simply reacted against the "studied eulogium" of the nation, its heroes, and its institutions. Flint called for history that would be "sternly impartial and strictly true." Anything else, he declared, would only "serve to perpetuate error, and propagate distrust." But in 1828 Flint knew himself to be ahead of his time; "taste has not yet matured sufficiently," and, he continued, the historian probably does not exist that could write such a history.[2]

The problem of origins was beginning to agitate the curiosity of some European historians, but there is no evidence apparent that the stirrings in Europe inspired American historians to revise their approach to history. Historians on both continents put a relatively high premium upon facts, and both groups of historians studied the past of towns and villages, but there the resemblance ends.

[1] *Historical Magazine*, 2d ser., XI (May, 1871), 348. These historians, singly or as a group, are wholly ignored in most accounts of American historical writing (Jameson, *History of Historical Writing in America*; Bassett, *The Middle Group of American Historians*; Gooch, *History and Historians in the Nineteenth Century*; H. E. Barnes, *History of Historical Writing* [Norman, Okla.: University of Oklahoma Press, 1937]). A few of the historians writing during the thirty years between 1850 and 1880, such as Dawson, Sabine, and Shea, are mentioned in Michael Kraus, *The Writing of American History* (Norman, Okla.: University of Oklahoma Press, 1953), pp. 114, 158, 162, 163.

[2] In Buley, *The Old Northwest*, II, 528.

European historians sought to understand the growth of the town as a key to an understanding of the growth of democracy in the nineteenth century. In 1854, G. L. von Maurer first advanced the theory that town government developed from the German "mark," land held in common by the village community. In the 1860's, Sir Henry Maine and Edward A. Freeman traced the development of English village communities. Maine's investigation was based on an idea advanced in an article in the *Nation* by Francis W. Allen, a professor of ancient history at the University of Wisconsin, who compared English and New England villages. But this approach to local history was not given much currency in the United States until the 1870's. American historians were not concerned with the town as a social and political unit; local historians were concerned only with the past of a particular town.

One source of the changing approach to history in America lay in the fact that the younger group of historians was much further removed from the American Revolution than their predecessors. Men like Richard Frothingham, a Massachusetts businessman and amateur historian, found that when they had chosen a subject they were forced to repeat stories told many times before or to delve into documents in search of fresh material. Men like Henry Dawson and George Moore of New York were jealous of their state's reputation and sought evidence in old newspapers and letters to aid them in exposing unmerited reputations and in justifying and increasing the reputation of New York state. Charles Deane, Henry Adams, and others who were caught up in the sectional struggle tried to "break some glass" by launching a critical attack upon heroes and legends of the South. Still other men, like Justin Winsor and John W. Draper, read the work of the English historian Henry T. Buckle and saw the potential value of a collection of facts, in the faith that a sufficient number of facts, rightly arranged, would lay bare the laws of human society. But whatever their intentions, they shared a reverence for data, for the publication of unexpurgated letters and documents, and for the straightforward presentation of events as they happened. They abhorred eulogy and practiced critical analysis.

In 1849, Richard Frothingham, the treasurer of the Middlesex Canal Company and occasional Massachusetts legislator, was one of the first of the genus of critical historians to receive acclaim and vituperation for his use of documentation. He applied his energies to an account of the often-repeated history of the siege of Boston during the revolution and of the battles of Lexington, Concord, and Bunker Hill. Frothingham admitted that, had he been less skeptical "as to tradition" and had credited "a larger portion of personal anecdote," his work might have been "less reliable" but more amusing and more acceptable to the general public. Frothingham found in the history of the battle of Bunker Hill an especial challenge, for over the event lay the confusing charges and countercharges, the heated disputes between generals and old soldiers, politicians and local historians.

The controversy began in February, 1818, when the *Analectic Magazine*, which devoted many pages to boastful accounts of military prowess, published a description of the battle of Bunker Hill and gave credit to General Israel Putnam of Connecticut as commander of the heroic American troops. In the March issue of *Portfolio*, General Henry Dearborn disagreed and set forth the claims of Colonel William Prescott as commander during the battle. The next month, Daniel Putnam, son of General Putnam, published in the same journal an indignant rebuke. In June, Dearborn printed a "vindication" and mustered documents to prove his case for Prescott. John Lowell, a Federalist lawyer and essayist, then entered the lists to champion Putnam's cause. Even Daniel Webster, with a strong article in the *North American Review*, entered the controversy on Putnam's behalf. The fight took on a political hue when old Federalists lined up solidly behind Putnam and the Republican party backed Prescott. Putnam seemed to be the final victor when a local historian, Samuel Swett, canvassed many of the survivors of the battle and published the results of his inquiry in a monograph defending Putnam's right to the nation's acclaim, duly granted him by textbook writers and general historians who accepted Swett's conclusions.[3]

Frothingham assured the readers of *The Siege of Boston* that he did not intend to make his pages "a pillory of error for a respected pioneer enquirer," but he could scarcely avoid doing so. Step by step, as the young historian marshaled his evidence and recapitulated the scene, Swett's account of the battle of Bunker Hill lost credence. The most telling feature of Frothingham's book was not the new material he introduced but his critical and discriminating use of evidence long known. Frothingham brought to history a lawyer's consciousness of the evaluation of evidence. He made distinctions in the kinds of testimony and their relative value that few American historians had noted (at least consciously). He threw out as "little good" the unsupported reminiscences of "old soldiers" who took part in the battle, and he warned that all contemporary material must be used with "much caution and discrimination." He gave much weight to a letter written by Colonel Prescott to John Adams, at the request of Adams, recapitulating the event several weeks after the battle. Because Prescott wrote shortly after the event, before there was an inkling of the future dispute or of the glory to be affixed to the battle, and at a time when Prescott could not know that the letter would be used for anything more than the personal enlightenment of John Adams, the statements carried their own validity.[4]

Frothingham's book was a penetrating treatment of a famous episode in American history and a step beyond the filio-pietistic writings of the elders and of his contemporaries. Although the book was not recognized as an innovation,

---

[3] Richard Frothingham, *History of the Siege of Boston, and of the Battles of Lexington, Concord, and Bunker Hill* (Boston, 1849), p. iii; Frothingham, *The Command in the Battle of Bunker Hill* (Boston, 1850), pp. 4–5.

[4] Frothingham, *Siege of Boston*, p. 6; Frothingham, *The Command*, p. 4; Frothingham, *Siege of Boston*, p. 30.

Frothingham's fellow historians were impressed by it and reviewers praised it. Washington Irving, in process of composing a biography of Washington, wrote Robert C. Winthrop that he had consulted Frothingham's history and acknowledge that it merited "the character you gave it, as being the best thing written about the Bunker Hill period." Henry B. Dawson, a New York historian and the author of *Battles of the United States*, obtained possession of the Wayne papers and told Jared Sparks that he hoped to do for the battle of Saratoga what Frothingham had done for the battle of Bunker Hill. Dawson, later, as editor of the *Historical Magazine*, counted Frothingham among the "new school of historians" who were not awed by their ancestors and who made judicious use of their sources.[5]

In the 1850's many more historians broke the spell of ancestor-worship. A lingering spirit of reverence did not prevent them from investigating and from revealing what they found. Charles Deane, Nathaniel B. Shurtleff, Edmund B. O'Callaghan, and John Romeyn Brodhead, among others, represented in the fifties the critical spirit of the dedicated historian. These men sought the necessary facts for a critical annotation of the documents they published. They shunned the practice of "polishing" letters and documents, a habit to which Jared Sparks had been prone, and without qualms set down every misspelling, every coloquialism, every slip of the pen. Charles Deane, a self-educated Boston businessman and long-time secretary of the Massachusetts Historical Society, edited with meticulous care the first edition of William Bradford's *Of Plymouth Plantation*, a manuscript he discovered in the library of the Bishop of London. Nathaniel B. Shurtleff, a Boston physician, accomplished the tremendous task of transcribing, annotating, and publishing five large volumes, *Records of the Governors and Company of Massachusetts Bay in New England*, and a year later began publication of *Records of the Colony of New Plymouth in New England*.[6]

Meanwhile, kindred spirits were at work translating, editing, and publishing the documents of the early history of New York. In the fifties, Edmund Bailey O'Callaghan, an Irish physician who migrated to New York by way of Canada, was hard at work translating and publishing Dutch documents relating to New Netherlands. O'Callaghan first became interested in New York history while digging among documents at Albany for background material for a series of articles on the New York anti-rent war. Having discovered a wealth of relatively unknown material, he determined to write a history of the Dutch colony. He published his three-volume history in 1845 and 1846, and was ap-

[5] In *Proceedings of the Massachusetts Historical Society* (Boston, 1884), II, 175; Henry B. Dawson to Jared Sparks, March 5, 1859, Sparks Papers, Massachusetts Historical Society; *Historical Magazine*, 2d ser., IX (October, 1870), 220.

[6] Bradford, *History of Plymouth Plantation*, ed. Charles Deane. For biographical sketch of Deane see *Proceedings of the American Antiquarian Society*, N.S., II (Boston, 1889); Nathaniel B. Shurtleff (ed.), *Records of the Colony of New Plymouth in New England* (8 vols.; Boston, 1855–57); Charles K. Bolton, "Nathaniel Bradstreet Shurtleff," *DAB*, XVII, 141–42.

pointed by the New York legislature to edit the Dutch records in the state archives.

In 1818, the New-York Historical Society, through the ministrations of DeWitt Clinton, persuaded the New York legislature to publish records concerning New Netherlands. The legislature appointed a scholar of Dutch ancestry, Francis Adrian Van der Kemp, to translate them. Van der Kemp, all-too-conscious of the "slur" cast upon the Dutch founders of New York by Washington Irving's satire, revised his translation to show that phase of New York history in a better light. O'Callaghan carefully checked and amended Van der Kemp's work before he began publication of an eleven-volume edition of the papers, *Documents Relating to the Colonial History of the State of New York*, which contained, in addition to the records at Albany, the bulk of the material collected by John R. Brodhead in a four-year tour of European archives sponsored by the New York legislature. Such historians as Bancroft and Parkman recognized the painstaking research of O'Callaghan and Brodhead. Parkman was a debtor to O'Callaghan for his discovery of the significance of reports and narratives by missionaries in New France, later published in seventy-three volumes as *Jesuit Relations*, for an understanding of colonial history, and for guidance in locating other French documents that became the foundation for his work, *The Pioneers of France in the New World*.[7]

The early history of New England fell under the scrutiny of the critical eye of one of her sons, Peter Oliver. Oliver was a descendant of one of the leading families in Massachusetts which remained loyal to the crown and went into exile in England during the War for Independence. Peter Oliver was a clergyman of the Episcopal church and had no love for the church of his ancestors. In 1856, he wrote *The Puritan Commonwealth* in which he exposed to public view the evils of Massachusetts' theocracy before the revocation of the colony's charter in 1684. Oliver's book, if it were to be answered at all, could not be dismissed as a display of bad temper, for he substantiated his epithets by quoting the documents of New England's hallowed writers, from Winthrop and Bradford down to Hutchinson. John Wingate Thornton, a Congregational minister and long a member of the Massachusetts Historical Society, in a pamphlet review of Oliver's book, answered in kind. Thornton had a thorough knowledge of Puritan history to bolster his acute criticism of Oliver's work. John Gorham Palfrey, in the following year, 1858, emphasized the positive aspects of Thornton's defense of Puritan history.[8]

---

[7] For biographical material see A. Everett Peterson, "Edmund Bailey O'Callaghan," *DAB*, XIII, 613; also Francis Shaw Guy, *Edmund Bailey O'Callaghan* ("The Catholic University of America Studies in American Church History," Vol. XVIII [Washington, D.C., 1934]); Edmund Bailey O'Callaghan, *Documents of New York* (10 vols.; Albany, 1853–58); Guy, *O'Callaghan*, p. 63.

[8] Peter Oliver, *The Puritan Commonwealth* (Boston, 1856); John Wingate Thornton, *Peter Oliver's Puritan Commonwealth Reviewed* (Boston, 1857); Thornton, *The Pulpit of the American Revolution* (Boston, 1860), pp. ix–xxxviii; Charles K. Bolton, "John Wingate Thornton," *DAB*, XVIII, 503.

John G. Palfrey, a Unitarian minister and a classmate of Jared Sparks at Harvard, considered himself one of the group of historians led by Sparks and Bancroft. In one way he could never be part of that group, for they were national historians and he was a sectional historian whose only interest in national history was to see that New England was credited with a lion's share of the development of the nation. And yet Palfrey combined successfully the filiopietism of Sparks and Bancroft and the critical spirit of the group of local historians. It is true that he defended the Puritans of Massachusetts Bay Colony in their treatment of Roger Williams and Anne Hutchinson, but his defense was not eulogy of the one and excoriation of the other; it was a reasonable attempt to explain the actions of the rulers of the colony. Palfrey was one of the first historians to point out that Roger Williams was not expelled for his religious beliefs but because he questioned the right of the settlers to occupy Indian land, thus raising a threat, if not to the existence of the colony, certainly to its future expansion. Palfrey pointed out that Anne Hutchinson's teachings in the theocratic society of the Massachusetts Bay Colony gave every indication of leading toward revolution or anarchy, neither of which the leaders of the colony could afford with the threat of war with the Indians imminent.

Palfrey's critical powers were at their best when he did not feel compelled to defend the Puritans. An intensive piece of detective work enabled him to discover the origin of a round fieldstone tower in Newport, Rhode Island. Antiquarians, and local tradition, generally attributed it to early Norse explorers, but Palfrey concluded that it was a part of a mill built about 1677 by a Benedict Arnold, who was a governor of the Rhode Island colony. Palfrey published a fourth and a fifth volume after the Civil War, toward the end of his life. They were inferior to his earlier histories because he failed to maintain the same standard of careful research and fine writing.[9]

In other parts of the country amateur scholars were beginning to scrutinize with critical eyes the history of their state or locale and to write with less florid pens of what they found.

William Adee Whitehead, an insurance broker and the corresponding secretary of the New Jersey Historical Society, which he helped to found in 1845, started his long career of editing the New Jersey historical collections by printing in 1846 his own monograph, *East New Jersey under the Proprietary Governments*. In this work Whitehead furnished much new information on colonial history and on the special problems of proprietary government. Whitehead became the leading authority on New Jersey history and continued to unearth and publish materials for that history.

In the Midwest, Lyman C. Draper was busy in Wisconsin building the collections of the "most lively historical society in the country" and the most famous collection of western Americana. Draper, like many western historians felt that his mission was to rescue the heroic western pioneers from un-

[9] John Gorham Palfrey, *History of New England during the Stuart Dynasty* (Boston, 1859), I, 470, 489; II, 57–59; James T. Adams, "John Gorham Palfrey," *DAB*, XIV, 169–70.

deserved oblivion and to give them their just place beside the settlers of James-town and Plymouth and the heroes of the revolution. His mission was not unique, but his method of carrying it out was unusual. Draper wanted to be certain that the reputations of his heroes were based firmly on fact, that no one could dispute their claim to fame. He believed that the role of the historian was "to represent with truth and clearness, the relations in which man exists," and he maintained that history is a science "dispersing the clouds which often envelope truth." Draper spent his life collecting material on western pioneers and determining its validity.[10]

One historian of the West, John Wesley Monette, preceded Draper as a critical scholar. Draper took as his field the Mississippi Valley. His pioneer heroes—George Rogers Clark, John Sevier, Daniel Boone—were associated with the territories of Kentucky and Tennessee, but Draper's field of research for the State Historical Society of Wisconsin was the old Northwest. The area as a whole, both geographically and economically, was a logical unit for study for the period of his interest (1775-1848). Draper came upon this unit largely by accident, but John Monette, a Mississippi physician, came upon it through his study of geography. In 1846, Monette published as a by-product of his geo-graphical studies a careful and comprehensive *History of the Valley of the Mis-sissippi*. He wrote at the period of culmination of the long-cherished dream of control by the United States of the entire Mississippi Valley, from the Great Lakes to the Gulf of Mexico, and at the time when a new dream was burgeon-ing, a system of railroads connecting Atlantic and Pacific coasts. Monette saw the Mississippi Valley as a geographic, economic, and historical unit centering upon the river. He assumed, as Stephen Douglas had declared, that in the valley lay the heart, strength, and future of the nation. In his history, Monette wrote that the jealous East, in control of the government, had tried to "embarrass the West in every way." He decried the deed of John Quincy Adams, who sacri-ficed our claim to Texas in 1819, and applauded the Texas revolt and its final annexation to the United States.[11]

In the 1850's there were in the South a number of local historians who shared the intent of historians of the northern and western states, who searched for facts substantiated by irreproachable documents. In 1851, Albert James Pickett

---

[10] *Proceedings of the New Jersey Historical Society* (Newark, 1846), I, 5–6; William Adee Whitehead, *East New Jersey under the Proprietary Governments* (Newark, 1846). Whitehead also edited and published some manuscripts dealing with the history of New Jersey, *The Papers of Lewis Morris, Governor of New Jersey* (Newark, 1852) and *Contributions to the Early History of Perth Amboy and Adjoining County* (Newark, 1856). A. Van Doren Honeyman, "William Adee Whitehead," *DAB*, XX, 130–31; Joel Munsell to Lyman C. Draper, Septem-ber 10, 1855, Draper Correspondence, Wisconsin State Historical Society Library; in Hessel-tine, *Pioneer's Mission*, p. 193.

[11] Monette, *History of the Mississippi*; Herbert H. Lang, "Nineteenth Century Historians of the Gulf States," (Ph.D. dissertation, University of Texas, 1954), pp. 139–40; Monette, *History*, I, 100 n.; II, 483–84. James H. Perkins should be mentioned here with Draper and Monette as a historian of the Mississippi Valley. In the main, his work was a compilation of secondary sources; Perkins, *Annals of the West*.

attempted to raise Alabama out of historical obscurity by publishing a *History of Alabama*, a carefully documented and detailed account. Pickett shared Monette's belief in the destiny of the United States, but perhaps his enthusiasm ran away with him when he declared that Alabama had "a more varied and interesting" history than any other state.[12]

Before the close of the decade, three southern historians brought out volumes which in no way compromised with the current fad, the twisting of historical truth in a defense of slavery. Charles Étienne Arthur Gayarré had studied documents in Louisiana and in the archives of Europe in order to chronicle the Spanish and French domination of Louisiana. His study clearly showed that the Spanish played the greater part in the development of Louisiana; the French too often neglected their colonies. The Spanish recognized its economic potential at the mouth of the Mississippi and saw the Louisiana territory as a strategic link in their control of the Gulf of Mexico.[13]

In the year following publication of Gayarré's history of Louisiana, a lawyer, Henderson Yoakum, published a history of Texas. Yoakum, who had moved to Texas from Tennessee, wrote a meticulous account of the settlement of the state from 1685 to the time of its annexation. Yoakum's respect for authentic documents is borne out by the preface, in which he bemoans his lack of success in an effort to consult certain materials he considered of significance. His history contains a list of manuscript collections and their locations and describes what each contributes to an understanding of Texas history.[14]

In North Carolina, Francis Lister Hawks of the Protestant Episcopal church began his long career as historian with the publication in 1858 of a two-volume history of North Carolina during the colonial period, from the founding and through the proprietary phase to 1729. During the nineteenth century, it was considered the standard history of the early years of North Carolina. Shortly after publishing this work, Hawks returned to New York, his native state, where he prepared to write a history of the Protestant Episcopal church in America, based on materials acquired in 1836 while in London.[15]

At the time that Hawks was preparing to move to New York, Edward Duffield Neill, a Congregational minister, was preparing to move to the South. In 1858 he had published a complete history of Minnesota. Three years later he was to become the chaplain of a Minnesota regiment, but for most of the Civil War he served as an assistant secretary on Lincoln's White House staff and

---

[12] Albert James Pickett, *History of Alabama and Incidentally of Georgia and Mississippi from the Earliest Period* (Charleston, S.C., 1851), p. 24; Lang, "Nineteenth Century Historians," pp. 1–31; Hallie Farmer, "Albert James Pickett," *DAB*, XIV, 569–70.

[13] Charles Étienne Arthur Gayarré, *History of Louisiana* (4 vols.; New York, 1854–66); Lang, "Nineteenth Century Historians," pp. 223, 237.

[14] Henderson Yoakum, *History of Texas, from Its First Settlement in 1685 to Its Annexation to the United States in 1846* (New York, 1855), I, Preface; II, III; Lang, "Nineteenth Century Historians," 256–91; Herbert P. Gambrell, "Henderson Yoakum," *DAB*, XX, 612–13.

[15] Francis Lister Hawks, *History of North Carolina* (3 vols.; Fayetteville, N.C., 1857–58); J. G. DeR. Hamilton, "Francis Lister Hawks," *DAB*, VIII, 416.

remained in that position during Johnson's administration. In Washington, Neill wrote two volumes on the early colonial history of Maryland and Virginia and another on *The English Colonization of America during the 17th Century*. With Francis Parkman, Neill was one of the first to make use of the as-yet-unpublished *Jesuit Relations* as a source, although as early as 1845 O'Callaghan had pointed out to the New-York Historical Society the value of these manuscripts. John Gilmary Shea, a Catholic historian, published his translation of a part of the *Jesuit Relations* in 1858, the same year in which Neill's *History of Minnesota* appeared.[16]

As historians sought the facts of American history, they found it necessary to deal with the history of foreign countries. This was especially true of Gulf State historians and those of the old Northwest. Buckingham Smith, a Florida lawyer, in preparing to chronicle the history of Florida, became interested in early Spanish explorations. In 1850, as secretary to the United States legation in Spain, he had access to Spanish archives which included a wealth of material on the early history of Florida. Smith transcribed many documents relating to the history of the Spanish in America, thus being of aid to Francis Parkman and other interested historians in the United States, and translated, edited, and published two manuscripts, travel accounts by sixteenth-century Spanish explorers, Álvar Núñez Cabeça de Vaca and Fernando de Soto. Smith anotated and verified the substance of each by painstaking, ponderous research and rigorous criticism.[17]

Others were interested in the history of the Spanish in America because it was a part of the history of their state, as in the case of Gayarré and Smith, or because the Mexican war and Prescott's history of Mexico stimulated their interest, or, finally, because there was perennial curiosity about the discovery and exploration of the American continent. Robert A. Wilson, a New York lawyer interested in the war with Mexico, wrote an account of the career of the Mexican dictator, Santa Anna. During the course of his labors, he made an effort to reconstruct the Spanish conquest of Mexico. Wilson was fascinated by the story the documents revealed and appalled by the discrepancies between his reading and the history written by Prescott. In 1859, he published a *New History of the Conquest of Mexico*, in which he took Prescott to task for his uncritical acceptance of the Spanish view gleaned from accounts written by Cortez and his contemporaries. Wilson attempted to verify the account written by Bartolomé de Las Casas, the historian of Columbus' expeditions, who

[16] Edward Duffield Neill, *Terra Mariae, Threads of Maryland Colonial History* (Boston, 1867); Neill, *History of the Virginia Company of London* (Albany, 1869); Neill, *English Colonization* (London and New York, 1871); Solon J. Buck, "Edward Duffield Neill," *DAB*, XIII, 408–9.

[17] Buckingham Smith, *The Narrative of Álvar Núñez Cabeça de Vaca* (New York, 1851). For biographical material see James Alexander Robinson, "Buckingham Smith," *DAB*, XVII, 243–44; George Fairbanks, *The History and Antiquities of the City of St. Augustine, Florida* (New York, 1858), p. 1.

appeared to be anti-Spanish, because he was a severe critic of the Spanish Indian policy.[18]

Just as Wilson was led to revise the history of the Spanish conquest of Mexico, others sought to clarify accounts of early explorers. Samuel L. M. Barlow, a New York merchant and collector, was not satisfied with Washington Irving's eulogistic biography of Christopher Columbus. Barlow published nothing himself, but he encouraged others to do so. Among his protégés was Henry Harrisse who devoted his life to a study of European discoveries and explorations in the New World. In 1866, after careful work and research, Harrisse published a critical bibliography of works about Columbus and followed it with essays upon the early explorers, culminating in a two-volume biography of Columbus, "the most important critical study ever devoted to the life of Columbus."[19]

By the mid-fifties, the critical spirit had begun to permeate the sacrosanct realm of biography. In 1856, Henry S. Randall, a New York lawyer, published a three-volume biography of Thomas Jefferson. While not escaping the spell of his subject, Randall produced a carefully documented book that was a long step nearer a realistic portrait of Jefferson than had been George Tucker's two-volume idealized biography. Randall declared that he would "seek the naked Truth" and "scorn the consequences." His book was, he feared, critical of Jefferson and might arouse the ire of the South, a fear that Randall confessed to his Virginia friend, Hugh Blair Grigsby. Grigsby, a gentleman farmer and amateur historian, had published several works of historical criticism. He had attacked the traditional pose of the Virginia cavalier, found additional evidence concerning the Mecklenburg Declaration of Independence, and published an exhaustive account of the Virginia ratifying convention of 1788. Grigsby's acute criticism of William Wirt's popular biography of Patrick Henry so intrigued Randall that he proposed to write a critical biography of the revolutionary hero.[20]

So prevalent was the revolt against idealized biographies in the decade of the fifties that even a popular writer like James Parton could declare that "to suppress the good qualities and deeds of a Burr is only less moral than to suppress the faults of a Washington. . . ." Parton, a New York journalist, had begun his career as a biographer by writing a sprightly account of the life of Horace Greeley. In 1858 he published a biography of Aaron Burr. For years Burr had

[18] Robert A. Wilson, *New History of the Conquest of Mexico* (New York, 1859). One contemporary reviewer placed Wilson's book in the current of critical spirit of the period; *Knickerbocker Magazine*, LIII (April, 1859), 410.

[19] Henry Dawson to Charles Deane, September 20, 1872, Deane Papers, Massachusetts Historical Society; Edward G. Bourne, in J. N. Larned (ed.), *The Literature of American History* (Boston: Houghton Mifflin Co., 1902), p. 777; Henry Harrisse, *Christophe Colomb* (2 vols.; Paris, 1884–85).

[20] Henry S. Randall, *Life of Thomas Jefferson* (3 vols.; New York, 1858). For further biographical material on Randall and Grigsby, see *Correspondence*, ed. Frank J. and Frank W. Klingberg, Introduction, pp. 1–17.

been presented as the personification of evil in history books and biographical dictionaries which sought to teach moral lessons from the experience of the past. Parton's biography showed that "Aaron Burr was no angel; he was a man and a filibuster." Some critics praised the book, but more damned it, as one reviewer suggested, because "it was injurious to the cause of morals to show the good in the life of a wretched man." As the audacious author discovered, most readers liked history and biography which conformed to the accepted canons.[21]

Although the critical spirit had not yet influenced the guardians of public taste, it spread through the ranks of local historians. These men, though separated by distance and specialized interests, were drawn into close fraternity by a shared love of history. In Wisconsin, far from the cultural centers and great libraries of the East, in a country only recently wilderness, Lyman C. Draper carried on a voluminous correspondence with almost every major and minor historian in the United States. He sought information and aid from historians all over the country and returned the favors when he could, often lending manuscripts on western history from his growing collection. Hugh Grigsby, on his Virginia plantation, kept in touch with what was going on among American historians with a corresponding membership in the Massachusetts Historical Society. Buckingham Smith, as secretary to the American ambassador in Madrid, kept informed of historical scholarship in the United States by correspondence. Because he had access to Spanish archives he was able to perform research chores for historians at home. For the most part, these men were local historians, but they were by no means in isolation.[22]

The *Historical Magazine*, founded in 1857, was intended as a parent journal for this community of historians; through the aegis of two of its editors, John Gilmary Shea and Henry Barton Dawson, it became in the decade of the sixties the embodiment of the current critical spirit. The magazine was the inspiration of Charles B. Richardson, a Boston publisher, and two other members of the publishing committee of the New England Historical and Genealogical Society. Richardson surveyed the number of societies devoted to history scattered over the county—there were fifty-four in 1857—and saw a need for a scholarly journal that would serve as a medium of communication for all men whose prime interest was the study of history. The New England Historical and Genealogical Society encouraged the new publication, and the society president, John Ward Dean, became the first editor.

During the first two years of publication, the magazine was a hodgepodge of data in an effort to please as many subscribers as possible. It reprinted large

[21] James Parton, *Life of Aaron Burr* (New York, 1858); in Milton E. Flower, *James Parton, the Father of Modern Biography* (Durham, N.C.: Duke University Press, 1951), p. 43; Julius W. Pratt, "Aaron Burr and the Historians," *New York History* (October, 1945), pp. 447–70.

[22] See Draper Correspondence, Wisconsin Historical Society; Hesseltine, *Pioneer's Mission*, pp. 63–68; Peter Force, personal correspondence, Library of Congress; Hesseltine and Gara (eds.), "The Historical Fraternity: Correspondence of Historians Grigsby, Henry, and Draper," *Virginia Magazine of History and Biography*, LXI (October, 1953), 450–71.

parts of addresses given at meetings of historical societies. "Notes and Queries," pages named for the English periodical, were dedicated to antiquarian
curiosities and questions of genealogy of interest to the "general reader." The
genealogist-editor hoped that this feature would be "useful to historians at the
South and West, who, while tracing an ancestry or historical investigation of
New England derivations, may be unable to prosecute their inquiries in person
upon the spot."

In 1858, when Richardson moved his publishing business to New York, the
magazine emanated from his new establishment. A single copy of the *Historical
Magazine*, bound in blue paper, was thirty-two pages long and included the
main article, "Notes and Queries," reprints of a few documents presented
without introduction or annotation, several "historical curiosities," the reports
of correspondents on the meetings of historical societies, and notices of books.
The start was inauspicious, but the subscription list grew and encouraged
Richardson to continue publication.[23]

In 1859, John Gilmary Shea became the editor of the magazine. Shea, an
extremely energetic little man with a narrow face, an abundance of tumbled
black hair, and a drooping mustache, poured forth a succession of books and
articles, most of which demanded meticulous research, year after year. A sec-
ond-generation Irish Catholic, Shea grew up in the environs of New York City
and studied and practiced law until 1848 when he joined the Society of Jesus.
As a novice he served two years at the recently established St. Mary's College
in Montreal. With the encouragement of Father Felix Martin, the president
of the college and the leading Catholic historian of Canada, he began to delve
into Father Martin's rich collection of accounts of early Jesuit missionaries in
America. Edmund B. O'Callaghan, Shea's close friend, early pointed out the
significance of this source for American history, but it remained for the young
Jesuit to make use of this material and, later, in 1858, to publish a translation
of *Jesuit Relations*.[24]

In 1852, Shea completed and published his first book, *The Discovery and
Exploration of the Mississippi Valley*. It was a series of carefully annotated,
original accounts of the early French explorers—Marquette, Allouez, Membre,
Hennepin, and Anastase Douay. Shea, in the course of his work, came upon
and published hitherto lost accounts of the explorations of John Nicolet, "the
first discoverer of the Northwest." Shea's decision to abandon the priesthood
allowed him to devote his life as a Catholic layman to the task of recording the
history of the Catholic church in America. He announced his choice of mission
in 1852 at a time when a resurgent anti-Catholicism was abroad and, presently,
would create near panic on the American political scene.[25]

[23] *Historical Magazine*, I (Boston, 1857), Introduction, 1; *ibid.*, XI (New York, 1865),
inside back cover.

[24] *Ibid.*, III (New York, 1859), Introduction; Peter Guilday, *John Gilmary Shea: Father of
American Catholic History, 1824–1892* (New York: The United States Catholic Historical
Society, 1926), pp. 9–68.

[25] *Historical Magazine*, I (Boston, 1857), 175; Guilday, *Shea*, p. 22.

Shea's position as self-appointed Catholic historian made him no less a possessor of the critical spirit than contemporary historians similarly possessed, but loyalties differed. Most historians of the day gave first allegiance to place. The Catholic historian labored to uncover the truth of the past; he sought no laws of human existence and hoped to avoid the substitution of "theories or party views for a real picture of the historical facts." As a result, Shea often incurred the wrath of churchmen who accused him of poking into old closets and exposing Catholic skeletons. In 1858, Shea published a bibliographical study of all those Catholic Bibles which had appeared in America and, by meticulous comparison, found them in error; there was no accurate English translation of the Catholic Bible. His old friend O'Callaghan had been at work on a similar study at the behest of James Lenox, then actively engaged in assembling a library of Americana, but O'Callaghan, fearful of the havoc that might follow, did not expose the errors he discovered. Shea answered Catholic attacks upon Henry de Courcy's *History of the Catholic Church in the United States*, which he had translated from the French in 1856 and to which he had added much from his own research.[26]

As editor and part-owner of the *Historical Magazine*, Shea did little to change the format of the journal but much to improve its quality. Before his editorship, the lead articles were generally unanotated summaries of addresses given before historical societies. Shea solicited articles from scholars all over the United States; the articles he obtained were fresh and usually had not been published before. In the volume for 1860, Shea included a diary of the American Revolution kept by a citizen of Newport, Rhode Island, at the time of the British occupation, documents from George Bancroft on colonial history, and documents from Buckingham Smith relating to the states of Spanish origin. He also published the results of Henry C. Murphy's researches in the archives at Leyden on the Pilgrim community in Holland.

Shea was at work upon projects of his own and published his work in book or pamphlet form. Only rarely did one of his articles appear in the *Historical Magazine;* such was an account of the history of the Chicago area between 1673 and 1725, based upon the records of French explorers. Another branded as myth an incident in the life of Columbus that involved an affair with the belle of the Canary Islands, Beatrice Enriques. Other articles were devoted to the linguistics of various Indian tribes of the North. In 1866, after seven years as editor of the *Historical Magazine*, Shea relinquished the post.[27]

Local historians all over the United States helped to raise the standards of

[26] John Gilmary Shea (ed.), *History of the Catholic Church in the United States* (New York, 1856); Guilday, *Shea*, pp. 63–66.

[27] Shea secured such articles as Henry C. Murphy's "Contributions to the History of the Pilgrim Fathers, from the Records at Leyden," Historical Magazine, IV (January, 1860), 4–6; George Bancroft's "Inauguration of the Perry Statue," *ibid.* (November, 1860), 326–28; James Lenox's "A Bibliographical Account of the Voyages of Columbus," *ibid.*, V (February, 1861), 33–38; Peter Force's "Letters to Joseph Galloway from Leading Tories in America," *ibid.*, V (September, October, December, 1861), 271–73, 295–301, 356–64.

historiography and critical scholarship; but only a few, like Shea, managed to remain objective through the holocaust of the Civil War. Most local historians would have seconded Lyman Draper, who said that he had "not by word or deed contributed in any manner to the terrible state of things now existing," and would have sympathized with Hugh Blair Grigsby and his view of the war as "a sign of a terrible epoch upon the heart of one who loved his whole country."[28] Invariably, the patriotism of local scholars stemmed from their love of their native ground. "My allegiance," said Doctor J. G. M. Ramsey as Tennessee withdrew from the Union, "has always been . . . first to my native Tennessee and second and through her to the United States."[29]

Historical study was at a halt during the Civil War as historians sought to serve the cause of their states. Ramsey stopped work on the second volume of his history of Tennessee to become an official of the Confederacy. Draper collected materials on the war and corresponded with soldiers from Wisconsin. The crippled Grigsby was forced to seek news of the war from Tazewell, his plantation home. Southern historical societies were dissolved or suspended activity for the duration, and the meetings of the northern societies, when held, were sparsely attended. The advent of the war forced the suspension of the writing of critical and local history and postponed indefinitely the writing of a national history.

[28] Hesseltine, *Pioneer's Missioner*, p. 197; Grigsby to Randall, March 18, 1861, *Correspondence*, ed. Klingberg and Klingberg, p. 183.

[29] Ramsey to Draper, February 12, 1861, Hesseltine (ed.), *Ramsey Autobiography and Letters*, p. 99.

---

14 THE SECTIONS DISPUTE ABOUT THE NATION'S HISTORY, 1850–60

Dr. James G. M. Ramsey declared in 1859, "We are now more heterogeneous than France and England and can no longer be a united people."[1] By 1859, as Ramsey implied, there was no national institution, no national culture, and no national history in which the great desire for union and conciliation could find expression against "the wild and furious spirit of Sectionalism."[2] New Englanders claimed to have written the country's history. Whether it was truly the nation's history, or the chronicles of New England writ large, did not

[1] Dr. James Gettys McGready Ramsey to Lyman C. Draper, April 16, 1859, Hesseltine (ed.), *Ramsey Autobiography and Letters*, p. 98.

[2] Henry Stephens Randall to Hugh Blair Grigsby, December 14, 1859, *Correspondence*, ed. Klingberg and Klingberg, p. 172.

matter; as long as Americans accepted it without serious objection, it passed for national history. But during the decades between 1830 and 1860 historians from other sections of the country began to challenge the dominance of New England. These challenges, far from being signs of progress toward a truly national history, were the first signs of disintegration. Historians, increasingly, devoted their efforts to attempts to prove that the nation owed its existence to the particular diligence, virtue, and patriotism of various, specific groups. This breakdown of New England's claim upon the nation's history was the result of the awakening self-consciousness of other regions as the goal, control of the nation, became more and more important to them.

As the years passed, an ever-increasing number of volumes purportedly written in the name of national history brought forth divisive tensions in the sectional struggle for power. These histories, treating "national subjects," were sectional in bias; the writers found new ways to prove their locality superior to all others in nurturing and maintaining the spirit of liberty and uncovered obscured facets of the revolutionary struggle. In 1842, Henry Cruger Van Schaack, a New York lawyer, wrote a biography of his grandfather, Peter Van Schaack, an ardent Whig who turned Tory upon the outbreak of hostilities. There was nothing remarkable about the biography except that it was seen to be the first sympathetic account of a Tory to appear since the war. In thus delineating a neglected aspect of history, the biography encouraged local historians to re-examine and bring into print the internal struggle for power in other states before and during the American Revolution.[3]

Five years later a Maine politician, Lorenzo Sabine, compiled two volumes devoted to *Biographical Sketches of Loyalists of the American Revolution*. Sabine had written a substantial life of Edward Preble for *The Library of American Biography*, but his prime qualification to write of the loyalists was his contact with sons and relatives of the American ex-patriots on the border of Maine and Canada. While attempting to dispel the popularly held belief that the American colonists rose up as one people against British tyranny, Sabine emphasized the patriotism of the people of New England by pointing out that "the adherents of the crown were more numerous at [*sic*] the South and in Pennsylvania and New York, than in New England." Sabine chose especially to destroy the patriotic reputation of South Carolina, the fountainhead of nullification and the home of John C. Calhoun: "It is hardly an exaggeration to add that more Whigs of New England were sent to . . . [South Carolina's] aid, and now lie buried in her soil, than she sent from it to every scene of strife from Lexington to Yorktown."[4]

[3] Henry C. Van Schaack, *The Life of Peter Van Schaack, LL.D., embracing Selections from his Correspondence and other Writings during the American Revolution* (New York, 1842); Charles Francis Adams, "Review of the Life of Peter Van Schaack," *North American Review*, LV (July, 1842), 99–113; also "Review of Sabine's The American Loyalists," *North American Review*, LXV (July, 1847), 138–59.

[4] Lorenzo Sabine, *Biographical Sketches of Loyalists of the American Revolution* (Boston, 1847), I, 38–39; Elizabeth Donnan, "Lorenzo Sabine," *DAB*, XVI, 276–77.

If Sabine wanted to stir reaction to his book, he chose an excellent way to do it. Champions of the South, and especially of South Carolina, published heated rejoinders and carefully documented retorts. William Gilmore Simms, the South Carolina novelist and leader of the movement to create a southern culture, wrote a fellow novelist Nathaniel Beverly Tucker in this vein: "Have you seen the . . . [*Southern Quarterly Review*] for July last containing an article entitled 'South Carolina in the Revolution'? I could wish you to read that. You will see how much of a Southron I am and how little of a Yankee."[5] The article, by Simms himself and published in extended form in 1853, set out to be a critique of Sabine's work but was, in fact, a scathing denunciation of the author for "gibbetting . . . the unfortunates, for whom their children should desire only silence and obscurity," a tirade against New England writers in general, "by whom most of our popular histories have been prepared," and a glowing defense of South Carolina's role in the American Revolution.[6]

This controversy supplied ammunition for a heated fight in Congress over the admission of Kansas as a state. Senator Charles Sumner, of Massachusetts, a master of vitriolic oratory, rose in the Senate chamber in May, 1856, to denounce the "crime against Kansas" and those senators who opposed its entry into the Union. Sumner attacked his foes by questioning the patriotism of the states they represented. He vented his bitter sarcasm upon Senator Andrew P. Butler of South Carolina. "Coming, as he announces, 'from a state'—Ay, Sir, from South Carolina—he turns with lordly disgust from Kansas. Pray, sir, by what title does he indulge in this egotism? Has he read the history of 'the state' which he represents?" Sumner spoke of the "shameful Imbecility" of South Carolina during the revolution, basing his remarks on the pages concerning South Carolina in Sabine's *American Loyalists*.[7] Two days later, Preston Brooks, a congressman from South Carolina and a nephew of Senator Butler, strode up to Sumner in the Senate chamber and gave the senator a thorough caning. When the news spread, the House of Representatives, split between horrified northerners and elated representatives of the South and West, proceeded to take action against the miscreant. The Massachusetts delegation denounced Brooks as unfit to hold public office; his champions made an elaborate and eloquent defense, not of his actions, but of the honor and patriotism of South Carolina, based upon the critique by Simms of Sabine's work.[8]

The Sumner-Brooks incident was graphic illustration of the support historiography lent to the sectional dispute and of the clash between national his-

[5] Simms to Nathaniel Beverly Tucker, May 6, 1849, *The Letters of William Gilmore Simms*, ed. Mary C. Simms Oliphant, Alfred Taylor Odell, and T. C. Duncan Eaves (Columbia, S.C.: University of South Carolina Press, 1952–56), II, 511; *Southern Quarterly Review*, XIV (July and October, 1848), 37–76, 262–337.

[6] Simms, *South Carolina in the Revolutionary War* (Charleston, S.C., 1853), pp. 5–6, 11, 22.

[7] Charles Sumner, "Crime Against Kansas," *Congressional Globe*, Appendix, 34th Congress, 1st sess. May 19, 1816, p. 531.

[8] Josiah J. Evans, untitled speech, *ibid.*, June 23, 1856, pp. 701–7; L. M. Keitt, untitled speech, *ibid.*, July 16, 1856, pp, 833–39.

tories written to support sectional bias and local pride. Less dramatic but no less significant was the gradual realization by the people of the South that almost every volume of national history, and particularly those used in the schools, originated "in the North, the *far* North." A writer for *DeBow's Review* wrote indignantly, "What is to be done with geographies that tell pupils 'states are divided into *towns* and counties' . . . with histories that are silent about Texas?"[9]

A war between the states was a distinct possibility at the time the Compromise of 1850 salved sensitive tempers, and it was not surprising that southerners began to press for southern school books written by southern authors. One writer warned that if a time should come when the South would have to "rally as one man, and resist or perish," the southern savior would not be "found among the 'curled darlings' who imbibed their education at the feet of some abolition Gamaliel of the North; but the 'true man' " would rise from the working classes and be someone "who had sat on the bench of the free school, and obtained his first ideas of the world . . . from books and from teachers that taught him the history of the South and the destiny of the South."[10]

Another writer complained that southern boys were expected to learn American history "from Peter Parley," and southern statesmen were forced to glean their history from "Bancroft and Sparks; unless, indeed, they prefer the historical speeches of Webster and Horace Mann." The first step in remedying this situation, the writer declared, was to require all public schools by law to use histories of the southern states and of the United States "prepared by native hands only."[11]

Such drastic action was unnecessary, for certain publishers had become aware that they could no longer sell the same history of the United States to all sections of the country. In 1860, A. S. Barnes and Burr, New York publishers, were advertising "school books by Southern authors" and a national history with "special adaptation to the youth of our land, in all parts of the Union."[12] Some authors, among them William Gilmore Simms and Charles Bonner, directed their works to sectional markets. Simms could scarcely hope that his popular text of South Carolina history would sell outside the state, but certainly Charles Bonner might have expected his two-volume work, *A Child's History of the United States*, to appeal to a large audience. Instead, he limited his market to the South, if only by his choice of words. Northern school boards might adopt a text which contained mention of "the glorious Henry Clay," but they surely would not accept a text that spoke of the tariff as a tool of northern

---

[9] "Southern School Books," *DeBow's Review of the Southern and Western States*, XIII (September, 1852), 259, 262.

[10] *Ibid.*, p. 265.

[11] "Pickett's History of Alabama," *Southern Quarterly Review*, XXI (January, 1852), 187.

[12] A. S. Barnes and Burr, advertisement, *DeBow's Review*, XXVIII (June, 1860), back pages.

manufacturers who intended to rob the people, or one that admonished northerners for judging South Carolina "too harshly."[13]

As the relations between North and South grew strained, both the authors of textbooks and American historians felt the despotism of sectional pride. Those writers who dealt fearlessly with controversial matters could expect the abuse of critics and damning reviews from all sections but that in which their opinion was in favor. Others, who dreamt of popular acclaim and unqualified adulation, avoided insofar as possible all controversial subjects. Reviewers, then as now, were rarely objective in their judgments. Histories were not appraised for their accuracy or the quality of truth they uncovered, but for how fervently they advanced the claims of one region at the expense of another.[14]

The South and the West had no general historians of the United States whom they could crown with literary laurels, but their reviewers covered this lack with the generous and extravagant praise they bestowed on any author who wrote or spoke favorably of southern or western local history. Thus they would rave about an address entitled "The Literary Progress of Georgia," which did little more than list obscure authors who chanced to live in that state, and exclaim over Albert J. Pickett's *History of Alabama*, a defense of southern expansion.[15]

Articles in *DeBow's Review* and the *Southern Quarterly Review* attempted to make the lack of a national historian in the South a sign of democratic virtue, for the "Stately historian," it was hinted, was far too preoccupied with "the grand hero to deal with the struggling myriad below."[16] But the concept of the hero was not an overwhelmingly significant part of current views of American history; histories of cities and towns and westward expansion were the material from which to extract the story of the United States. "Ours is a curious history of a perpetual colonization," explained a writer for *DeBow's Review*. "A History," he continued, "of incessant transition to which we owe the constant development of the picturesque and salient; the due consequence of the hourly recurring conflict between art and nature, civilization and the savage."[17] According to journals like *DeBow's Review*, local histories were needed to chronicle the development of America.

Northern journals were equally incontinent, meting out praise and blame in accord with sectional bias. They heaped encomiums upon Bancroft for each new volume of his *History*. A sketchy and heterogeneous compilation of docu-

---

[13] Simms, *The History of South Carolina, from its first European Discovery to its Erection into a Republic; with a Supplementary Chronicle of Events to the Present Time* (Charleston, S.C., 1840), p. vii; John Bonner, *A Child's History of the United States* (New York, 1856), I, 264–65.

[14] H. S. Randall to H. B. Grigsby, November, 14, 1856, September—, 1857, *Correspondence*, ed. Klingberg and Klingberg, pp. 66, 105; see n. 15.

[15] "Domestic Histories of the South," *Southern Quarterly Review*, XXI (April, 1852), 508; "Review of Albert J. Pickett's History of Alabama," *ibid.* (January, 1852), pp. 182–83.

[16] *Ibid.*, p. 185.

[17] "Domestic Histories," *Southern Quarterly Review*, p. 509.

ments, *The Spirit of '76 in Rhode Island,* by Benjamin Cowell, elicited the praise of a writer for the *Democratic Review,* who claimed it to be a "severe rebuke to those infamous men, who, for purposes merely selfish, lay their sacrilegious hands upon the most noble political structure ever reared by man, and dare breathe the word disunion among the descendants of those heroic men."[18] Critics writing in the *North American Review* used the columns at their disposal to vent their distrust and dislike of the southern states.[19]

While critics bickered, two national historians who should have garnered acclaim received nothing more than abuse and neglect. Richard Hildreth and George Tucker lent themselves to the sectional dispute, and as a result their histories of the United States suffered.[20] Both Hildreth and Tucker might have had great success in the regions from which they came, but the histories they published contained flaws which made it unlikely that they would be honored as sectional champions. Hildreth's book, condemning slavery and heavily weighted with New England material, was far too critical of Puritan rule to be accepted by scions of Puritan descent. Tucker, on the other hand, defended slavery and was sympathetic to the minority position of the South; but he spoke as a nationalist, and his defense of slavery was, at best, half-hearted. Slavery, he wrote, was dying; the problems in its wake could be solved by a vigorous colonization program; the question of slavery was not worth the passions it aroused.

Richard Hildreth published the first volumes of his history in 1849, a year after the last volume of *The Library of American Biography* had appeared and shortly after the publication of the third volume of Bancroft's *History.* Patriotic historians held full sway. When, in the ninth volume, Bancroft came to write of the American Revolution, he criticized the conduct of some individuals; but few sons of New England found cause to complain of Bancroft's glowing tributes to their ancestors. Richard Hildreth was not in tune with these proponents of "a colonial golden age of fabulous purity and virtue."[21] He had often attacked the uncritical type of patriotic oration and literature that cloaked the nation's past in purest white.

Hildreth stood apart from his contemporaries not only in his critical attitude toward the past but in his philosophy. He was a follower of the English classical

[18] "Review of Benjamin Cowell's *Spirit of '76 in Rhode Island,*" *Democratic Review,* XXVII (November, 1850), 476.

[19] A reviewer in the *North American Review,* in speaking of the histories of Virginia and Georgia, wrote, "An ignorance of . . . fundamental moral and economical law early involved in its disastrous consequences the property and population of the southern colonies and entailed evils which impede their progress and hang like threatening clouds over their prospects. . . ." *North American Review,* LXVII (October, 1848), 295. On the southern side, see James P. Holcombe's blasts at Bancroft in *Sketches of the Political Issues and Controversies of the Revolution* (Richmond, 1856); or the extravagant praises heaped upon Gayarré's *The Spanish Rule in Louisiana* in *DeBow's Review,* XIII (October, 1852), 383.

[20] Richard Hildreth, *History of the United States* (New York, 1849), p. 52; George Tucker, *History of the United States to the end of the 26th Congress in 1841* (Philadelphia, 1856–57).

[21] Hildreth, "National Literature," *American Monthly Magazine,* I (July, 1829), 380.

economists and liberals, Adam Smith and Jeremy Bentham. He could speak of the existence of slavery as preventing the "carrying out of the principles of the Revolution, that assimilation and true social union, toward which the States have constantly tended"; he could give hearty approval to Hamilton's funding plan; but he parted company with the rising industrialists in New England upon the tariff issue. He favored free trade and, before 1849, loudly proclaimed his belief, thus setting himself apart from those who otherwise might have been his supporters. While the *History* did not sin in this respect, Hildreth had, and that in itself would explain the cold reception his historical work received.[22]

Reviewers in the South ignored Hildreth's history; those in the middle states praised it for impartiality but were repulsed by its cold, matter-of-fact style. Among New England reviewers, few praised the *History*; some damned it with faint praise and others simply damned it. One critic declared that Hildreth had committed "high treason against the truth" in his treatment of colonial New England theocracy.[23] Later, Hildreth admitted that he had felt the pain of many barbs from the critics of the "region of set formality and hereditary grimace."[24] Hildreth, in his approach to history, was spiritually akin to a group of critical historians who rose in the fifties and flourished in the seventies, who, if they did not imitate his work, showed how much they admired it. His history was solid and withstood all vicissitudes, gaining popularity in the eighties among professional historians who used it as a text and believed they saw in it the genesis of scientific history in America.[25]

George Tucker's *History* enjoyed neither contemporary nor posthumous fame. Compared to Hildreth's work, it was flimsy stuff. Tucker, writing in the historical present, produced a fast flowing and superficial narrative based largely on Hildreth's and Bancroft's volumes and on the annual messages of presidents and the acts of Congress. He terminated his four-volume chronicle at 1841, twenty years beyond Hildreth's terminal date. It was an essay of an old Jeffersonian attempting to bring his country to its senses and to the tenets of Jefferson. Tucker declared that the "question of African slavery" was "not solid ground" for the apprehension that the nation would split. He showed how the nation had weathered other storms safely; how it had made rapid and steady progress in its political, cultural, and material growth; and what great things were yet to come. "But," he warned, "it must never be forgotten that the realization of these splendid visions depends upon the continuance of our political union." Tucker's warning and his work were ignored by southerners,

[22] Hildreth, *History*, I, 399–409; II, 457–59, 526–59.

[23] Francis Bowen, "Hildreth's History of the United States," *North American Review*, LXXIII (October, 1851), 413–37. A southern reviewer wrote, "Never before was history so prostituted to gratify personal or party malevolence." "Hildreth's History of the United States," *DeBow's Review*, X (May, 1851), 599.

[24] Hildreth, *History*, I, ix–x.

[25] For more on Hildreth see Donald E. Emerson's *Richard Hildreth* (Baltimore: Johns Hopkins University Press, 1953); Emerson, "Hildreth, Draper, and 'Scientific History,'" *Historiography and Urbanization*, ed. Eric F. Goldman, pp. 139–70.

who were demanding of authors more vociferous support of their "peculiar institution," and by northerners, who were becoming increasingly tight-fisted in their praise for things southern.[26]

But with the firing upon Fort Sumter and the secession of the southern states, national history writing came to a halt. With patriotic pride, historians like Lossing and J. S. C. Abbott championed their side and broadcast their bias while writing chronicles of the great war. They discovered a heroic theme, the struggle between "the agents of slavery and freedom." Abbott, maintaining that he was an impartial recorder of the events of the Civil War, nonetheless characterized it as a "slave-holding rebellion against the rights of humanity. . . ."[27]

Benson J. Lossing discovered the existence of a long-standing "conspiracy against the Nationality of the Republic," which he had hitherto neglected in his histories, and traced its existence as far back as the Constitutional Convention.[28] Later, other historians pushed the history of the struggle back to the founding of the colonies. Lossing consciously wrote "to educate the public *out* of the wicked sophistries of the Calhoun school."[29] In the South, Edward A. Pollard, the editor of the *Daily Richmond Examiner*, published a running history of the war from the secessionist's point of view and sought to justify the "Lost Cause."

Historians of the nation were fighting the war in their books, and none left any doubt as to which side was favored. The dream of an impartial, true, and epic narrative history shattered with the rending of the nation. *Harper's New Monthly Magazine* only a few years before had announced optimistically that history would soon become a science, "fixed like chemistry."[30] Now *Harper's* expressed disillusionment with the potential science of history after viewing the productions of the fifties and sixties. "How hard it is," wrote George W. Curtis, "to know the truth when we have all the documents and live among the men and events! But when a hundred years hence any man's interpretation of them must be trusted, is it not clear that we should not be too swift to believe, until we know exactly the sympathies and character of the historian?"[31]

[26] Tucker, *History*, I, iii–iv; IV, 399–434; L. C. Helderman, "A Social Scientist of the Old South," *Journal of Southern History*, II (May, 1936), 148–74.

[27] John Stevens Cabot Abbott, *The History of the Civil War in America* (Springfield, Mass., 1863–65), I, Preface.

[28] Lossing, *The Pictorial History of the Civil War* (New York, 1866–68), I, 18.

[29] Lossing to Draper, November 25, 1866, Draper MSS.

[30] "Editor's Table," *Harper's Magazine*, X (May, 1855), 835.

[31] Editor's Easy Chair," *Harper's Magazine*, XXIV (May, 1862), 846–47.

PART FOUR

Localism

The Lost Cause, 1860–84

---

15 CIVIL WAR: A NATIONAL THEME PLAYED WITH
SOME DISCORD, 1861–76

The Civil War ended for at least twenty years all effective efforts to write histories of the nation and of national events that would be acceptable to the country as a whole. Many men and several women felt called upon to produce histories during this period, but this impulse was not always born of a curiosity to discover what had happened and why; they believed they knew the answers to these questions. The mission of the historians of the United States during the time of the Civil War and the Reconstruction period was to establish a record, to glorify or justify a cause, and to claim a due share for section, county, town, regiment, and individual in the great national struggle.

In spite of this factional approach, the disputes about the causes of the war, and the relative contribution of various groups in its prosecution, in most written accounts there was an underlying agreement. Almost universally, whether advocates of "the Lost Cause" or "the Cause of Liberty," historians agreed that the war was a great national trial, that the country was a stronger one for having undergone it, and that because of the struggle patriotism had been strengthened and not weakened. As heated tempers cooled and the urge to revive old arguments grew weaker, this latent agreement became more explicit and North and South found a new synthesis.

The immediate effect of the Civil War was to intensify the urge to write about it. Southerners saw historiography as a chance to establish the rectitude of the cause for which they fought and to save their honor from the ruins of defeat. And from this concern for the record of the "Lost Cause" grew a broad and lasting interest in the writing of history of all magnitudes, from general histories to monographs on local colonial settlements. Northerners wrote histories with the same aplomb with which they erected monuments dedicated to the triumphant cause of the Union. Westerners who had claimed a share in the building of the nation by recounting their pioneer feats in subduing the Indians and settling the wilderness now hastened to present evidence of their patriotism during the national crisis; and if they could not claim equality with the seaboard states in creating the nation, they could claim an equal share in preserving it. Historians of states, towns, and regiments took it for granted that their cause was right, just, and glorious, and, with few exceptions, they made little effort to justify their side but went immediately about the task of claiming a due share of glory for their locality.

The secession of the southern states wrought an immediate change in the attitude of writers toward the production of American histories. The southern market was closed to the northern historian; he no longer had to avoid such controversial issues as slavery and varying interpretations of the constitution, nor need he preach democratic patriotism in an effort to appeal to readers in all parts of the country. Until the outbreak of the Civil War, those historians who directed their work to a broad market had avoided the subject of American history. John Stevens Cabot Abbott, a Congregational minister, had made a reputation by the production of histories dealing with European subjects. Joel Tyler Headley, a minister who was also a popular historian, dealt with European topics or such noncontroversial subjects as *Washington and his Generals* and the *American Pulpit in the Revolution*. Benson J. Lossing, an engraver, who published illustrated histories of the United States, chose to deal primarily with battle scenes in which he could display to good advantage American courage and patriotism. With the firing upon Fort Sumter, historians in the North vigorously espoused the Union cause. Abbott and Headley turned to the United States as the subject for their histories, and Lossing transformed democratic virtues, hitherto granted Americans everywhere, into purely northern attributes.

John S. C. Abbott was typical of this group of national historians who thirsted after a popular market. Abbott, a minister's son, grew up in Maine, graduated from Bowdoin in 1825, and after three years at Andover Seminary went from one pastorate to another organizing Sunday schools. He began his literary career with the zeal and worthy intentions of a Christian evangelist. His first book, published in 1833, expressed the tenor of his thought in its title, *The Mother at Home, or the Principles of Maternal Duty Familiarly Illustrated*. He produced inspirational literature in popular form until 1850 and then began to write biography and history. Although he had changed the subject of his writing, he had not abandoned his "message": He continued to preach the brotherhood of man and the virtues of hard work and piety. Near the end of his life, he declared, "I have written fifty-four volumes. In every one it has been my endeavor to make the inhabitants of this sad world more brotherly, better and wiser."[1]

Abbott, like many of his colleagues, praised the conservative virtues embodied in orthodox Congregationalism and the Whig and Republican parties, to which he gave his allegiance and support. In 1850, Harper and Brothers accepted Abbott's biography of Napoleon and published it serially in their re-

[1] In Stanley P. Chase, "John Stevens Cabot Abbott," *DAB*, I, 23.

cently established periodical, *Harper's New Monthly Magazine*. The biography was popular both as a two-year serial and as a two-volume book. It raised the ire of Horace Greeley, and of Edwin Godkin, the founder of the *Nation*, who abhorred the attempt to make a popular hero of a despot and tyrant. But to Abbott the "message" was the important part of his writing, and he chose the best vehicle, the one that would carry his message to the most people. He had selected Napoleon as the subject of his biography because there was a great deal of interest in the old emperor in the 1850's when people were watching and trying to predict the actions of his nephew, Louis Napoleon, then president of the Second French Republic.[2] Abbott continued to write on European subjects, *The Empire of Austria* (1859) and *The Empire of Russia* (1860), until the outbreak of the Civil War.[3]

In the great conflict to preserve the Union, Abbott found a theme befitting his talents; in 1863, he began issuing periodically a *History of the Civil War in America* in numbers of twenty-five to fifty pages each. In this history, which he assembled by pasting together hastily excerpted and paraphrased articles from magazines, he proclaimed the Union cause to be that of all mankind—freedom against tyranny, virtue against a corruption bred by easy living in a slave-supported economy. After the Civil War, Abbott considered American history a rich vein from which to mine other books; and he continued to write European histories.[4]

Other writers who had been producing histories for the popular market before the war seized upon the Civil War as a subject certain to sell books. William M. Thayer, a Congregational minister and an editor of *The Home Monthly*, presented the theme of "rags to riches through virtue and thrift" in biographies of Amos Lawrence, "the poor boy and merchant prince" and Mary Lyon, "the poor girl's true woman," before the Civil War. In a subsequent biography, the reward of virtue was the office of President, in *The Pioneer Boy and How he Became President*. Thayer continued to write books about the war and produced, among others, *A Youth's History of the Rebellion*, which he declared would show the children of the nation the sacrifices their fathers had

[2] See the comments of Charles Kendall Adams in *A Manual of Historical Literature* (New York, 1888), pp. 366–67. Somewhat later, Edwin L. Godkin spoke of Abbott as representative of a particularly offensive type of popular historical writer. "I single out Abbott for special hostility, not because I think he is himself or his books worth half a page, but because his 'histories' are fair specimens of a kind of literature of which there is an immense quantity issued every year and which the half educated look on as 'solid reading.' I suppose neither you nor I have any idea of the enormous number of respectable people who think his history of Napoleon and his history of the Rebellion solid works, and it is sickening to see him treated in the newspapers with great deference as 'Abbott the historian.' " Godkin to George E. Norton, January 18, 1865, in *Life and Letters of Edwin Lawrence Godkin*, ed. Rollo Ogden (New York: Macmillan Co., 1907), II, 33.

[3] Abbott also published a history, *Italy* (New York, 1860).

[4] Abbott declared, "This slave holding rebellion against the rights of humanity, is the greatest crime on earth. In recording its events, candor does not demand that one should so ingeniously construct his narrative, as to make no distinction between virtue and vice" (*History of the Civil War in America*, I, iv).

made in order to preserve the Union and thereby heighten the patriotism of the rising generation.[5]

Joel Tyler Headley, another established author of history and biography, seized upon the great rebellion as a topic and took up his pen in the Union cause. Headley was a Congregational minister, a native New Yorker, who held for five years a pastorate in Stockbridge, Massachusetts. In 1842, he suffered a nervous breakdown, gave up the ministry, went to Italy, and began his life's career by writing a travel account of Italy. Before the war, Headley wrote a biography of Napoleon, as Abbott had done; in a sense he was publisher Charles Scribner's answer to the House of Harper. Headley was among those who saw some possibilities for popular sales in subjects from American history. He published *Washington and his Generals* in 1847 and followed it in 1853 with a history of the War of 1812. In both works he vilified the British and praised American courage, and carefully avoided any criticism of states or sections.[6] During the Civil War, Headley, whom some people called "a rather hard old fellow," came to justify his reputation. In a history of *The Great Rebellion*, he put the blame on the South, and throughout the volumes he tendered no mercy, no sympathy, and no justice to the Confederacy, seeing only perfidy and treason.[7]

While Abbott, Thayer, Headley, and others were clipping newspaper and magazine articles to compile a history of the war, Benson J. Lossing toured the battlefields, following his thoroughly tested method of gathering first-hand material. Lossing, an engraver, had written and illustrated a good many histories; all centered on the nation's battles and preached patriotism. Like Abbott, Thayer, and Headley, Lossing did not publicly espouse the Union cause before the outbreak of war. He joined the Republican party sometime in the late fifties, but his partisanship did not influence his writing until the southern states left the Union.

In 1862, Lossing began a series of magazine articles concerning the history of the great struggle between slavery and freedom, tracing it from the colonial period. He obtained a correspondent's pass to visit the battlefields; many of the scenes he had visited on earlier trips to gather material for his books, a *Field Book of the Revolution* and a *Field Book of the War of 1812*. He interviewed gen-

---

[5] William Makepeace Thayer, *The Poor Boy and Merchant Prince . . . The Life of Amos Lawrence* (New York, 1857); Thayer, *The Poor Girl and True Woman . . . Life of Mary Lyon* (New York, 1857); Thayer, *The Pioneer Boy and How he Became President* (New York, 1863); Thayer, *The Bobbin Boy* (New York, 1860). Thayer preceded Horatio Alger in use of the rags-to-riches theme. Although he was not as popular as Alger, still he enjoyed fair success. The theme as well as its popularity are definite indications of how much industrialization was taken for granted in the 1850's. Verne Lockwood Samson, "William Makepeace Thayer," *DAB*, XVIII, 412–13.

[6] Joel Tyler Headley, *Napoleon and his Marshalls* (2 vols.; New York, 1846); Headley, *Washington and his Generals* (2 vols.; New York, 1847); Headley, *Second War with England* (New York, 1853); Roger Burlingame, *Of Making Many Books* (New York: Charles Scribners' Sons, 1946), pp. 58, 76.

[7] Headley, *The Great Rebellion* (Hartford, 1866), I, 9.

erals and examined their papers, as William Gordon had done during the American Revolution. He sketched the camps, the fields, and the men, and in 1863 he began to issue a history of the Civil War. Lossing's history was no less harsh on the "Southern conspiracy" than other histories appearing in the North at the time. Shortly after the war, Lossing declared that he had written so to educate "the public mind *out* of the wicked sophistries of the Calhoun school, *into* the sober and beneficent doctrines of government put forth by Washington and Hamilton, and other fathers of the Republic."[8]

Death and the exigencies of war silenced the few established historians in the South. George Tucker died just before the war, and during the war William Gilmore Simms wrote no history. In the North, the most prominent historians, George Bancroft, Francis Parkman, and John Lothrop Motley, favored the Union cause and contributed to Union propaganda, but none chose the Civil War as a theme.[9]

Biographers also felt the impact of the war. Some laid aside their pens for more active duties, others chose more immediate topics. William Cabell Rives, a student of Jefferson and a powerful Jacksonian Democrat in Virginia, had been working since 1845 on an exhaustive biography of James Madison. He chose his subject with the hope of discovering in Madison's papers further indications of the intent of the authors of the Constitution and in an effort to restore the national reputation of a friend and fellow Virginian.[10] Rives published the first volume in 1859, but in the following year he put aside the project to work for peace and union. When Virginia seceded, he took a part in the Confederate government; after the war, he sought to lose himself in the unfinished biography. He brought Madison to 1797 in the third volume, but died before attempting the fourth and final volume. His biography of Madison, a product of the ante-bellum constitutional controversy, became a casualty of the fire it sought to quench, and it stands as an unfinished monument, a model of the prewar "life and times" biography.

[8] Lossing to L. C. Draper, November 25, 1866, Draper correspondence; Lossing, *Pictorial History of the Civil War* (issued serially, beginning in 1863; published in book form, New York, 1866–68); Van Tassel, "Lossing," *American Quarterly*, VI, 43.

[9] Thomas J. Pressly discusses the ideas of these historians on the war as expressed in articles and speeches in *Americans Interpret Their Civil War* (Princeton: Princeton University Press, 1954), pp. 7–10.

[10] William Cabell Rives, *History of the Life and Times of James Madison* (3 vols.; Boston, 1859–68). The Federalist-Whig interpretation of the Constitution and plaudits for Alexander Hamilton as its "father" seemed to be gaining a permanent place in American historiography by repetition. For example, George Ticknor Curtis, son-in-law of Joseph Story, a prolific legal scholar and constitutional lawyer, presented this view, with the aid of Daniel Webster, in a series of public lectures in 1849–50 for the Lowell Institute in Boston. Curtis later published *A History of the Origin, Formation, and Adoption of the Constitution of the United States* (2 vols.; New York, 1854–58), in which he expanded the lectures. Curtis used only the published official documents, took a highly legalistic approach to history, and managed, nonetheless, to make Hamilton a hero and the father of the Constitution. A number of scholars other than Rives took exception to this interpretation. See Hugh Blair Grigsby to Henry Stephens Randall, July 31, 1858, *Correspondence*, ed. Klingberg and Klingberg, pp. 142–43.

In New York, when war broke out, another biographer, James Parton, was hard at work on a life of Benjamin Franklin. The critics, in the North and abroad, had praised his three-volume biography of Andrew Jackson in which he had portrayed the man not as "a model to copy, but a specimen to study."[11] Parton chose Franklin as his next subject because the man intrigued him and because he was a figure of national interest. But when the war intervened Parton put aside his biography of Franklin. Unlike Rives, Parton had to live by his writing, and with a journalist's sense of the timely he began a study of Benjamin F. Butler's administration of New Orleans. He interviewed the blustery political general and published in 1864 a glowing defense of the administration. In the same year he rushed into print his biography of Franklin; the result was disappointing. Not only was the sale poor, but the biography itself fell far short of the standard Parton had set himself before the Civil War.[12]

The war brought out the sectional partisanship of some national historians and apparently silenced others. It also proved a stimulus to journalists, who began to write popular histories. The decade before the war had been a period of phenomenal growth and development for the newspaper. The weekly paper, owned, edited, and printed by a single man, was giving way to the large metropolitan daily, owned by an individual or corporation interested less in the support of a political party than in the profits to be gained from a wide circulation and the patronage of advertisers. Writing for such a journal as the New York *Times* or *Tribune* became a full-time job, and editing the work of a staff of specialists. Even in the early days of American journalism, such columnists as Nathaniel P. Willis and Fanny Fern discovered the ease with which they could make books by pasting old columns together.[13] During the war, newspaper correspondents wrote day-by-day accounts of the conflict, and it was not long before this material was used again in histories of campaigns, biographies of generals, and chronicles of the war. Reporters and editors of both the Union and the Confederacy entered the field of historical writing and soon surpassed in popularity men like Lossing, Barker, Sears, Abbott, and Headley.

It was a relatively simple task for an editor or a correspondent to collect material and produce a history of the war. Elliot G. Storke, editor of *Family Farm and Garden*, might have been speaking for many of his colleagues when he wrote, "At the opening of the Great Rebellion, we began to arrange and record its important events. By the time Lee met Grant at Appomattox in 1865, Storke had enough material to issue, in two volumes, *A Complete History of the*

[11] James Parton, *Life of Andrew Jackson* (New York, 1861), I, ix–xi; III, 694–95. A good, recent estimate of Parton's *Jackson* in relation to Jackson historiography is Charles Grier Sellers, Jr., "Andrew Jackson versus the Historians," *Mississippi Valley Historical Review*, XLIV (March, 1958), 615–34.

[12] James Parton, *General Butler in New Orleans* (New York, 1864); *Life and Times of Benjamin Franklin* (2 vols.; New York, 1864). Contemporary critics praised the *Franklin* and subsequent biographers have been gentle in their comments. See Flower, *James Parton*, pp. 58–77.

[13] Flower, *James Parton*, pp. 20–21, 22–23.

Great American Rebellion, embracing its Causes, Events and Consequences, with Biographical Sketches and Portraits of its Principal Actors and Thrilling Incidents of Land and Naval Heroes.[14]

Other reporters were clipping, collecting, and compiling material to appear in book form during and immediately after the war. Frank Moore, editor of *Putnam's Monthly Magazine*, published *The Rebellion Record* (1862–66) at the rate of two volumes a year. His aim was to issue periodically a systematized and digested history of the war, "sifting fact from fiction and rumor; presenting the poetical and picturesque aspects, the notable and characteristic incidents, separated from the graver and more important documents."[15] *The Rebellion Record* and a similar production, *Harper's Illustrated History of the Rebellion*, served as source material for shorter histories until the 1880's, when *Century Magazine* published its four-volume work, *Battles and Leaders of the Civil War*, and the War Records Office began publishing . . . *Official Records of the Union and Confederate Armies.*[16]

In the Confederacy, too, newspaper men began to produce histories of the war. Edward A. Pollard, an editor of the *Daily Richmond Examiner* and an ardent secessionist, published the first volume of a *Southern History of the War: the First Year of the War* in 1862, and published the second and third volumes in 1863 and 1864. To Pollard, as to other southern historians, the southern cause was the preservation of the Constitution in its original purity; the South, they argued, had fought changes in the Constitution made by grasping and materialistic elements in the North, until there seemed no way to avoid the eventual tyranny of the industrial North except by leaving the Union.[17]

James Williams of Tennessee, a former diplomat and a writer for the *Index*, the London propaganda organ of the Confederacy, also published histories of the war, *The South Vindicated* (1862) and *The Rise and Fall of "The Model Republic"* (1863), designed to explain the history of the southern cause to the British and to muster support for the Confederacy.[18] Among other southern journalists writing accounts of the conflict was "Parson" William G. Brownlow, editor of the *Knoxville Whig*, whose *Sketches of the Rise, Progress and Decline of Secession* was published in 1862. Brownlow emphasized the inner struggle that had taken place in the South over the question of secession. It was a story northerners wanted to read, and Brownlow sold some three hundred thousand

[14] (Auburn, New York, 1865), I, Preface.

[15] Moore continued to insist that it was his intention to sum up the history of "the most extraordinary and unjustifiable conspiracy and rebellion which the world had ever witnessed." Frank Moore, *The Rebellion Record* (New York, 1862–66), I, iv.

[16] *Harper's Pictorial History of the Great Rebellion*, ed. Alfred H. Guernsey and Henry M. Alden (2 vols.; New York, 1866) (4 vols.; New York, 1884–87) (128 vols.; Washington, D.C., 1880–1900).

[17] Edward A. Pollard, *Southern History of the War* (Charleston, 1865), I, 107–8; J. G. DeR. Hamilton, "Edward Alfred Pollard," *DAB*, XV, 47–48.

[18] Pressly, *Americans Interpret Their Civil War*, pp. 66–68.

copies. Brownlow's success encouraged imitators, and there followed a legion of Civil War histories compiled by northern journalists.[19]

The discordant notes of these wartime propagandists would be echoed by American historians for nearly a century, but both North and South agreed that the Civil War was a great national event, to rival the American Revolution as a subject for historians. The war had disrupted the development of historical studies; critical and local scholars had all but ceased their "delving and rummaging" in the dust of the past. Journalists found a way to market old articles and took to writing history, thus challenging the dominance of the minister and lawyer in the field of national historical writing. But, above all, a new national theme was born. Local and would-be national historians in the North and in the South, no matter how they accounted for the war and whether they considered it a triumph or a catastrophe, agreed that only glory was due those who had participated in the struggle and that henceforth American history would be written to celebrate the event.

[19] E. Merton Coulter, *William G. Brownlow: Fighting Parson of the Southern Highlands* (Chapel Hill, N.C.: North Carolina University Press, 1937), pp. 208-20.

16 LOCAL HISTORY GOES TO WAR, 1861-76

While scholars and journalists recorded, supported, and glorified the Union or the Confederacy, local historians were hard at work compiling community records of the national crisis. Just as the Civil War introduced the journalist into historical writing, so it encouraged the writing of regimental history. The histories of regiments were not devoted to discussion of the planning of battles and of military tactics but were an extension of local history—local history gone to war. They were the stories of and monuments to the men of Illinois, Massachusetts, Alabama, and Virginia. In the record of their regiments lay the claim of states and local communities to a share in the glory of the great national struggle. "No general history," one local historian asserted, "can do the individual states justice; nay, no complete, comprehensive history can be written until at the end of the war, the states have made up their annals. For these the Irvings, Bancrofts and Prescotts of the Union must wait. In each state should be written the deeds of its sons, the achievements of its regiments, the deeds of its officers and citizen soldiery."[1]

The Civil War was fought by citizen armies. Men recruited in a certain locality were formed into regiments and generally remained together throughout the war. Thus, three-month enlistees from the western counties of Pennsyl-

[1] T. M. Eddy, *The Patriotism of Illinois* (Chicago, 1865), I, 9-10.

vania formed the Eleventh Regiment of Pennsylvania Volunteers; at the end of the three months the regiment was discharged; most members then re-enlisted in the same regiment for three years. In the strictest sense, every state, county, and town was represented by its male citizens in military units which served on the battlefield as extensions of the local community.[2]

Histories of towns and states published during and shortly after the war were simply histories of regiments. Thomas M. Eddy, a minister and editor of the *Christian Advocate*, published in 1865 a two-volume history, *The Patriotism of Illinois*, as "a record of the part our noble state has borne in the great struggle to maintain our glorious government." The author's sole concern was to re-count the history, regiment by regiment, of Illinois' troops in the war.[3] The same was true of P. C. Headley's *Massachusetts in the Rebellion* (1866), Fearing Burr and George Lincoln's *Town of Hingham in the Late Civil War* (1876), and other regimental histories that followed to the battlefield the names of the state or town of their origins.[4]

John W. Barber and Henry Howe, who in 1860 published a documentary his-tory, *Our Whole Country*, after the war considered the idea of publishing his-tories of the North, the West, and the South. They intended to divide the con-tents of *Our Whole Country*, add material on the Civil War, and issue three separate volumes. They published only one, *The Loyal West in the Times of the Rebellion* (1865), the last half devoted to regimental history, classified by town and county, with intent to demonstrate the courage and patriotism of "the Loyal West" on the field of battle as further evidence of the greatness of the "empire" that had grown up "on the sunset side of the Alleghenies. . . ."[5]

Many regimental histories were not written by military men.[6] Chaplains to the regiments, civilians employed by the state Adjutant General's office, jour-nalists, and at least one woman wrote books of this kind.[7] The problems of logistics, tactics, and strategy were recounted in volumes about large military units, the brigade, the division, the corps, by high ranking officers. These units were too large and included men from too many localities to become the sub-jects of histories of appeal to local pride. Officers gave their allegiance to larger

[2] Samuel P. Bates, *History of the Pennsylvania Volunteers, 1861–1865* (Harrisburg, 1869), I, 245.

[3] Eddy, *op. cit.*, p. 8.

[4] Fearing Burr and George Lincoln, *Town of Hingham in the Late Civil War, with Sketches of its Soldiers and Sailors* (Boston, 1876).

[5] John W. Barber and Henry Howe, *Our Whole Country* (New York, 1860); Barber and Howe, *The Loyal West in the Times of the Rebellion* (Cincinnati, 1865), p. 5.

[6] General James D. Cox observed: "One's first impression would be that regimental his-tories . . . are among the most authentic sources of the war history. It does not turn out so. They are almost all devoted to what we may call the domestic side of their experience." J. D. Cox, "Bibliography of the Civil War," in Larned (ed.), *The Literature of American History*, p. 216.

[7] Mrs. Ellen Williams, *Three Years and a half in the Army; or a History of the Second Colorados* (New York, 1885).

segments of the army, but the regiment received the allegiance of the enlisted man, for he might serve in many divisions and in several armies, but as a rule he served in but a single regiment.[8]

For the most part, the authors of regimental chronicles did not attempt to record the events leading up to the war; they began with the onset of hostilities and took it as obvious that the cause for which the regiments fought was both honorable and glorious. One author was typical of most when he declared that he did not propose "to describe the movements of armies, or chronicle the results of campaigns, except to illustrate more fully the doings of the regiment."[9] Not particular men, whose names were rarely mentioned, but the regiment was always the hero of the story; for all served honorably, and individuals were not singled out for special mention. The record of desertion, plain and undenied in the muster rolls appended at the end of the volume, was not mentioned in the narrative.

The historian sometimes referred to the regiments by their wartime nicknames, the Rhode Island Twelfth as "the flying regiment," the New York Ninth as "Hawkins' Zouaves." The regiment always "tasted victory" and "won the commendation of its superior officers" as if it were an individual; in this way each soldier and the relatives of soldiers in battle could share in the glory of the regiment and its heroes.[10]

No matter how unmilitary and how like reminiscences these regimental histories seem, in order to write them the authors required access to official documents. They had to have accurate muster rolls, for it was to the soldiers and their families that they hoped to sell their books—indeed, this list of names gave the history its *raison d'être*. Most of the regimental historians wrote their works only after the state legislatures published the Adjutant General's report. In some instances they used the original papers. If, as in the case of many southern states, records were missing, they wrote the War Records Office in Washington for access to or copies of the papers relating to the military history of the state. The passion for materials on local troops in the Civil War, and the pressure of local veterans' organizations and regimental historians, moved state legislatures to rescue and publish many documents of the war.

In 1864, the state legislature of Pennsylvania acted to initiate the preparation for publication of the war record of each Pennsylvania regiment. Nothing more was done until veterans and politicians urged Governor Andrew G. Curtin to appoint Samuel P. Bates, a well-known educational reformer and state superintendent of schools, to gather the necessary data. Bates found that there

[8] F. A. Shannon, *The Organization and Administration of the Union Army* (2 vols.; Cleveland: Arthur H. Clark Co., 1928).

[9] George W. Powers, *The Story of the Thirty-eighth Regiment of Massachusetts Volunteers* (Cambridge, Mass., 1866), Preface.

[10] William Swinton, *The History of the New York Seventh Regiment during the War of the Rebellion* (New York, 1870). Swinton asserts in his Preface that it is his policy not to mention names of members of the regiment.

had been good reason for not implementing the act, for records had not been kept or were missing from the Adjutant General's office. Bates was an indefatigable worker; although the government War Office refused him permission to see the records pertaining to Pennsylvania troops, he was able to collect enough material from former officers and from the published annual reports of the Adjutant General to fill five thick volumes, a *History of the Pennsylvania Volunteers*. By legislative act in 1867 the volumes were published as a tribute to the services of Pennsylvania men in the war and "as a mark of the appreciation in which their valor is held."[11]

Minnesotans were extremely slow in recording the history of their regiment. John B. Sanborn, the "Commander General of the Minnesota Commandary of the Military Order of the Loyal Legion of the United States," deplored this neglect. Sanborn lamented that the state of Minnesota had "made no proper record of, and claimed no preëminence from the fact that the first offer of volunteers to the President of the United States for the war was from her governor . . . and the first regiment of volunteers for three years was organized by the state. . . ." He called for the support of the legion to remedy the situation, and soon regimental histories began to appear.[12]

While local veterans' organizations and others interested in regimental history were applying pressure to their various states to get documents and histories published, national veterans' organizations urged the federal government to publish the long-promised records of the Union and Confederate armies. The Loyal Legion, which was modeled after the Order of the Cincinnati, the Society of the Army of the Potomac, and the Society of the Army of the Tennessee, as well as the Massachusetts Military Historical Society and the common soldier's organization, the Grand Army of the Republic—all were, in part, concerned to keep alive the past in the public mind. At each meeting the members relived "the exciting scenes of the past" and thus were "rebaptized with that spirit of patriotism and devotion to the country that characterized our people in the early days of the war."[13]

In order to satisfy the hunger for stories of the war, veterans who had addresses to give, articles to write, or histories to prepare saw the value of having documentary sources readily available. The one great mine of material, aside from the state Adjutant Generals' offices, was the War Records Office in Washington. General Henry W. Halleck was the first to propose a special depository of the military records of the war when he had difficulty in obtaining material for a report he was to make. In 1865, Secretary of War Edwin M.

---

[11] Samuel P. Bates, *History of the Pennsylvania Volunteers*, I, Preface; Hiram H. Shenk, "Samuel Penniman Bates," *DAB*, II, 53.

[12] John B. Sanborn, "Remarks of the Past Commander General," in *Glimpses of the Nation's Struggle, a Series of Papers read before the Minnesota Commandery of the Military Order of the Loyal Legion of the United States* (St. Paul, 1887), pp. 406–7.

[13] *Ibid.*, pp. 404–5; *Report of the Proceedings of the Society of the Army of the Tennessee at the First Annual Meeting Held at Cincinnati, Ohio, Nov. 14 and 15, 1866* (Cincinnati, 1877), p. 8.

Stanton set up the Archives Office of the War Department, which was used at first as a depository for captured Confederate records.

The first task of the members of the Archives Office was to research for evidence implicating Jefferson Davis and other Confederate leaders in the plot to assassinate Abraham Lincoln; the second was to sort, arrange, and file the confiscated records. In 1866, Congress passed legislation providing for the publication of "the official history of the rebellion." The object of the Senate Committee on Military Affairs was to "perpetuate the proud record made by the armies of the republic in their efforts for the maintenance of the Union, and to furnish a means for historical reference . . . [which would] find its way as such into every library at home and abroad, and mould the judgment of history."[14] Though implying otherwise, the committee had every intention of publishing Confederate records. The job of editing the "official history" was the responsibility of the Adjutant General's office, which was to work in conjunction with the Archives Office, but perhaps as a consequence of bureaucratic apathy, nothing was done toward publication.[15]

Impatiently, veterans' organizations demanded that these records be published and deluged the Archives Office with requests for information. The general policy of the Archives Office, which was to refuse to give out such information, only served to increase public clamor. In 1874, a Democratic Congress passed a law providing for the publication of the records of both Union and Confederate armies. The War Department reorganized the Archives Office and renamed it the War Records Office. Captain Robert N. Scott, former aide-de-camp to General Henry W. Halleck, was placed in charge of the office and of editing the official history. Scott threw the records open to anyone who wished information and appointed a former Confederate general, Marcus J. Wright, as special agent of the War Department to collect from the southern states Confederate records of the Civil War. In 1880, the first volume of *The War of the Rebellion* was issued by the Government Printing Office.[16]

In the nineties, a fresh rash of regimental histories rolled off the presses. In general, these latter-day histories were more accurate than those produced before the smoke of battle had cleared. Writers like William R. Hartpence, who published a *History of the Fifty-First Indiana Veteran Volunteer Infantry* (1894), and Charles E. Davis, whose *Three Years in the Army: the Story of the Thirteenth Massachusetts Volunteers* appeared in 1894, had an opportunity to consult published accounts and documents and to collect the diaries and letters of

---

[14] *Senate Miscellaneous Documents*, No. 102, 39th Congress, 1st sess., I, 1240.

[15] *The War of the Rebellion: A Compilation of the Official Records of the Union and Confederate Armies* (Washington, 1880), I, Introduction.

[16] Dallas Irvine, "The Genesis of the Official Records," *Mississippi Valley Historical Review*, XXIV (1937), 221–29; Irvine, "The Archive Office of the War Department, Repository of Captured Confederate Archives, 1865–1881," *Military Affairs*, X (Spring, 1946), 93–111; Carl L. Lokke, "The Captured Confederate Records under Francis Lieber," *American Archivist*, IX (October, 1946), 277–319.

those who had participated in the war and had preserved evidence of their share in the great catastrophe.

The regimental histories of the Civil War which continued to appear into the early twentieth century were generally better written and more accurate than the earlier products, but they did not differ in kind. They were peculiarly the product of the Civil War, when local and state individuality was retained in the fighting forces. The desire of northern and southern veterans to record their share in the great struggle, as well as the necessity of reconciling a returning southern electorate, forced the War Department to publish a huge collection of official documents, making what might have been the victor's official history an unprecedented mine of source material for the war as a whole and a symbol of the national character of the struggle.

The regimental histories themselves added little to the military history of the war; they were the products of a democratic era, when the structure of the army reflected the structure of the country, when individualism and local loyalty could not be submerged even during a national crisis, and when a private could refuse to obey an officer ("I'll see you in hell first!") without fear of certain retribution. These volumes are extensions of local history and "social histories" of common men at war.[17]

[17] Using these regimental histories as a main source, Bell I. Wiley wrote two very successful social histories of "men at arms," *The Life of Johnny Reb* (New York: Bobbs-Merrill Co., 1943) and *The Life of Billy Yank* (New York: Bobbs-Merrill Co., 1952). Bruce Catton made effective use of regimental histories in writing of the Army of the Potomac in various works, including *A Stillness at Appomattox* (New York: Doubleday & Co., Inc., 1953).

---

17 THE NATIONAL PAST: A BASIS FOR REUNION, 1866–76

In 1866, George Bancroft, his sense of nationalism justified by the Civil War, dedicated the ninth volume of his epic *History of the United States* to "freedom and union."[1] But Bancroft's history was no more acceptable to local critics than it had been before the war, because he continued to generalize from the history of the New England states and rode roughshod over the past of other regions.

[1] Bancroft, *History*, IX, 5. For southern criticism see *Southern Review*, IV (1868), 225. Another southerner, goaded anew by Bancroft's continued production, lamented that the historian could no longer be caught up in his errors on southern history. Thomas H. Wynne, secretary of the Virginia Historical Society, had seen the records of the trial of Nathaniel Bacon's associates, destroyed during the Civil War. Wynne declared that when Bancroft was "preparing his account of this portion of his *story* of the United States and he made notes of the same yet when he [Bancroft] published his book he misstated the facts in the grossest manner." Wynne to L. C. Draper, April 4, 1868, in Hesseltine and Gara (eds.), "Postwar Problems of a Virginia Historian," *Virginia Magazine of History and Biography*, LXI (April, 1953), 194.

Bancroft's effort to restore the bonds of union was a method many historians were to attempt during the violent years of Reconstruction. Only an uneasy reconciliation could be effected in a chronicle of the Civil War, for most patriots believed that history was the ultimate tribunal.

Northern writers, attempting to glorify the Union cause, made the war an epoch in the continuing battle for human freedom, as did Henry Wilson in his three-volume hymn to radical Republicanism, *The History of the Rise and Fall of the Slave Power in America* (1872). Southern champions of the "Lost Cause" felt that they would fail in their duty to posterity if they permitted "the false allegations of the Northern historians to be accepted as true without attempting a refutation and vindication."[2] The "refutations and vindications" appeared in a steady stream as southerners, never before known as authors of histories or of other forms of literature, were impelled to vindicate, or justify, the cause of the South. Alexander H. Stephens, the former vice president of the Confederacy, defended the course taken by the southern states in a two-volume work, *The Constitutional View of the War Between the States* (1868–70). Jefferson Davis, once president of the Confederacy, refused to admit defeat and sought to rally Confederate veterans to the battle of history. Davis followed his own precepts in *The Rise and Fall of the Confederate Government*, a vindication of the Confederate cause and a refutation of the aspersions cast upon his administration by fellow southerners. Others, with less stake in the reputation of the Confederacy, professed the belief that God would not abandon a just cause; and when right was triumphant, they would be on record as defenders of the faith.

The generals, no less than the politicians, had a claim to history; and both northern and southern military leaders, having hung their swords above the mantlepiece, picked up their pens to tell of their part in the war. In 1869, Generals Dabney H. Maury, Braxton Bragg, Simon Bolivar Buckner, and Pierre G. T. Beauregard met in New Orleans to form the Southern Historical Society, to collect and preserve records "illustrating the nature of the struggle from which the country has just emerged, defining and vindicating the principles which lay beneath it. . . ."[3] The society showed little vigor until 1873, when delegates from twelve southern states met in Virginia to reorganize the group and to propose branches in every southern state. The society assembled a valuable collection of Confederate materials, but publications under its aegis, far from vindicating the honor of the South, became a forum used by military leaders to defend their reputations on the battlefield against the recriminations of former comrades in arms. The society's northern counterpart, the Military History Society of Massachusetts, founded in 1876, was used for the same purpose by Union commanders.[4]

[2] R. Randolph Stevenson, *The Southern Side; or Andersonville Prison* (Baltimore, 1876), p. 6.

[3] Southern Historical Society, *Papers*, I (Richmond, 1876), 41.

[4] Military Historical Society of Massachusetts, *Papers*, I (Boston, 1881), 1–3, *passim*.

Although there was never a backslapping unanimity among historians about the Civil War, a movement toward reconciliation did occur, closely paralleling the political reunion of 1877, when southern politicians swapped their votes for power and patronage, and 1884, when the Democrats, reunited, again became a national party. The first signs of reconciliation came in the late seventies and the eighties. Regimental histories, North and South, were noticeably less denunciatory of the former enemy than were more general histories of the war. Some noted the bravery and courage of the opposing side; but then soldiers who have known the realities of war have always been less vindictive than civilians. Sherman's troops, before leaving Raleigh, burned a cartload of New York newspapers that denounced the easy terms Sherman had given Confederate General Joseph E. Johnston.[5] Officers were eager to hear both sides of historic battles in order to confirm judgments made in the field. The *Historical Magazine* published documents on the war submitted by both northern and southern officers.

As the fires of hate began to die, a spirit of reconciliation rose among the people of North and South. The popular journals printed articles, stories, and reminiscences of Confederate and Union officers. In 1879, the *Philadelphia Weekly Times* published a series of such articles in a large volume, "with a view of correcting many of the grave errors of the hastily compiled, heedlessly imperfect, and strongly partisan histories which appeared during and soon after the close of the war."[6] The *Century Magazine* published a "war series" in the early eighties and republished them in book form as *Battles and Leaders of the Civil War* (1884–87). The editors of these volumes claimed that the series "exerted an influence in bringing about a better understanding between the soldiers who were opposed" in the Civil War.[7] The publication of the first volume of *The War of the Rebellion* set to rest southern fear that the federal government would seek to distort the history of the war by withholding from publication Confederate records in its possession.[8]

Although historians did not slough off their wartime bias, their textbooks and national histories gave evidence of mellowing and provided an opportunity for reconciliation. In 1872, George F. Holmes, a professor of history and literature at the University of Virginia, an exponent of Comtian positivism, and a professional textbook writer, published a *School History of the United States of America* which avoids the recriminations of earlier southern histories and has as theme the inevitability of the conflict. In a chapter dealing with the Missouri

[5] Dixon Wecter, *When Johnny Comes Marching Home* (New York: Charles Scribner's Sons, 1942), p. 109.

[6] *The Annals of the War Written by Leading Participants North and South* (Philadelphia, 1879), pp. i–ii.

[7] Robert Underwood Johnson and Clarence C. Buel (eds.), *Battles and Leaders of the Civil War* (New York, 1884–86), I, 1.

[8] *The Proceedings of the Southern Historical Convention, which assembled at the Montgomery, White Sulphur Springs, Virginia, on the 14th of August, 1873, and of the Southern Historical Society as reorganized, with the Address by General Jubal A. Early, delivered before the Convention on the first day of its session* (Richmond, 1873).

Compromise and the administrations of Monroe and John Quincy Adams, Holmes, writing of the Compromise of 1820, declared that "it was foreseen that the time must arrive when the objects of the Compromise would be frustrated." And he speaks further of a "rush of events toward a bloody war of sections." The war was bound to occur, Holmes maintained; it wrought destruction and deep wounds, but because of it the United States became a stronger nation, with a "fuller consciousness of national power and large capacities for national grandeur."[9] Horace Scudder, a product of the Boston Latin School and Williams College, an author and later an editor of the *Atlantic Monthly*, wrote a *History of the United States* (1884) in which he made no mention of a conspiracy of slaveholders but emphasized how inevitable was the outbreak of the Civil War.[10]

Nor were the officers and textbook writers the only ones imbued with the spirit of reconciliation; a new group of national historians hastened the trend. In 1870, James Schouler, a Boston lawyer from Ohio, proposed to write a history of the United States. The author of a number of legal textbooks, Schouler postponed his historical project in order to edit the *United States Jurist*, to initiate "the legal profession of the whole country" in the rapidly developing realm of national jurisprudence.[11] Progressive deafness made an active legal career difficult for him, and he turned back to his historical project. In 1880, Schouler published the first of a seven-volume *History of the United States of America Under the Constitution*, covering the period between 1783 and 1877. Unlike Bancroft's work, Schouler's was intended as a truly national history. He wrote as if a representative of the federal government, using as his primary sources government documents and the personal papers of presidents.

James Schouler maintained his prejudices against the South and its "peculiar institution." He did attempt to minimize his anti-southern bias, and did so by emphasizing the conflict of ideals, placing blame less on individuals than on the circumstance which hurtled the North and the South into war. Schouler attempted to do full justice to both factions and to avoid the terms "conspiracy" and "reason" in order not to give the "false impression that the crime of a few Southern leaders produced the real mischief."[12] He was not always successful in his aim, but the attempt was made. Later, historians James Ford Rhodes and John Bach McMaster emulated Schouler, with scarcely more success. Some few historians, in the name of "objective science," began to search for patterns,

---

[9] Samuel G. Mitchell, "George F. Holmes," *DAB*, IX, 164; George F. Holmes, *A School History of the United States of America from the Earliest Discoveries to the Year 1870* (New York, 1872), pp. 4, 216, 260.

[10] Horace E. Scudder, *A History of the United States* (New York, 1884), p. 25.

[11] Lewis Ethan Ellis, "James Schouler," in Hutchinson (ed.), *Jernegan Essays*, p. 86.

[12] James Schouler, *History of the United States of America under the Constitution* (New York, 1880–1913), V, 509–11; William A. Dunning, "James Schouler's History of the Civil War, 1861–1865," *Truth in History and Other Essays* (New York: Columbia University Press, 1937), pp. 173–77; Pressly, *Americans Interpret Their Civil War*, pp. 129–31.

trends, and forces that might explain the coming of the war. Dr. John W. Draper, influenced by the English historian Henry T. Buckle, pioneered in applying a scientific method to the writing of a history of the Civil War and hypothesized a "climatic determinism" which made the war inevitable.[13] Others would propose that geographic, economic, and cultural "climates" determine war. But whatever the hypothesis, the assumption was the same—that war was somehow inevitable. In this way they avoided the question of blame. To such interpretations both North and South could agree.

The Civil War settled into the stream of American history, a memorable family quarrel in which all felt they had played an honorable role; and they wrote that, terrible and tragic though the conflict had been, it had tested and strengthened the sinews of the nation. Historians again wrote histories of one nation, and local chroniclers, at first satisfied to report the contributions to Confederate or Union cause of local regiments, began to rewrite local histories to chronicle civilian efforts during the war as well as to rehearse the whole story of the community's past.

The Civil War wrought havoc among national historians. For a time they were, in fact, sectional historians, but with the sanction of political reunion, the return to power of the Democratic party, proponents of the New South in control in southern states, and the spirit of conciliation among veterans of the war, historians began to write upon national subjects, and their works again promoted patriotism and nationalism.

Although Civil War histories gave some basis for agreement and reconciliation, many people looked to the Revolutionary War as the common memory that could best break down the barriers of sectional hatred and allow for a national reunion. Local historians in the North and South could not always agree upon rivaling claims of importance in the War for Independence, but they coincided in the choice of a common enemy—England—and a common goal— liberty.[14]

Soon after the Civil War ended, local historians resumed their rummaging among the materials pertaining to the revolutionary and colonial periods. Lyman C. Draper, the corresponding secretary of the State Historical Society of Wisconsin, turned his attention from the Civil War to his first interests, western pioneers and the border wars. Dr. J. G. M. Ramsey, a historian of Tennessee, his fortune gone, his spirit disconsolate, his house burned and with it the manuscript of the second volume of his work in progress, resumed his labors. In 1866, General D. H. Hill began to publish in Charlotte, North Carolina, a journal called *The Land We Love*, devoted largely to American his-

[13] John William Draper, *History of the American Civil War* (3 vols.; New York, 1867–70); Donald Fleming, *John William Draper and the Religion of Science* (Philadelphia: University of Pennsylvania Press, 1950), pp. 113–21.

[14] *American Historical Record*, I (January, 1872), 42; James A. Woodburn, "Promotion of Historical Study in America Following the Civil War," Illinois State Historical Society, *Transactions* (Chicago, 1922), pp. 38–41.

tory. It rang with an unmistakable echo of the rebel yell, but its purpose was to realign the South with the nation, and its pages were filled with historical articles dealing with the period of the American Revolution.[15] Southern historical societies began to revive or to be reorganized; county and town historical societies sprang up in great abundance in the Atlantic seaboard states. Most of these societies emphasized the colonial and early national periods in their publications and collections, as if seeking to recall a period of national harmony.

The greatest national effort to achieve reunion by recapturing the past came with the celebration of the centennial anniversary of the Declaration of Independence. In 1871, Congress authorized a national centennial exposition to be held at Philadelphia in 1876. The following year, Congress created the United States Centennial Commission, which included two representatives from each congressional district. To publicize the occasion, the commission rallied the support of businessmen, journalists, and politicians.[16] The purpose of the centenary was to display to the world what progress the country had achieved in one hundred years of independence and democracy.[17] It was to be a truly "national celebration, in which the people of the whole country should participate."[18] Inevitably, historians were to have major roles in the celebration. Alfred T. Goshorn, director general of the exposition, sent out a circular to all the state and territorial governors urging them to have historical studies written so that the country might display "a correct history of the birth and progress of the several communities that have contributed during the century to the growth and strength of the Union of States." Under this official stimulus, many state governments authorized or encouraged the writing of histories. The state of Kansas, for example, hired someone to write the history of each of its counties.[19]

In festive spirit, the nation celebrated the centennial anniversary of the Declaration of Independence. Fairs, expositions, and flights of oratory hailed a century of progress and the natural grandeur of the Union. The national exposition boosted the sales of local merchants and quickened staid old Philadelphia. During the course of the exposition, the United States accepted the gift from France of the Statue of Liberty, and enthusiastic members of the Pennsylvania Historical Society inaugurated their journal, the *Pennsylvania Magazine of History and Biography*. In the same year, James Austin Stevens, librarian of the New-York Historical Society, helped to found an organization

[15] *The Land We Love*, II (December, 1866), 129–45; III (September, 1867), 381–400; IV (December, 1867), 135–36; Hesseltine (ed.), *Ramsey Autobiography*, pp. 233–34.

[16] Joseph R. Hawley, "Report of the President of the Commission," United States Centennial Commission, *International Exhibition 1876*, II (Washington, D.C., 1880), 2–11.

[17] *Ibid.*, p. 31.

[18] *Ibid.*, p. 10.

[19] Goshen's circular and a short account of the effect of the centennial on Kansas history are given in James Malin's "Notes on the Writing of General Histories of Kansas, Part Four," *Kansas Historical Quarterly*, XXI (Summer, 1955), 415–18.

called the Sons of the Revolution and a year later undertook the ambitious task of establishing and editing the *Magazine of American History*. Centennial orators no sooner delivered their addresses than some industrious publisher put out a a collection of the speeches for sale to an uncomplaining public.

Historians hastened to complete books on every aspect of American history to take advantage of the promotional boost offered by the centenary. Fresh scholarship was no requisite for publication; George Bancroft issued a centenary edition of his *History of the United States;* Benson John Lossing compiled the *American Centenary*, a historical survey which emphasized material and industrial progress. Moses Coit Tyler, a journalist and an English professor at the University of Michigan, hurried to complete his literary history of the American colonies to take advantage of the centennial year.

But the flurry of the centenary soon passed, and the national spotlight turned toward the heated presidential contest between Rutherford B. Hayes and Samuel J. Tilden. Although the interest aroused in the subject of American history had some lasting effects, for the most part it left undisturbed the trends already evident in American historical writing.[20]

In 1876, Americans found salve for spiritual wounds and a way to rekindle national feeling by asserting their attachment to the nation's past and singing patriotic hymns to the American Revolution, but the writing of the history of the newly unified country was not to be left in the charge of local amateurs, ministers, lawyers, or journalists, nor would the reuniting of North and South be accomplished under their auspices. The task of writing the history of the United States was taken up by historians who were nationalists by training. In German and American universities they had acquired an understanding of the growth of the nation-state and thus became nationalists in their approach to the study of history. And, almost by necessity, they gave their undivided allegiance to the nation since they had severed or seriously weakened their local roots by taking up a profession that could only be practiced in widely scattered academic communities and that often involved a series of moves during the course of a successful career. As members of the new group of historians prepared to re-examine the past, local historical studies continued to develop along the lines that had emerged in the decade before the Civil War.

[20] There is no adequate treatment of the effects of the centennial celebrations on historical writing in the United States. *Pennsylvania Magazine of History and Biography*, I (1877), Preface; William Bristol Shaw, "John Austin Stevens," *DAB*, XVII, 617; Benson John Lossing, *American Centenary* (New York, 1876).

18 CULMINATION OF THE CRITICAL SPIRIT, 1866–84

The clamor of politicians, businessmen, and journalists preaching national patriotism and reverence for the founding fathers in an effort to divert attention from the livid wounds of war and the pain of Reconstruction, drowned out the voices of critical historians. Many scholars imbued with the criticial spirit, who had laid down their tasks during the war, resumed their historical labors after Appomattox. Some new historians who appeared in the postwar years contributed to the growth of critical historiography and to its final synthesis in Justin Winsor's *Narrative and Critical History of America*. John Gilmary Shea had nursed the flame of critical scholarship through the war years, publishing with great regularity issues of the *Historical Magazine*. In 1866 he relinquished his charge, and the journal eventually passed into the hands of an aggressive scholar, Henry B. Dawson.

Shea raised the standards of the *Historical Magazine* and made it a forum for critical scholars; Dawson made it a tool of historical criticism. The magazine was edited for a few months in 1866 by Henry R. Stiles, of Windsor, Connecticut. Stiles was preoccupied with another project, a history of Brooklyn, New York, and very quickly decided to give up the added chore of editor. In the June issue, Stiles informed his readers of the change of ownership and assured them that Henry B. Dawson's reputation as a historian would be "ample guarantee for the future of the *Historical Magazine*." Dawson's reputation, Stiles might have explained, was based on his meticulous scholarship and biting criticism of the scholarship of others.[1]

Dawson, a thin, nervous man with long, straight hair, unkempt gray beard and intense eyes, was born in 1821 in England. His family emigrated to the United States in 1834 when he was thirteen. With only a meager education, he worked at many jobs without enthusiasm and with little success. Toiling as a clerk in a number of business establishments, he interested himself in politics as a Free Soiler and Republican. In 1854, David T. Vallentine, veteran clerk of the Common Council of New York City, induced Dawson to write a historical article on City Hall Park for a city manual he was editing. Dawson's essay, a scholarly effort, asserted New York's prominent role in the revolutionary movement. Historical research, Dawson decided, would be his vocation. Henceforth, he would concentrate all of his energy in this field of endeavor. In 1858 he produced a heavily annotated and documented, two-volume history of the *Battles of the United States*. Dawson was a prolific author of papers which

---

[1] *New England Historical and Genealogical Register*, XVIII (July, 1864), 316; *Historical Magazine*, X (June, 1866), 200.

he delivered before the New-York Historical Society. In 1865, he edited a small town newspaper, the *Yonkers Gazette*, which he very nearly turned into a historical journal, to the disgust of some of his readers, and in which he first essayed some of the ideas he was later to develop as editor of the *Historical Magazine*.[2]

As his first act, Dawson enlarged the book review section, making it one of the strongest features in the magazine. Dawson was a fearless and somewhat harsh reviewer, and his standards were high for works that professed to be the product of research and claimed the prestige of scholarship. "What is known to be historically untrue," Dawson declared, "the *Historical Magazine* will fearlessly expose and condemn, no matter by whom it may have been uttered." He criticized some of the work of George Bancroft, John Lothrop Motley, and the senior Charles Francis Adams, as well as the work of writers of less prominence. He disagreed with Bancroft's contention that the thirteen colonies were already a nation in embryo, and he pointed out Bancroft's error in presenting men like John Jay and Alexander Hamilton as of one mind during the revolution with men like Samuel Adams and Patrick Henry. Dawson struck at the heart of Motley's address on "Progress and American Democracy" before the New-York Historical Society when he suggested that American democracy had faced questions every bit as important as that which concerned slavery in the South.

In 1870, Dawson assailed Charles Francis Adams' scholarship when the former ambassador sought to outline the history of the American struggle for neutrality. Adams praised George Washington for originating the policy in his Neutrality Proclamation; Dawson pointed out that Congress had long discussed and projected such a policy for the United States and cited in proof dates and pages in the secret journals of Congress. Adams referred to the chaos engendered by the faulty Articles of Confederation, and the peace, order, and prosperity which followed the establishment of the Constitution; Dawson disagreed, suggesting that the disorder was caused by the effects of war; as for the order purportedly effected by the Constitution, Dawson pointed to the near-disintegration of Congress in 1792, the Whiskey Rebellion, and the New Hampshire riots.[3]

Dawson continued Shea's efforts to obtain for the magazine original articles

[2] There is no adequate biography of Henry Dawson, but material may be found in John Ward Dean's "A Memoir of Henry Barton Dawson, Esq.," *Historical Magazine*, IV, 2d series (December, 1868), 257–61; J. Thomas Scharf, *History of Westchester County, New York* (Philadelphia, 1886), I, 612–16, a copy of J. W. Dean's sketch with material added on Dawson's later life; John A. Todd, "Henry B. Dawson," *New England Historical and Genealogical Register*, XLIV (July, 1890), 235–48; Robert E. Moody, "Henry Barton Dawson," *DAB*, V, 152. There are other sketches in nineteenth-century biographical dictionaries, but all drew their information from the first three sketches and supply no more. For a more extensive discussion of Dawson and his work see Van Tassel, "Henry Barton Dawson: A Nineteenth Century Revisionist," *William and Mary Quarterly*, 3d series, XIII (July, 1956), 319–41.

[3] *Historical Magazine*, X (July, 1866), 201–2; Dawson, "The Motley Letters," *Historical Magazine*, IX, 2d series (March, 1871), 163–70; Dawson, "Charles Francis Adams' *The Struggle for Neutrality in America*," *Historical Magazine*, IX, 2d series (February, 1871), 129–50.

and unpublished documents. He was such an active solicitor that by the time he published the final issue in 1875, almost every contemporary scholar working in the field of American history had contributed something to its pages. The majority of the documents and articles published in the magazine related to the Revolution and to the Civil War.[4]

Dawson's journal served as a forum for historical controversy. George H. Moore, the librarian of the New-York Historical Society, carried on a long debate with the *Boston Daily Advertiser* over the existence of slavery in colonial Massachusetts. The newspaper claimed that slavery was never legal in Massachusetts; Moore produced documents to prove that at one time it was. A phase of the Reed controversy also appeared in the pages of the *Historical Magazine*. Joseph Reed, a prominent Pennsylvania statesman during the American Revolution, often had to defend his patriotism and military reputation against the attacks of political opponents. In the fifties the arguments of Reed's detractors found favor with some historians and were accepted by Bancroft who added to the ninth volume of his *History of the United States* some documentary evidence which he believed supported the accusations. William B. Reed, Joseph's son, wrote a series of articles for the *Historical Magazine* defending his father's memory, in "reply to Mr. George Bancroft." Later, the articles were republished at greater length in pamphlet form and answered by Bancroft in another pamphlet. Reed published a rejoinder. In 1876, William S. Stryker, later to become State Archivist of New Jersey and known for pioneer translations of German records of Hessian soldiers in the revolution, reviewed the controversy and proved that Bancroft had been led to confuse Joseph Reed and a Colonel Charles Reed who deserted to the British in 1776. Bancroft acknowledged his error and revised the text and defamatory note in the centenary edition of his history.[5]

Many controversies enlivened the pages of the *Historical Magazine*, stimulated research, and sharpened the critical faculties of the disputants. Dawson himself supplied a good deal of the controversial material. In 1866, the year of the Methodist centenary, Dawson prepared to write a series of articles on the history of the Methodist church in America. He announced his intention to forestall the efforts of "inconsiderate speakers and writers" who would

[4] For example, John R. Brodhead, "The Government of Sir Edmund Andros over New England in 1688 and 1689," *Historical Magazine*, I, 2d series (January, 1867), 1–14; Peter Force, "Henry Laurens in England," *Historical Magazine*, I, 2d series (March, 1867), 129–35; E. E. Bourne, "First Christian Worship in New England," *Historical Magazine*, II, 2d series (July, 1867), 1–3; J. Hammond Trumbull, "Indian Names in Virginia," *Historical Magazine*, VII, 2d series (January, 1870), 47–48; Lorenzo Sabine, "Moose Island and its Dependencies; Four Years under Martial Law," *Historical Magazine*, VII, 2d series (April–May, 1870), 317–34.

[5] George H. Moore, "Slavery in Massachusetts," *Historical Magazine*, X (1866), Supplement 2, 105–8; Moore, "Mr. Moore's Reply to his Boston Critics," *Historical Magazine*, X (1866), Supplement 6, 186–87; Charles F. Dunbar, "Slavery in Massachusetts," *Boston Daily Advertiser*, September 12, 1866, in *Historical Magazine*, X (1866), Supplement 5, 138; William B. Reed to John C. Hamilton, August 26, 1859, in *Historical Magazine*, X (1866), Supplement 6, 177; Dawson, "Review of President William B. Reed," *Historical Magazine*, XI (April, 1867), 251; Richard B. Morris, "Joseph Reed," *DAB*, XV, 452–53.

claim for the pioneers of the Methodist church "what they would disclaim were they living." The articles drew fire from historians all over the country, and most of the attacks were published in the *Historical Magazine*. Dawson also published letters written by Citizen Edmond Genêt, the French envoy to the United States in 1793, which reflected upon the reputations of Rufus King and John Jay; the letters brought no refutation but inspired a bitter rebuke to the magazine from Boston newspapers.[6]

Prominent scholars and some popular writers testified to the usefulness of the *Historical Magazine* as an aid in keeping abreast of recent research and discovery in the field of historical study. James Parton, "the father of American biography," declared the magazine indispensable to the historian. Francis Parkman affirmed Parton's judgment, as did others.[7] Historians gave testimony that the *Historical Magazine* was a useful aid to scholarship; its victims bore scars that proved it an effective champion of the critical spirit. One careless researcher, after suffering exposure in one of Dawson's reviews, wrote to say that he would rather have his books ignored than to have them reviewed in the pages of the *Historical Magazine*. The *Boston Evening Transcript*, representative of the New England conservative tradition, deplored the critical bent of an increasing number of American historians. "We cannot forbear to deprecate," the Boston paper scolded, "the denationalizing tendency of any and every attempt to diminish reverence for the fathers of the Republic, who, whatever may have been their personal errors, as citizens and patriots have become historically preëminent all over the world; and whose example and writings are sacred precedents to lovers of Freedom and humanity. It is especially unworthy of historical students and societies to sanction that 'folly which is the martyrdom of fame.' " The article included a series of examples and ended with the shock-filled accusation that "an American historical magazine defended the insulting conduct of Genêt at the expense of Rufus King and other high minded Federalists." This was the complaint of patriots in many parts of the country, but the trend continued, only suffering a setback when the *Historical Magazine* ceased publication in 1875. The centennial celebrations, a year later, encouraged the filio-pietists to seek control of historical journals.[8]

[6] Dawson, "What are the Methodists Celebrating?" *Historical Magazine*, X (August, 1866), 259–60; Dawson, "The Early Methodists and the American Revolution," *Historical Magazine*, X (December, 1866), 361–68; "Early Methodists and the American Revolution," in *The Methodist*, March 30, April 13, April 27, 1867, in *Historical Magazine*, XI (May, 1867), 291–97; Dawson (ed.), "Selections from the Papers of Citizen Genêt," *Historical Magazine*, II, 2d series (July, September, 1867), 38, 155–60.

[7] James Parton to Dawson, September 17, 1867, J. Wingate Thornton to Dawson, September 14, 1867, Benson J. Lossing to Dawson, February 18, 1867, all in *Historical Magazine*, II, 2d series (November, 1867), Extra no., 322–24; George Hannah to Dawson, June 22, 1869, Dawson miscellaneous MSS, New York Public Library.

[8] Charles Whittlesey, "An Indignant Historian still more Indignant," *Historical Magazine*, III, 2d series (May, 1868), 320; in *Historical Magazine*, I, 2d series (January, 1867), 14–15; Dawson, "The Progress of Despotism," *Historical Magazine*, III, 3d series (December, 1874), Extra II, 397–407.

Henry Dawson had assumed full responsibility for the editing and publishing of the *Historical Magazine* at its purchase in 1866 and had made it a moderately successful business venture; but circumstances conspired against him. Although he found it necessary to raise the subscription rate from two to five dollars in 1872, the number of subscribers continued at a peak of eight hundred, some four hundred more than that claimed by the tottering old *North American Review*.

In 1868, Dawsor contracted malaria, which continued to recur periodically and slowed his work. In 1873 he fell and broke his hip, an accident which left him a cripple. He was rapidly going into debt. His illness and the accident put the magazine behind schedule, an inadvertence which Dawson tried valiantly to make up to his subscribers. In 1875, the New York Post Office refused to carry the magazine at second-class rates, maintaining that because it appeared only erratically it could not be considered a periodical and could not be classed as second-class matter. Dawson was not able to afford the extra mailing cost. With a closing blast at the post office, he ceased publication of the *Historical Magazine*, and historical scholars in America lost one of their tangible national bonds.[9]

As Dawson's forum for critical scholars ceased, an unusual phenomenon appeared in local historical writing, under the sponsorship of a group specializing in the production of town, county, and regional "memorial" histories. The organizers made use of local antiquaries, paying them a certain sum for articles which the editor-author combined with a long historical sketch of the state, not always giving credit to the contributors. They appealed to local pride to sell subscriptions and sometimes were able to gain subsidies from municipal and state governments. Among the leaders in enterprises of this sort were John Thomas Scharf of Baltimore and Clarence F. Jewett of Boston.

Scharf was a native of Baltimore, the son of a local lumber merchant. He was just two months past his eighteenth birthday in July, 1861, when he enlisted in a Maryland artillery regiment. He fought as a member of the Confederate Army until 1863, then transferred to the Navy. He was captured on the first leg of a secret mission to Canada and pardoned in 1865 by President Johnson. Next, Scharf studied law, but soon began writing for the Baltimore newspapers and gave up the law for a career in journalism.[10] In 1874 he made a foray into historical writing with the publication of the *Chronicles of Baltimore*, a volume of social history and a "repository of valuable knowledge." Two years later, during the centennial year, the Maryland legislature subsidized Scharf's history of the state by guaranteeing to buy three hundred copies.

[9] Dawson, "The Progress of Despotism," p. 397; Dawson to Charles Deane, October 16, December 13, 1875, in Deane MSS, Massachusetts Historical Society. There is no positive evidence to indicate that the *Historical Magazine* was suppressed for political reasons, but Dawson's vigorous attacks on prominent Republicans, his opposition to the war and to Reconstruction measures, as well as his unpopular interpretation of Constitutional history, might well have influenced the Republican Postmaster's decision.

[10] W. Stull Holt, "John Thomas Scharf," *DAB*, XVI, 419–20.

The three-volume *History of Maryland from the Earliest Period to the Present* appeared in 1879. Scharf appealed to the state pride of local historians in the preface: "Not only aliens, but even her own sons, have been very imperfectly informed of Maryland's true history; and she has been denied her due meed of honor, both abroad and at home. Yet no land has a history more worthy of being studied and laid to heart by its children."[11]

But a motive other than state pride inspired Scharf's production of historical surveys. Unlike the majority of historians, he was able to make a profit on his labor. Legislatures subsidized his work, and his breezy journalistic style and deft use of newspaper material, making his volumes largely a series of anecdotes, were popular, Also to his advantage were low publishing costs, efficient sales methods, and the degree of public interest in American history current at this time.[12]

Having made a success of his history of Maryland, Scharf organized the efforts of local historians and produced city, county, and state histories up and down the Atlantic seaboard. Having added his name to Thompson Westcott's work, Scharf arranged for the publication of the Philadelphia historian's long-nurtured history of the Quaker City, and Henry Dawson was persuaded to submit his last monograph as one of many contributions to Scharf's *History of Westchester County, New York*.[13]

The Maryland entrepreneur was not alone in utilizing the labor of antiquarians in producing local histories. A California businessman, Hubert Howe Bancroft, called upon a staff of local specialists to aid him in a twenty-one-volume *History of the Pacific States*.[14] Bancroft's work differed markedly from the general run of co-operatively written local histories published during the last decades of the nineteenth century. He spoke out against a proclivity of local historians, to accept politically established state boundaries as limits for research, and urged them to disregard the confines of national borders for a concept both historically and geographically sound, a view of the Pacific coastal region extending from Alaska through Central America. The completed work represents, as Bancroft hoped it would, a summation and critical digest of all published knowledge concerning the natural, cultural, and political history of the Pacific coast.

Bancroft grew up in Granville, Ohio, and as a youth earned his keep by peddling books. In 1852 he went to California to sell books in that storied land

---

[11] J. Thomas Scharf, *The Chronicles of Baltimore* (Baltimore, 1874), p. vii; Scharf, *History of Maryland from the Earliest Period to the Present* (Baltimore, 1879), I, vi.

[12] Holt, "Scharf," *loc. cit.*

[13] Scharf, *History of St. Louis City and County* (Philadelphia, 1883); Scharf and Thompson Westcott, *History of Philadelphia* (3 vols.; Philadelphia, 1884); Joseph Jackson, "Thompson Westcott," *DAB*, XX, 14; Scharf, *History of Westchester County*.

[14] Bancroft decided during the production of these volumes to issue everything he and his assistants had written, including *Native Races of the Pacific States of North America* (5 vols.; New York, 1874–76), along with other works, in a comprehensive edition, *The Works of Hubert Howe Bancroft* (39 vols.; San Francisco, 1882–90).

of gold and fabulous wealth. A determined and sound businessman, he established himself in San Francisco and proceeded to print, publish, and retail books. In 1859, for commercial reasons, he determined to collect all available books and pamphlets dealing with the Pacific Coast for reference in compiling a *Hand-Book Almanac for 1860* and to help him in deciding what new books to publish. He first believed such a collection could be assembled very quickly, and expressed surprise when he found he had accumulated seventy-five titles. In 1862, when his collection had grown to a thousand volumes, he recalled, "I fancied I had them all."[15] But he quickly discovered his error and continued to collect Californiana with omnivorous zeal, although he had long since lost sight of his practical intention. In building a complete reference collection, Bancroft thought first of content and not bindings or rare editions. As the West Coast bibliophile became absorbed in the hunt, he found that books on Panama and Mexico contained material on California, that books on Canada and Alaska referred to Washington and Oregon. In 1869 his collection had grown to fifty thousand volumes. Bancroft discerned a pattern reflecting the historical development of a region unified geographically and historically by its dependence upon a common commercial highway, the Pacific Ocean, a region, it is true, of great diversity, the unity of which would grow less apparent after 1869, when transcontinental railroads opened a highway to the East Coast.

Once Bancroft completed his huge collection, he set out to refine this vast store of raw material. At first he projected an encyclopedia of the Pacific Coast, but for practical reasons (and because he had visions of eventual literary achievement) he gave up the idea. He proposed instead to write a comprehensive history of the entire western half of the North American continent, a project worthy of fame and, it seemed to him, no less ambitious than the work of Edward Gibbon, Francis Parkman, and George Bancroft. He had little illusion of the profit and popularity his project would gain him; he knew there would be none; he sought recognition as a scholar and a literary figure and wished to be known and respected among the elite of the world's learned men.[16]

Hubert Howe Bancroft never won the respect and recognition he yearned for. From 1874 to 1876, when he published the first five volumes of his series *Native Races of the Pacific States of North America*, the critics acclaimed his "boldness of design" and his thorough and exhaustive treatment of the subject, but other reviewers expressed some doubt as to the merits of the co-operative methods of research and writing that Bancroft so efficiently employed in his "literary workshop." Between 1882 and 1890 Bancroft published, on an average,

[15] Hubert Howe Bancroft, *Literary Industries* (San Francisco, 1890), p. 177.

[16] *Ibid.*, chap. ix, "Desperate Attempts at Great Things," pp. 218–44. See also the fine description of Bancroft's trips East to gain a favorable reception for his *Native Races* from the learned men of Boston and New York, in John Walton Caughey, *Hubert Howe Bancroft; Historian of the West* (Berkeley and Los Angeles: University of California Press, 1946), pp. 140–56.

two and three volumes a year. The critics' applause turned to denunciation; far from writing careful appraisals of the volumes, they discussed the dubious ethics of a man who would take credit for the work of others. At his death, some professional historians wrote memorial tributes to the man, but refused him priase for his historical studies, though some gratitude was expressed for his selfless labors in assembling an unparalleled library of books on the West.[17]

At the same time critics were denouncing Bancroft's methods, many were welcoming the young men, fresh from European "seminaries," who were establishing similar "literary factories" at eastern universities. None of the younger historians leaped to the defense of Bancroft by pointing out the similarity of his methods and, for example, those of Leopold von Ranke, who made use of the efforts of generations of graduate students in the writing of his universal history, or with the methods of many other scholarly co-operative projects of the period. Bancroft was a businessman, an amateur historian; reviewers compared his methods with those of the factory and pointed out the low wages paid his workers.

Another characteristic detrimental to a favorable reception was that, in spite of the quantity and coverage of Bancroft's work, it was local history, and worse, *western* local history. Bancroft was interested in the Pacific Coast, not for what the study might explain about the development of the nation, but for its own sake. On the other hand, the philosopher Josiah Royce, who worked in Bancroft's library, reached many of the same conclusions in his one-volume history of California as did the historian. Nevertheless, Bancroft's seven volumes on California received far less scholarly acclaim than did the young man's single volume. Royce gave his book a national orientation, making it "a study of American character."[18]

Contemporary critics and historians did not recognize Bancroft's history as a culmination of all prior Pacific Coast scholarship, systematized by a unique concept of the area's regional unity. Perhaps they could not acknowledge his achievement because they objected to his more readily discernible faults.

In Chicago, the Historical Publishing Company was filling library shelves with middlewestern state and county histories. The company supplied local historians with forms and format, which they were to fill in with appropriate facts, commencing with a general history of the state, an account of the geography and Indians of the county, and of the political history of the county and of each town in the county, always taking particular notice of firsts—first settlers, first school, first church, and so on. Some of the local researchers grew so proficient in filling in the blanks that, like Consul W. Butterfield, who

[17] Caughey, *op. cit.*, pp. 382–90.

[18] *Ibid.*, p. 272; Josiah Royce, *California: a Study of American Character* (American Commonwealth Series [Boston, 1886]).

produced the histories of seven Wisconsin counties in as many years, they became professional historians.[19]

In New England, Clarence Frederick Jewett, an enterprising Boston publisher, promoted the writing of town and county histories. He had already published several local histories, one of which was a co-operative work, before he approached Justin Winsor, librarian of Harvard, to edit a history of Boston. A prominent librarian and founder of the American Library Association, Winsor was very much interested in American history. In 1849, he had written a history of his home town of Duxbury, Massachusetts. Inspired by the centennial anniversary of the American Revolution, Winsor published *The Reader's Handbook of the American Revolution* in 1879. The Harvard librarian accepted Jewett's proposition and solicited contributions on all phases of Boston's history from friends and acquaintances. In three years Winsor brought the project to completion and saw through the press the four heavy volumes that make up the *Memorial History of Boston*. At the time that the first volume appeared, Jewett suggested a new project to the busy Winsor. The publisher proposed to sponsor a history of the United States compiled in the same manner as the history of Boston. Winsor accepted the job as editor and set about the task of outlining and contacting men to write the various chapters.[20]

When he undertook Jewett's assignment in 1880, Justin Winsor had some very definite ideas as to what the nature and purpose of the work should be. He had no intention of making the projected volumes a "model for the general writing of history based on co-operative and critical methods." "There is no substitute," he maintained, "for the individuality of an historian." Winsor proposed a summary of the work that had been done in every field of American history. Each chapter was to be a monograph by a scholar "most entitled to be heard" on the particular phase of history to be covered; each monograph was to be a summary of all scholarly knowledge of the subject, and appended would be an exhaustive critical bibliography of all primary and secondary sources.[21]

Winsor drew up a prospectus for a *Narrative and Critical History of America* and sent it to historical societies throughout the country. The Massachusetts

[19] There were many more companies and men producing co-operative "memorial" or "vanity" histories than can be listed here. There was, for example, a very industrious itinerant minister, Charles Richard Tuttle, who wrote or compiled twenty-five books, eight of them ponderous state and local histories published within the short span of three years (1873–76). For detailed discussion of Tuttle and other "vanity" histories of Kansas see James C. Malin, "Notes on the Writing of General Histories of Kansas, Part Five: The 'Vanity' Histories," *Kansas Historical Quarterly*, XXI (Winter, 1955), 598–643.

[20] Charles K. Bolton, "Clarence Frederick Jewett," *DAB*, X, 66–67. For biographical information on Justin Winsor see John A. Borme, "The Life and Letters of Justin Winsor" (Columbia University, 1950), MSS thesis, on University Microfilm; James Truslow Adams, "Justin Winsor," *DAB*, XX, 403–4; Edward Channing, "Justin Winsor," *American Historical Review*, III (January, 1898), 197–202.

[21] Winsor, *Narrative and Critical History of America*, VIII (Boston, 1884–89), 509–10.

Historical Society, of which Winsor was a member, looked with favor upon the project; after observing that Jared Sparks had cherished a similar plan in the last year of his life, the members voted to set up a committee of four to aid and advise the editor in his ambitious undertaking.[22] Winsor now began the arduous task of corresponding with potential contributors, of obtaining their consent, and of collecting and editing their contributions. Of the thirty-nine men who wrote chapters for the *Narrative and Critical History*, only eight were of New England; the rest were scattered over the country. The great majority were from the Atlantic states, so it is not surprising that the emphasis of the history falls on colonial America. Charles Deane, corresponding secretary of the Massachusetts Historical Society, wrote the chapter on New England in the colonial period; Edward D. Neill, then president of Macalester College at St. Paul, Minnesota, was called upon to do the chapter on the proprietary colonies. With one exception, southern historians wrote the chapters on the southern colonies. (John Gilmary Shea of New Jersey was asked to write the chapter on Florida.) William F. Poole, a Chicago librarian and the author of monographs on witchcraft in New England and on the Northwest Ordinance and the editor of the *Guide to Periodical Literature*, did the chapter on the West. Most of the contributors were local historians, but included among them were Sydney Howard Gay, who wrote a five-volume *Popular History of the United States* to which William Cullen Bryant lent his name, and Nathaniel Shaler, a geographer.[23]

When the *Narrative and Critical History* was completed in 1889, it was considered a monument to the work of scholars in American history. More particularly, it was a monument to the critical historians who rose and flourished in the decades between the publication of the last volume of Sparks's *Library of American Biography* and the appearance of the *Narrative and Critical History* and dominated for some forty years the realm of American historical scholarship. Most reviewers believed, as did Winsor himself, that the work was a plateau from which historians would look back to view the path along which they had come and ahead to see what paths led on to greater heights. The contributors to the *Narrative and Critical History* could not know that they had scaled a peak that others would not climb, though they might seek to obscure it in the shadows of the dazzling range they hoped to conquer.

[22] Massachusetts Historical Society, *Proceedings*, XVIII (Boston, 1880–81), 288.

[23] Contributors to the *Narrative and Critical History* were, in the order of their contributions, Justin Winsor, Clements R. Markham, Henry W. Haynes, George E. Ellis, Charles C. Smith, Sydney H. Gay, Edward Channing, John G. Shea, Edward E. Hild, Charles Deane, William W. Henry, Robert A. Brock, Benjamin F. DeCosta, Franklin D. Dexter, John Austin Stevens, William A. Whitehead, Gregory B. Keen, Frederick D. Stone, William T. Brantly, Nathaniel S. Shaler, George Dexter, Edmund F. Slafter, Edward D. Neill, George Stewart, Jr., Berthold Fernow, Andrew W. Davis, William T. Rivers, Charles C. Jones, Jr., Mellen Chamberlain, George W. Cullum, William T. Poole, Edward F. Lowell, John Jay, George T. Curtis, Alexander Johnston, James Russell Soley, and James B. Angell.

19 DENOUEMENT: THE TRIUMPH OF NATIONAL HISTORY, 1876–84

In 1884 an epoch of American historiography reached its climax. As if to herald a new era, a small band of zealous young scholars, fresh from German seminars and armed with the twin gospels of evolution and the scientific method, organized to propagate and give a new direction to "American history and history in America."[1] At first they attracted little public attention because, for the country at large, 1884 was a year of national unification. Grover Cleveland led the newly united Democratic party into power, and each issue of *Harper's Weekly* displayed some new evidence that "the South has become a part of the modern world," that "there is no longer a North or a South in business or in society."[2] Even so, this popular weekly overlooked one proof of national union—the formation of a national historical association.

During the closing days of the summer season at Saratoga Springs, New York, just as the band was leaving the Grand Union Hotel and as the public schools were about to open, scholars, teachers, college presidents, and ministers converged on the resort, taking advantage of the end-of-season hotel rates to hold their conventions. Former President Rutherford B. Hayes presided over the meeting of the Prison Association. The Honorable John Eaton, United States Commissioner of Education, presided over the Social Science Association and sponsored the formation of a new group, soon to become the American Historical Association.[3] Led by a master promoter, Herbert Baxter Adams, who taught at Johns Hopkins, supported by the universities, and taking advantage of the popular awe of science in their struggle to dominate the field of historical scholarship in the United States, the historians concerned had but a single idea and a missionary zeal to make it a cohesive and potent force. They saw history as continuous development, made manifest in the growth of political institutions. In theory, at least, their method of study was that of the natural sciences; though they had no hope of formulating historical laws based on information obtained from repeated and controlled experiments, they could gather sufficient data from the past to test certain historical hypotheses.

These pioneer scientific historians founded their studies upon an a priori

[1] Herbert Baxter Adams first used this phrase in "The New Historical Movement," *Nation*, XXXIX (September 18, 1884), 240, a description of the organization of the American Historical Association. He later used it in his reports of the early meetings, and it appears in the association's charter, passed by Congress in 1888.

[2] *Harper's Weekly*, XXVII (December 27, 1884), 856.

[3] New York *Times*, September 9, 1884; New York *Independent*, September 18, 1884.

thesis, and consequently their work did not result in tests of tentative theories but in repetitious statements in support of the unproven major premise. They viewed history as the study and record of social evolution. Like the biologists after Darwin who sought to trace to its origin each living species of plant and animal, the new historians, working from the assumption that local political and cultural institutions were basic social units, proceeded to trace each line of descent. As historians of the United States, their prime concern was the genealogy of democratic institutions. In the course of revealing logical sequences, they recorded institutional changes, placing emphasis upon demonstrable continuity.

Such historians as Andrew D. White, Herbert B. Adams, Alexander Johnston (the first popular textbook writer of the group), and John Fiske, in the course of public lectures on American history, assumed or implied that the historian need only point out the similarities of early institutions to succeeding ones to prove cause and effect. In fact, causation could be taken for granted; as every university scholar knew, causality was one of the "laws of evolution" or, as most Americans believed, the keystone of the "law of inevitable progress."[4]

Scientific historians would acknowledge no lineal, spiritual, or intellectual connection between themselves and the early romantic nationalists, dubbed "literary historians," in spite of the apparent similarity of their point of view. Among the "romantics," Bancroft, Parkman, Prescott, and Motley displayed in their works an intense nationalism and a faith in progress, the organic development of nations, and the inherent superiority of the Anglo-Saxon or Teutonic race, and made prodigious use of original sources, characteristics common to the younger generation of historians. But the new scholars emphasized differences (or "faults"), in the conviction that their own development sprang from the main stem of European historiography only recently transplanted to American soil. The older historians had a transcendental faith in progress; the new group argued from demonstrable facts which supported the hypothesis of social and natural evolution, a concept that they quite unscientifically equated with the idea of progress.[5]

[4] Only the original "scientific" and professional historians were in any degree unanimous in viewing history as a social science. This was in part because many of these men had gone to Germany to study government and international law. The German universities were then approaching these subjects historically, as were Sir Henry Maine and Edward Freeman in England. When the scholars returned to American universities they established "departments of history and political science." Many of these men thought of themselves as political scientists. The second generation of historians tended to be more orthodox in their approach to history as the study of the unique event or series of events in time. Like Frederick J. Turner in his revolt against contemporary emphasis on the "germ theory," they accepted the theory of continuity, but instead of proving lineal connections, they concentrated upon explaining change. See discussion in Herman Ausubel's *Historians and Their Craft: A Study of the Presidential Addresses of the American Historical Association, 1884–1945* (New York: Columbia University Press, 1950), pp. 17–49.

[5] David W. Noble, *The Paradox of Progressive Thought* (Minneapolis: University of Minnesota Press, 1958), pp. 3–33, 246–56.

The critical younger generation summed up its major attack in the epithet "literary historians." As literary artists the great mid-century historians received the respect of the newcomers, but history was no longer to be considered a branch of literature; it was a science whose practitioners marshaled and classified data and published monographs modeled after the laboratory report of the natural scientist. When George Bancroft died in 1891, Herbert B. Adams preserved a newspaper obituary in which Bancroft is eulogized and a funeral oration delivered for "the school of which he was the last representative." Adams heavily underscored the declaration that "The limelight of the stage on which such an historian marshalls his figures is a sore temptation to produce dramatic effects and picturesque situations. He is but too apt to scarifice accuracy to a phrase, and his historical perspective is the deluding perspective of the scene painter."[6]

The new historians firmly disavowed kinship with the literary historians, and for the vast body of amateur historians they had only a withering contempt. Historical societies were either "provincial" or pronounced dead, and their miscellaneous collections, John Franklin Jameson proclaimed, "are to us the poke bonnets and spinning wheels of all garrets." Recognition was granted only to those scholarly historians who were imbued with the critical spirit. No attempt was made to explain their existence in a hitherto unenlightened country.[7]

The differences between the critical historians and the scientific historians were more real than was first apparent and boded ill for the hope of future harmony unless one or the other dominated the scene. The critical historians were students of a particular geographic or political area, usually either their home state or town; they studied its past to acquire information about its history and not to document generalizations or to trace national development. That one group was composed of amateurs of history and the other of trained professionals was to be manifest as the younger group grew in number, organization, and confidence. Trained historians exhibited professional self-consciousness in the energetic drive to establish new organizations and new journals as well as in exuberant references to themselves and their growing ranks as a "noble army of Doctors."[8] In the eighties, both groups emphasized their

---

[6] Newspaper clippings from an unidentified source, in American Historical Association Papers, Library of Congress. For a summary of the attacks on George Bancroft as well as additional sources see A. S. Eisenstadt, *Charles McLean Andrews* (New York: Columbia University Press, 1956), pp. 164–65.

[7] Jameson, *The History of Historical Writing in America*, p. 88.

[8] Herbert B. Adams advised Jameson to borrow money if necessary in order to finish graduate training so that he might join "the rank and file of professional teachers." H. B. Adams to J. F. Jameson, August 6, 1880, in Jameson Papers, Library of Congress. Jameson later wrote in the same vein, hoping that a student would complete his work, "that he may be duly enrolled in that noble army of doctors who are now instructing and converting New England." J. F. Jameson to H. B. Adams, April 30, 1890, *ibid*. The same professional esprit de corps is reflected in many of the letters published in W. Stull Holt (ed.), *Historical Scholarship in the United States, 1876 to 1901* (Baltimore: Johns Hopkins University Press, 1938).

similarities. The older group was flattered to see young men entering the field and hoped the new historians would carry on their work. The scientific historians, eager for national dominance over the field of history, were in need of the backing and support of the older men and did everything in their power to secure that support.[9]

Henry Adams and Herbert B. Adams, proponents of the seminar method of teaching and studying history, followed the lead of such British scholars as Sir Henry Maine, James Bryce, and Edward Freeman in tracing the history of legal and political institutions to English and Germanic origins. They advocated the study of local institutions, but their viewpoint was to remain national. They agreed with Edward Freeman, eminent Oxford historian, who said, during a visit to America, "The local annals of Maryland or of any other State are something more than local history, something more than the history of the United States or of the whole English-speaking people. They are really contributions to the general science of politics. . . ." Herbert B. Adams declared that his monograph on Plymouth would be "for town history what Huxley's work on the Cray fish is for Biology, i.e., typical of many things besides those described." The monograph was intended as a case study, important not so much for its subject as for the broad general principles it proved or disproved.[10]

The new historians first turned their attention to local institutions. They were able to avail themselves of a wealth of materials accumulated by local chroniclers and historical societies and often found opportunities for publication. Herbert Adams and his students set out to ally the young professional group of historians with "the Historical Societies and *quasi*-historians in all the seaboard states."[11] Adams hoped to secure the "corporate influences of associations of men and money" and tried to win the blessing of, and thereby the prestige accorded to, "the father of American History," George Bancroft. Adams showered the old historian with requests for a portrait to hang in the seminar room at Johns Hopkins, asked for a manuscript for the new historical museum, and invited him to make a guest appearance at a meeting of the seminar, an appearance which "would do much for the future interests of historical inquiry in this University."[12]

[9] W. Stull Holt, "The Idea of Scientific History in America," *Journal of the History of Ideas*, I, No. 2 (June, 1940), 252–62; Herbert B. Adams to John Franklin Jameson, August 6, 1880, April 30, 1890, in Jameson Papers, Library of Congress.

[10] J. M. Vincent, "Herbert B. Adams, A Biographical Sketch," in *Herbert B. Adams: Tributes of Friends* (Baltimore: Johns Hopkins University Press, 1902), pp. 9–23.

[11] Adams to Samuel Green, September 22, 1879, October 14, 1881, in Green MSS, Massachusetts Historical Society; "Bibliography of History, Politics, and Economics, 1876 to 1901," in *Adams Tributes*, pp. 3–160; Adams to Daniel Coit Gilman, July 3, 1882, in W. Stull Holt (ed.), *Historical Scholarship*, p. 55.

[12] *Ibid.*, p. 56; Adams to George Bancroft, April 25, 1884, Bancroft MSS, Massachusetts Historical Society; Adams to Clarence W. Bowen, August 6, 1885, in American Historical Association Papers, Library of Congress; Adams to Bancroft, November 10, 1883, April 16, 1884, March 3, 1886, in Bancroft Papers, Library of Congress.

In 1884, Herbert B. Adams, Charles Kendall Adams, professor of history at the University of Michigan, Moses Coit Tyler, professor of history at Cornell, Frank B. Sanborn, secretary of the American Social Science Association, and John Eaton, its president, agreed that it was time to form a national historical association. Herbert Adams drew up a prospectus and called for an organizational meeting to be held in September, 1884, at Saratoga Springs, New York, in conjunction with the annual meeting of the American Social Science Association. The established organization consented to lend its name to the formation of the new association as well as the use of its halls for historical sessions. Adams sent copies of the prospectus to historians throughout the country, to all contributors to *Narrative and Critical History*, to members of state historical societies, and to a number of newspaper and magazine editors. The advance publicity was satisfactory to the little group of promoters. Adams himself wrote a glowing editorial in the *Nation* about the "new historical movement" and won a powerful convert in Clarence W. Bowen, amateur historian and editor of the New York newspaper, the *Independent*.[13]

The little group met on September 9. The prime movers, with a few others, met informally in one of the parlors of the United States Hotel a few hours before the public session to organize the association and to prepare for presentation a well-marked-out program for approval. Justin Winsor, the librarian of Harvard University, was temporary chairman until Andrew Dickson White, the president of Cornell University, was elected president of the association at the public session. Winsor, upon acceptance of temporary office, expressed the hope, on behalf of the "older men," that the younger members would continue the development of historical studies. The organization, successfully launched, declared its independence of its host, and forty men were enrolled as members of the new association. Only ten were trained historians, but they were to form the "inner circle" of the organization.[14] Like the men who sponsored it, the new society was to be nation-centered, not "narrow or provincial." In the *Nation*, Adams wrote that the American Historical Association was to be devoted to "history in general," as "the outgrowth of the catholic spirit represented by some of our American colleges and universities, where students from various sections learn national and liberal ideas and catch glimpses of the world through the science of history."[15]

The formation of the association and the ideas propounded by the new historians were a part of the growing nationalism of the time. Southern Democrats trooped back to the old party after a brief but effective defection to the Republi-

[13] Adams to Bowen, July 15, 1884, Moses C. Tyler to Bowen, July 16, 1884, in American Historical Association MSS; Adams to Gilman, August 8, 1884, in Holt (ed.), *Historical Scholarship*, pp. 71–72; Adams to Bowen, September 14, September 24, 1884, in American Historical Association MSS; *Nation*, Vol. XXXIX (September 18, 1884); *Independent* (New York), September 18, 1884.

[14] American Historical Association, *Papers*, I (New York, 1886), 5–40; Tyler to Bowen, September 15, 1885, American Historical Association MSS.

[15] "A New Historical Movement," *Nation*, September 18, 1884.

can party. The period of Reconstruction was over and the powerful exponents of the "New South" were extolling the virtues of industry. Protestant sects, split by the question of slavery, were in process of reuniting. Many learned societies were formed; the American Social Science Association was only a few years older than the historical association; the American Economic Association was established in 1885; and the Modern Language Association was organized in 1883. Andrew Dickson White, in his presidential address to the American Historical Association, acknowledged the founding of the association as a phase in the reunion of the northern and southern states as a homogeneous nation after the Civil War. Annual meetings of the association were often held in Washington in the early years to emphasize its "national character."[16]

But some members of the new organization were not satisfied to have it claimed to be national in name and membership; they asked for federal support and in 1887 began to work toward that end. In order to obtain from Congress a charter and a subsidy, they sought to demonstrate in a variety of ways that the association was truly representative of all American historians and historical organizations. If success depended upon complete harmony among the members, the plan was doomed from the start. Non-academic historians expressed their increasing dissatisfaction with the organization. Edward Eggleston, a novelist and a pioneer as a social historian of America, complained that the subjects discussed at their meetings did not interest him and that the association seemed "to be run in the interest of college professors only and to give those of us who are not of that clan the cold shoulder."[17] Others objected to the predominance of young men on the panels of the annual meetings. Herbert Baxter Adams was well aware of growing discontent and saw the need to mollify the non-academicians, who formed the largest part of the membership, by promoting election to the presidency of such scholars as George Bancroft and John Jay to give the lie to the rumor of an organization dominated by college professors, and made an effort to establish on panels, a balance between the "boys and the patriarchs," much to the disgust of his former student, John Franklin Jameson, who, like Adams himself, had no high regard for "*quasi*-historians."[18]

In spite of Adams' efforts, a movement to establish a national organization

[16] Andrew D. White, "Studies in General History and the History of Civilization," American Historical Association, *Papers*, I (New York, 1885), 21.

[17] *Congressional Record*, January 4, 1889; Adams to Bowen, September 13, 1889, American Historical Association MSS; Adams to Jameson, October 25, 1889, Jameson MSS; J. Franklin Jameson, "History of Historical Societies," *Seventy-fifth Anniversary Report of the Georgia Historical Society* (Atlanta: Georgia Historical Society, 1914), pp. 33–51.

[18] Adams to Bowen, October 19, 1889, American Historical Association MSS; Adams to A. D. White, February 4, 1890, in Holt, *Historical Scholarship*, p. 126; Adams to Jameson, February 5, 1890, in Jameson MSS; Jameson to Adams, February 21, 1890, in Holt, *Historical Scholarship*, pp. 127–28; George Brown Goode to Adams, February 10, 1890, in Jameson MSS; Charles Francis Adams to Jameson, October 6, 1892, Jameson MSS.

of historical societies was begun in 1889 and gained support. The pillars of the American Historical Association did not relish the thought of the establishment of a rival organization only a year after the association had obtained a national charter and federal subsidy. Adams immediately set out "to bring the State Historical Societies into line."[19] He drew up a circular and sent copies to all of the historical societies, asking their co-operation at annual meetings in filling part of the program devoted to state and local history. Furthermore, the association would make "every effort" to serve the needs of local historical societies. His foresight ended the movement for a national organization of historical societies, and local historians relinquished to the colleges their claim to dominance of the field of historical scholarship. The success of this maneuver gave support to the confident belief of trained historians that ultimately they would wrest historical writing and study from the control of the amateur. In 1887, Jameson, with unusual boldness, predicted that "the local antiquaries, the professionally literary men, and the men of wealth and leisure devoted to study, will no doubt continue to write historical books. But an increasing proportion of the annual product now comes from the teachers of history in the universities and colleges, and the signs are that the immediate future belongs to the professional class."[20]

The long age of the amateur historian in America was drawing to a close, but it left a legacy, the extent of which is partially indicated by the cramped, small print of the "critical bibliographies" that follow each chapter in the eight volumes of Justin Winsor's *Narrative and Critical History of America*. The men of the period not only made forays into almost every conceivable facet of America's history, but collected, preserved, and published in private and governmental series the documents essential to the study of American history. They organized societies which in early days enlisted the aid of members in accumulating materials which otherwise might have been lost. Scholars often find these collections curious, miscellaneous, "un-programmatic," but, as did Frederick Jackson Turner after burrowing in Lyman Draper's collections of manuscripts on western pioneers, finish by acknowledging the debt they owe the amateur historian.[21]

Important and vast as is the material legacy, a less tangible heritage is equally significant. Historical studies developed in America in response to contemporary needs. The growth of historiography followed closely, and sometimes kept pace with, the political, social, and economic development of the nation. Jefferson, by an act of will and the use of his considerable influence, attempted to "republicanize history," and orators and essayists demanded historical studies befitting the new republic. Amateur historians, patiently collecting

[19] George Brown Goode to H. B. Adams, February 10, 1890, in American Historical Association MSS, Library of Congress; Van Tassel, "The American Historical Association and the South, 1884–1913," *Journal of Southern History*, XXII (November, 1957), 474–75.

[20] Jameson, *History of Historical Writing*, pp. 158–59.

[21] Hesseltine, *Pioneer's Mission*, pp. 319–20, 357–59; Caughey, *Bancroft*, pp. 382–407.

and writing, created the body of a new and democratic history. They collected the papers and accounts of pioneers, businessmen, lawyers, and ministers, and they recorded the development of local administration, economy, schools, churches, and other mundane affairs once considered no part of European historical tradition. In the course of this attempt to preserve everything of importance to the community's past, the local chroniclers came to believe that the whole of human endeavor within set limits of time should be taken as the subject of historical study. Historical society charters proclaimed this concept; the large collections of material assembled by men like Hubert Howe Bancroft bear testimony to the pervasiveness of the idea, as do the innumerable dark and dusty volumes of town, county, and state histories. Trained historians rejected this concept of history, for they saw the value of a narrower vision. Only after many interpretative excursions would a later generation of historians rediscover a total view that could be adopted by right of inheritance.[22]

During the time they held the field, amateur historians, both popular and scholarly, often fell far short of the standards they had set themselves; nevertheless, in their own right they played a significant, supporting role in the social, political, and economic growth of the nation. History as they recorded it served to preserve a sense of continuity and an understanding of the historic mission of America for an otherwise heterogeneous and relatively rootless people. "The American mind," observed a writer in *The Nation* in 1877, "does not dwell on the past, does not easily recall it, forgets as freely as it forgives, and only by a miracle secures for its legislation and its institutions an historical development."[23] The statement is a fair description of an idea long popular; Americans may not dwell upon the past as do the citizens of older nations, but as a people who profess a deep regard for constitutional law and the basic rights of men they have taken care to safeguard the records of the birth and growth of the Union.

Historical studies justified the American Revolution, which otherwise might have been considered an illegal rebellion against established law and order, and proved it to have been a defense of constitutional rights and the rights of all mankind. Historians demonstrated that the War for Independence was the inevitable result of this defense of rights and thrust the awesome burden of continuing defense upon the shoulders of the citizens of the new nation. Thus it was taught, from the beginning, that the Republic was founded upon law, not revolution.

[22] Malin, "Notes on the Writing of General Histories of Kansas, Part Four," *Kansas Historical Quarterly*, XXI (Summer, 1955), 407–43; Van Tassel and Tinsley, "Historical Organizations as Aids to History," in Hesseltine and McNeil (eds.), *In Support of Clio*, pp. 127–52; W. Stull Holt, "Historical Scholarship," in Merle Curti (ed.), *American Scholarship in the Twentieth Century* (Cambridge, Mass.: Harvard University Press, 1953), pp. 83–110. Wendell H. Stephenson, "A Quarter Century of American Historiography," *Mississippi Valley Historical Review*, XLV (June, 1958), 3–22.

[23] "Notes," *Nation*, V (January 18, 1877), 24, 41.

Americans have never considered the right of revolution a part of the Bill of Rights. The most telling charge hurled at those who propose change has been the accusation of fomenting revolution. An equally strong defense has been the demonstration that changes of a radical nature are quite within the traditions of the United States when they serve to realize or safeguard the ideals upon which this country was founded. As the federal system grew in power, historical studies preserved the record of the independent heritage and individuality of the states. Historians fought on either side before and during the Civil War, bolstering the sanctity of the nation, the autonomy of the states. When the war ended, it was seen as a part of national tradition, a painful, essential trial, out of which a united country came victorious. It became a symbol of glory in which every faction could claim with pride its share. In these and other ways the amateur historian served the time in which he wrote.

In 1884, with the debut of the professional historian whose methods were critical and "scientific," whose subjects were local and whose spirit was national, the day of the amateur historian came to a close. Local historians henceforth would defer to the professional. Many scholars of the older generation, like Justin Winsor, welcomed the new group and into their hands gladly relinquished the future of American historical studies. George Bancroft, the elder statesman and "father of American history," blessed the new historians by becoming president of their association.

Men like Francis Parkman continued to work industriously to bring their private projects to a conclusion in accordance with first-laid plans. In the last days of December, 1884, after reading an advance copy of *Montcalm and Wolfe*, Henry Adams wrote the author, his friend Francis Parkman, of his admiration for the book, adding as if in gentle warning the prediction that "before long a new school of history . . . will leave us antiquated."[24] Not far off in Baltimore young Herbert Baxter Adams prepared a report for publication from the hastily penciled notes he had taken in September during the first meeting of the American Historical Association. Thus in the waning days of the old year, as Grover Cleveland and the victorious Democrats made preparations to assume control of the new national state, the professional historians prepared to assume the task of recording America's past. The long age of the amateur historian had ended.

[24] Henry Adams to Francis Parkman, December 21, 1884, in Harold Dean Cater (ed.), *Henry Adams and His Friends* (Boston: Houghton Mifflin Co., 1947), p. 134.

Appendix

AMERICAN HISTORICAL SOCIETIES, 1790–1890

The following list of historical societies is organized chronologically according to the date of founding. The societies are grouped by decades. The list includes only organizations which had as a major purpose historical work; most of the many patriotic, centennial, and monument societies are excluded. The location, town and state, of each society is given whenever that information is available. This list is not to be considered definitive, although an attempt has been made to include every noted American historical society.

The purpose of this appendix is to illustrate the rapid increase in local historical interest and activity in the decade preceding the Civil War and in the decades following the war. A glance at the geographical location of the societies will show that the western societies originated in urban (or potentially urban) centers. The great proliferation of town and county organizations occurs mainly on the East Coast in the vicinity of expanding industrial cities. Many of these societies were extremely short-lived and represented the enthusiasm of only a few men; nevertheless, the total picture is one of widespread and steadily growing interest in local history, perhaps a reaction to the compelling concern with the present and the strong currents of nationalism characteristic of the expanding urban industrial society.

1790–1820

1791
Massachusetts Historical Society, Boston.

1799
Connecticut Academy of Arts and Sciences, New Haven.

1804
New-York Historical Society, New York City.

1805
New England Society in the City of New York.

1812
American Antiquarian Society, Worcester, Mass.

1815
Historical Committee, American Philosophical Society, Philadelphia.
Literary and Philosophical Society of New York City.

1817
Religious Historical Society, Philadelphia.

1819
New England Society of Charleston, S.C.

1820–30

1820
Tennessee Antiquarian Society, Nashville.
Pilgrim Society, Plymouth, Mass.

1821
Essex Historical Society, Salem, Mass.

1822
Historical and Philosophical Society of Ohio, Cincinnati.
Maine Historical Society, Portland.
Rhode Island Historical Society, Providence.

1823
New Hampshire Historical Society, Concord.
Historical and Philosophical Society of New York, Schoharie.

1824
Historical Society of Pennsylvania, Philadelphia.
Society for the Commemoration of the Landing of William Penn, Philadelphia.

1825
Connecticut Historical Society, Hartford.
Worcester County (Mass.) Historical Society, Worcester.

1827
Antiquarian and Historical Society of Illinois, Vandalia.

1828
Historical Society of Michigan, Detroit.
Albany (N.Y.) Institute.

1830–40
1830
Indiana Historical Society, Indianapolis.

1831
Virginia Historical and Philosophical Society, Richmond.

1832
Albany (N.Y.) Historical Society.

1833
North Carolina Historical Society (Historical Society of the University of North
    Carolina), Chapel Hill.
East Tennessee Historical and Antiquarian Society, Knoxville.
Columbian Historical Society, Washington, D.C.

1834
Historical Society of Western Pennsylvania, Pittsburgh.

1835
Louisiana Historical Society, New Orleans.
American Historical Society, Washington, D.C.
Franklin Society of St. Louis, Mo.

1837
Antiquarian and Natural History Society of the State of Arkansas, Little Rock.
1838
Kentucky Historical Society, Louisville.

Historical and Philosophical Society of Ashtabula County (Ohio), Jefferson.
Vermont Historical Society, Montpelier.

1839
Western Methodist Historical Society, Cincinnati.
Vincennes (Ind.) Historical and Antiquarian Society.
Georgia Historical Society, Savannah.

1840-50

1840
American Statistical Association, Boston.

1841
Logan (Ohio) Historical Society, Westfall.
Historical and Geological Society of Norwalk Seminary, Norwalk, Ohio.
Marietta (Ohio) Historical Association.

1842
Mecklenburg (N.C.) Centennial and Monumental Association.

1843
Dorchester (Mass.) Antiquarian and Historical Society.
Illinois Literary and Historical Society, Upper Alton.
Middlebury (Vt.) Historical Society.
Iowa Historical and Geological Institute, Burlington.

1844
Maryland Historical Society, Baltimore.
Cincinnati (Ohio) Historical Society.
Red Jacket Historical Society, Buffalo, N.Y.
Vigo County (Ind.) Historical Society, Terre Haute.
Missouri Historical and Philosophical Society, Jefferson.
Historical Society of the University of North Carolina, Raleigh.

1845
New Jersey Historical Society, Trenton.
Newburgh (N.Y.) Historical Society.
New England Historic-Genealogical Society, Boston.
American Ethnological Society, New York City.

1846
State Historical Society of Wisconsin, Madison.
New England Society of Cincinnati, Ohio.
New Confederacy of the Iroquois, Rochester, N.Y.

1847
Historical Department of the Society of the Alumni of the University of Virginia,
   Richmond.

1848
Historical Society of the American Lutheran Church, Gettysburg, Pa.
St. Nicholas Society of the City of New York.

1849
Historical Society of Tennessee, Nashville.
Minnesota Historical Society, St. Paul.

1850–60

1850
Alabama Historical Society, Tuscaloosa.
Society of California Pioneers, San Francisco.
Protestant Episcopal Historical Society, New York City.

1851
Jeffersonville (Va.) Historical Society.

1852
Historical Society of the State of California, Inc., San Francisco.
Presbyterian Historical Society, Philadelphia.

1853
Newport (R.I.) Historical Society.
Old Colony Historical Society, Taunton, Mass.
Orleans County (Vt.) Natural and Civil History Society, Derby.

1854
American Baptist Historical Society, Philadelphia.
South Carolina Historical Society, Charleston.

1855
'Seventy-six Society, Philadelphia.

1856
Staten Island (N.Y.) Historical Society.
Chicago (Ill.) Historical Society.
Litchfield County (Conn.) Historical and Antiquarian Society, Litchfield.
State Historical Society of Iowa, Iowa City.
Historical Society of Florida, St. Augustine.

1857
Bradford Club, New York City.
Franklin Club, Philadelphia.
Fire Lands Historical Society, Norwalk, Ohio.
Cuyahoga County (Ohio) Historical Society, Newburg.

1858
Numismatic and Antiquarian Society of Philadelphia.
Wyoming Historical and Geological Society, Wilkes-Barre, Pa.
Tallmadge Historical Society, Tallmadge, Ohio.
Historical Society of Mississippi, Jackson.
American Numismatic and Archaeological Society, New York City.
Battle of Lake Erie Monument Association, Sandusky, Ohio.
Hawk Eye Pioneer Association of Des Moines County, Burlington, Iowa.
Louisa County (Iowa) Pioneer Settlers' Association, Iowa City.

1859
Dedham (Mass.) Historical Society.
Historical Society of New Mexico, Santa Fe.
Philomathic Club (became New Hampshire Antiquarian Society, 1873), Contoocook, N.H.
New England Methodist Historical Society, Boston.

Junior Pioneer Association of the City of Rochester and Monroe County (N.Y.), Rochester.
Holland Club, New York City.

1860–70

1860
Moravian Historical Society, Nazareth, Pa.
Rochester (N.Y.) Historical Society.
Ulster County (N.Y.) Historical Society, Kingston.
Yates County (N.Y.) Historical Society, Penn Yan.
Old Dominion Society of the City of New York.

1861
Tolland County (Conn.) Historical Society, Tolland.

1863
Long Island Historical Society, Brooklyn, N.Y.
Buffalo (N.Y.) Historical Society.

1864
New York Numismatic Society, New York City.
Arizona Historical Society, Prescott.
Delaware Historical Society, Wilmington.

1865
Narragansett Club, Providence, R.I.
Onondaga Historical Association, Syracuse, N.Y.
Furman Club, Brooklyn, N.Y.
Prince Society, Boston.
New Haven Colony Historical Society, New Haven, Conn.
Boston Numismatic Society.
Historical Society of Montana, Helena.

1866
Whitewater and Miami Valley Pioneer Association, Cleves, Ohio.
Houghton County (Mich.) Historical Society and Mining Institute, Houghton.
Arizona Pioneer Society, Prescott.
York Institute, Saco, Maine.

1867
Western Reserve and Northern Ohio Historical Society, Cleveland.
Historical Association of St. John's College, Fordham, N.Y.

1868
Southern Historical Society, Richmond, Va.
New England Society of Orange, New Jersey.
St. Louis (Mo.) Historical Society.

1869
Seneca County (Ohio) Pioneer Association, Tiffin.
Licking County (Ohio) Pioneer Society, Newark.
Pioneers' Association of Central New York, Syracuse.
New York Genealogical and Biographical Society, New York City.
Franklin Society, Chicago.

[185]

1869—*Continued*
Deutscher Pionier–Verein, Cincinnati.
West Virginia Historical Society, Morgantown.
Historical Society of Berks County (Pa.), Reading.
Dauphin County (Pa.) Historical Society, Harrisburg.
Old Residents' Historical Association, Lowell, Mass.

1870–80

1870
Old Settlers' Club of Milwaukee County (Wis.), Milwaukee.
Historical Society of Bradford County (Pa.), Athens.
Mad River Valley Pioneer and Historical Association, Sandusky, Ohio.
New Brunswick (N.J.) Historical Club.
Pocumtuck Valley Memorial Association, Deerfield, Mass.
Historical, Natural History, and Library Society, South Natick, Mass.

1871
Old Settlers' Society of Racine County (Wis.), Racine.
Franklin County (Ohio) Pioneer Association, Columbus.
New London County (Conn.) Historical Society, New London.
Backus Historical Society, Newton, Mass.
Pioneer and Historical Society of Oregon, Astoria.
Nashua (N.H.) Historical Society.
Northern New York Historical Society, Plattsburg.
Old Settlers' Association of Hennepin County (Minn.), Minneapolis.

1872
Old Settlers' Association of Sauk County (Wis.), Baraboo.
Western Ohio Pioneer Association, Bellefontaine.
Historical Society of Schenectady, N.Y.
Missouri Historical Society, St. Louis.
Oregon Pioneer Association, Salem.

1873
Pioneer and Historical Society of Pickaway County (Ohio), Circleville.
Cincinnati (Ohio) Pioneer Association.
Historical Society of Joliet, Ill.
Geauga County (Ohio) Historical Society, Cleveland.

1874
Old Settlers' Society of Lafayette County (Wis.), Darlington.
Historical Society of the Reformed Church in the United States, Lancaster, Pa.
Pioneer Association of Montgomery County (Ohio), Dayton.
Westchester County (N.Y.) Historical Society, White Plains.
Pioneer and Historical Society of Michigan, Detroit.
California Historical Society, San Francisco.
Society of First Steamship Pioneers, San Francisco.

1875
Historical Society of Galveston, Texas.
Ohio State Archaeological Convention, Mansfield.
Southern Historical Society, North Carolina Branch, Raleigh, N.C.
Mecklenburg (N.C.) Historical Society.

Maine Genealogical and Biographical Society, Augusta.
New England Numismatic and Archaeological Society, Boston.
Friends' Historical Association of Philadelphia.

1876
Bennington (Vt.) Historical Society.
Deutsche Gesellschaft von Pennsylvanien, Philadelphia.
Mahoning Valley Historical Society, Youngstown, Ohio.
Pilgrim Record Society, New York City.
Cass County (Mich.) Pioneer Association, Detroit.
Oldest Inhabitants' Association, Washington. D.C.
Old Settlers' Society, Springfield, Ill.
Connecticut Valley Historical Society, Springfield, Mass.
Military History Society of Massachusetts, Boston.
Worcester (Mass.) Society of Antiquity.
State Archaeological Society of Ohio, Newark.

1877
Vermont Numismatic Society, Montpelier.
Maumee Valley Pioneer and Historical Association, Toledo, Ohio.
Cuyahoga County (Ohio) Pioneer Association, North Solon.
District Historical Society of the Counties of Medina, Summit, and Wayne (Ohio),
    Wadsworth.
Albemarle (N.C.) Historical Society.
Livingston County (N.Y.) Historical Society, Geneseo.
Free Public Library, Reading Room, and Historical Association of St. Augustine, Fla.
Rumford Historical Society, Woburn, Mass.
Kansas State Historical Society, Topeka.
Pioneer Association of the Counties of Marin, Napa, Lake, and Mendocino (Cal.).

1878
Tennessee Historical Society, Nashville.
Battle Monument Association, Bennington, Vt.
Rhode Island Soldiers' and Sailors' Historical Society, Providence.
Cayuga County (N.Y.) Historical Society, Auburn.
Canton (Mass.) Historical Society.
Historical and Antiquarian Society of Old Newbury, Newburyport, Mass.
Old Residents' Association of the Grand River Valley, Grand Rapids, Mich.
Nebraska State Historical Society, Lincoln.
Wyoming (Pa.) Commemorative Association.

1879
Wisconsin Pioneer Association, Madison.
Pioneer Association of the Western Reserve, Cleveland.
Waterloo (N.Y.) Library and Historical Society.
Historical Society of Wilmington, N.C.
Old Settlers' Association of Oswego County (N.Y.), Fulton.
Oneida Historical Society, Utica, N.Y.
Genesee Valley Pioneer Association, Batavia, N.Y.
Archaeological Institute of America, Cambridge, Mass.
Mattatuck Historical Society, Waterbury, Conn.

1879—Continued
Weymouth (Mass.) Historical Society.
Early Settlers' Association of Cuyahoga County (Ohio), Cleveland.

1880–90
1880
Monument Association of the Capture of André, Tarrytown, N.Y.
Surveyors' Association of West New Jersey, Camden.
Pioneer Association of Will County (Ill.), Joliet.
Marshall County (Kan.) Pioneer Association, Atchison.
Louisville (Ky.) Southern Historical Society.
Boston (Mass.) Antiquarian Club.
Mahoning Valley Pioneer Society, Cleveland.
New England Society in the City of Broklyn, N.Y.

1881
Rutland County (Vt.) Historical Society, Castleton.
Washington County (Pa.) Historical Society, Washington.
New England Society of Pennsylvania, Philadelphia.
Rockland County (N.Y.) History and Forestry Society, Nyack.
Conecuh (Ala.) Historical Society.
Historical Society of the State of Arkansas, Little Rock.
Geographical Society of the Pacific, San Francisco.
Fairfield County (Conn.) Historical Society, Bridgeport.
Pioneer-Verein of Philadelphia.
Harvard Historical Society, Cambridge, Mass.

1882
Genealogical Association of Pennsylvania and New Jersey, Philadelphia.
Pioneer Association of Athens County (Ohio), Ames Township.
Historical and Scientific Society of Wilmington, N.C.
King's County (N.Y.) Genealogical Club, Brooklyn.
Webster Historical Society, Boston.
Bostonian Society, Boston.

1883
Washington County (Ohio) Pioneer Association, Marietta.
Huguenot Society of America, New York City.
Old Folks' Association of Charlemont, Mass.
Tri-State Old Settlers' Association of Illinois, Missouri, and Iowa, Keokuk, Iowa.
Maine Genealogical Society, Portland.

1884
Rhode Island Veteran Citizens' Historical Association, Providence.
American Catholic Historical Society of Philadelphia.
Bucks County (Pa.) Historical Society, Doylestown.
Early Settlers' Association of Cleveland, Ohio.
Historical Society of Newburgh Bay and the Highlands, Newburgh, N.Y.
Historical Society of Southern California, Los Angeles.
Old Settlers' Association of Lake County (Ind.), Crown Point.
Filson Club, Louisville, Ky.

Gorges Society, Portland, Me.
American Historical Association, Saratoga Springs, N.Y., 1884–86 (Washington, D.C., 1886—).
Salem County (N.J.) Historical Society, Salem.

1885
Barrington (R.I.) Historic-Antiquarian Society.
Ohio Valley Catholic Historical Society, Pittsburgh.
Richland County (Ohio) Historical and Pioneer Society, Mansfield.
Chautauqua Society of History and Natural Science, Jamestown, N.Y.
Holland Society, New York City.
Winchester (Mass.) Historical and Genealogical Society.
U.S. Catholic Historical Society, New York City.
Old Settlers' Society of Muscatine County (Iowa), Muscatine.
Boyle County (Ky.) Historical Society, Maysville.

1886
Otterbein University Historical Society, Waterville, Ohio.
Society of Old Brooklynites, Brooklyn, N.Y.
Suffolk County (N.Y.) Historical Society, Riverhead, Long Island.
Jefferson County (N.Y.) Historical Society, Watertown.
Ramsay County (Minn.) Pioneer Association, St. Paul.
Rehoboth (Mass.) Antiquarian Society.
Pioneer Law Makers' Association of Iowa, Des Moines.
Harford Historical Society, Bel Air, Md.
Berkshire Historical and Scientific Society, Pittsfield, Mass.
Concord (Mass.) Antiquarian Society.
Lexington (Mass.) Historical Society.
Lackawanna Institute of History and Science, Scranton, Pa.

1887
Ohio State Archaeological and Historical Society, Columbus.
Society for the History of the Germans in Maryland, Baltimore.
Ipswich (Mass.) Historical Society.
North Brookfield (Mass.) Historical Society.

1888
Milwaukee (Wis.) Pioneer Association.
American Society of Church History, New York City.
Anne Arundel County (Md.) Historical Society, Annapolis.
Orleans County (Vt.) Historical Society, Newport.

1889
Historical Society of Adams County (Pa.), Lancaster.
Ohio Church History Society, Oberlin.
Schoharie County Historical Society (N.Y.), Schoharie.
Minisink Valley Historical Society, Port Jervis, N.Y.
Westborough (Mass.) Historical Society.
State Historical and Natural History Society of Colorado, Denver.
Pejepscot Historical Society, Brunswick, Maine.
Huguenot Society of Charleston, S.C.

1890
Tarrytown (N.Y.) Historical Society.
Watertown (Mass.) Historical Society.
Hyde Park (Mass.) Historical Society.
University of Pennsylvania Archaeological Association, Philadelphia.
West Virginia Historical and Antiquarian Society, Charleston.

A Selective Bibliography

MANUSCRIPTS

American Historical Association Papers. Library of Congress. A huge collection consisting of 90 letter file boxes, 342 manuscript boxes, plus assorted packages of material covering the years 1884–1946. The collection is very meager for the first fifteen years of the association's existence. Committee records are often missing and in some cases may be found among the private correspondence of the men who served as chairmen.

George Bancroft Papers. Library of Congress. A minor collection of a few boxes of letters concerning political and personal matters, very little on historical work.

Bancroft Papers. Massachusetts Historical Society. A large collection covering a great variety of topics, but fairly well culled by Russell Nye and Mark DeWolfe Howe for material pertaining to the *History*.

Mathew Carey. Account books 1785–1821. American Antiquarian Society. Worcester, Mass.

Century Collection. New York Public Library. The correspondence and papers of the *Century Magazine*. Contains letters of Alexander Johnston, J. B. McMaster, and Edward Eggleston.

Henry B. Dawson Papers. New-York Historical Society. Contains two folders of letters and a MS of his history of the New York volunteer fire department. Other letters are scattered through the well-indexed collections of the society.

Dawson Papers. New York Public Library. One folder of miscellaneous letters.

Charles Deane Papers. Massachusetts Historical Society. A large collection. Much of it deals with society business, especially good for the purpose of this study from 1865 through the 1870's.

Lyman C. Draper Papers. Wisconsin State Historical Society. A very large collection of Draper's personal correspondence concerning his own project as well as official correspondence of the historical society. Contains letters from almost every American historian active between 1845 and 1890.

Charles Folsom Papers. Boston Public Library. A small collection containing a dozen letters from Jared Sparks, written in the 1840's, and two short notes from James Parton.

Peter Force Correspondence. Library of Congress. A very large collection containing 32 volumes of letters. Force corresponded with a great many historians in America between 1830 and 1868. Also contains much relating to the American Archives and the American Historical Society.

Francis Lister Hawks Papers. New-York Historical Society. A large collection; the bulk of it consists of letters and documents collected by Hawks. The correspondence deals primarily with church matters.

Historical Committee Papers. American Philosophical Society. Consists of two letter books and two volumes of minutes kept intermittently from 1815 to 1845.

Henry Holt Papers. Princeton University. A rich collection but somewhat disorganized and difficult to use. Early letterbooks are chronologically arranged with tables of contents to each volume, but there is no comprehensive catalogue for the collection. Contains a folder of Frederick Jackson Turner letters and some correspondence of J. B. McMaster and Alexander Johnston.

John Franklin Jameson Papers. Carnegie Institute, Washington, D.C. A collection rich in materials on all phases of historical activity in American from 1884 to 1937. Three filing cases of four drawers each are packed with correspondence, with a folder for each individual or institution.

Herbert H. Lang. "Nineteenth-Century Historians of the Gulf States," Ph.D. dissertation, University of Texas, 1954.

Jedidiah Morse Papers. New York Public Library. Five letters to Noah Webster in a miscellaneous collection.

Morse Papers. Sterling Library, Yale University. A very full and relatively untouched collection. Contains much about literary and religous matters in New England from 1770's to 1820, but little of interest for this study.

William Plumer Papers. Library of Congress. Contains the half-finished, unpublished MS of his history of the United States.

Robert Proud Commonplace Book. Boston Public Library. Contains some Greek translations and memoranda of a "short and thoughtful journey from Philadelphia to New England" in 1762.

Proud Papers. Pennsylvania Historical Society. Very small collection. Contains some letters to his brother, which mention work on his history of Pennsylvania.

Charles Scribner's Sons Archives. New York. Most of the early papers of Scribner's publishing house were burned in a fire, but some letters of Joel T. Headley remain, as well as the correspondence concerning Scribner's Civil War campaign series.

Buckingham Smith Papers. Library of Congress. Consists of five boxes of the personal correspondence of Smith, mostly letters from historians asking for information about material in the Spanish archives.

William Rudolph Smith Papers. Wisconsin State Historical Society. A small collection of a few scattered letters and the MSS volumes of Smith's history of Wisconsin.

Jared Sparks Papers. Massachusetts Historical Society. A vast collection. Thoroughly indexed, with detailed material on every project Sparks undertook. Occasionally he kept journals on trips, and the journals contain accounts of manuscript collections throughout the coastal states. Letters from every historian working between 1828–1855.

Mercy Otis Warren Papers. Massachusetts Historical Society. Two letter books of correspondence between Mercy Warren and Catherine McCaulay, 1774–1780's.

John F. Watson Papers. Pennsylvania Historical Society. Small collection; a few items dealing with the early history of the Pennsylvania Historical Society, a short MS account of the founding of the society.

Watson, "Annals of Philadelphia," MS, Vol. I, June, 1830. Pennyslvania Historical Society.

PERIODICALS

American Journal of Education. Boston, 1826–28.

American Journal of Education. Hartford, 1855–70.

American Monthly Register. Philadelphia, 1802–8.

Annals of the State Historical Society of Iowa. Iowa City, 1863–74.

Annual Register, or a View of the History, Politics, and Literature. London, 1759——.

Archaeologia Americana: Transactions and Collections of the American Antiquarian Society. Worcester, Mass., 1820–1911.

Boston Courier. Boston, 1786–89.

The Boston Gazette and the Country Journal. Boston, 1719–98.

Bulletin of the American Association for State and Local History. Washington, D.C., 1941——.

Collections of the Georgia Historical Society. Savannah, 1840–1916.

Collections of the Maine Historical Society. Portland, 1831–1906.

Collections of the Massachusetts Historical Society. Boston, 1792——.

Collections of the Minnesota Historical Society. St. Paul, 1850–1920.

Collections of the New Hampshire Historical Society. Concord, 1824——.

Collections of the New Jersey Historical Society. Newark, 1846——.

Collections of the New-York Historical Society. New York, 1811–59.

Collections of the South Carolina Historical Society. Charleston, 1857–97.

Collections of the Virginia Historical and Philosophical Society. Richmond, Va., 1882–92.

Collections of the State Historical Society of Wisconsin. Madison, 1889——.

Columbian. Philadelphia, 1787–95.

DeBow's Review. New Orleans, 1846–64, 1866–70, 1879–80.

Georgia Historical Quarterly. Savannah, 1917——.

Harper's New Monthly Magazine. New York, 1850——.

Historical Magazine. Boston and New York, 1857–75.

Independent Chronicle and the Universal Advertiser. Boston, 1786–89.

Knickerbocker Magazine. New York, 1833–65.

Memoirs of the Historical Society of Pennsylvania. Philadelphia, 1826–95.

New England Historical and Genealogical Register. Boston, 1847——.

New York History. New York, 1932——.

North American Review. Boston, 1815–1940.

Papers of the American Historical Association. New York, 1885–91.

Papers of the Southern Historical Society. Richmond, Va., 1876–1908.

Pennsylvania Magazine of History and Biography. Philadelphia, 1877——.

Proceedings of the Massachusetts Historical Society. Boston, 1879——.

Proceedings of the New Hampshire Historical Society. Concord, 1874–1917.

Proceedings of the New Jersey Historical Society. Newark, 1847——.

Proceedings of the American Antiquarian Society. Worcester, Mass., 1843——.

Proceedings of the American Philosophical Society. Philadelphia, 1838——.

Reports and Collections of the State Historical Society of Wisconsin. Madison, 1855–88.

Southern Literary Messenger. Richmond, 1834–64.

Southern Quarterly Review. New Orleans, 1842–57.

Transactions of the American Philosophical Society. Philadelphia, 1771——.

United States Magazine and Democratic Review. New York, 1837–59.

Virginia Historical Register. Richmond, 1848–53.

ARTICLES

ADAMS, CHARLES FRANCIS. "Review of the Life of Peter Van Schaack," *North American Review*, LV (July, 1842), 99–113.

ADAMS, HERBERT BAXTER. "The New Historical Movement," *Nation*, XXXIX (September 18, 1884), 240.

"Bancroft's *A History of the United States*," *Southern Literary Messenger*, I (June, 1835), 587.

"Bancroft's History," *American Quarterly Review*, XVI (September, 1834), 205–35.

BANCROFT, GEORGE. "American History," *North American Review*, XLVI (April, 1838), 475–87.

———. "Review of Force's Documentary History of the American Revolution," *North American Review*, XLVI (April, 1838), 481.

BARKER, EUGENE C. "The Changing View of the Function of History," *The Social Studies*, XXIX (April, 1938), 149–54.

BENTLEY, WILLIAM. "Remarks on the Remarks on a History of Salem," *Collections of the Massachusetts Historical Society*, VIII (Boston, 1802), 1–4.

BOWEN, FRANCIS. "Hildreth's History of the United States," *North American Review*, LXXIII (October, 1851), 413–37.

BRASCH, FREDERICK E. "The Newtonian Epoch in the American Colonies," *Proceedings of the American Antiquarian Society*, N.S., XLIX (October, 1939), 314–32.

BRUNHOUSE, ROBERT L. "David Ramsay's Publication Problems, 1784–1808," *Papers of the Bibliographical Society of America*, XXXIX (1st Quarter, 1945), 51–67.

CARTER, CLARENCE E. "The Territorial Papers of the United States: A Review and a Commentary," *Mississippi Valley Historical Review*, XLII (December, 1955), 510–24.

CARTER, JAMES G. "The Schools of Massachusetts in 1824," *Old South Leaflets*, No. 135 (Boston, 1903), pp. 1–24.

CASS, LEWIS. "Discourse," *Historical and Scientific Sketches of Michigan* (Detroit, 1834), pp. 1–20.

CHANNING, WILLIAM ELLERY. "Reflections on the Literary Delinquency of America," *North American Review*, II (November, 1815), 33–43.

"Circular Letter of the Historical Society," *Collections of the Massachusetts Historical Society*, II (Boston, 1793), 1–2.

COLBURN, H. TREVOR. "Thomas Jefferson's Use of the Past," *William and Mary Quarterly*, 3d ser., XV (January, 1958), 56–70.

"A Concise History of the Late War in America," *Columbian*, IV (March, 1789), 285–90.

CONKLIN, EDWIN G. "Brief History of the American Philosophical Society," *Year Book of the American Philosophical Society, 1952* (Philadelphia, 1953), pp. 13–42.

COPELAND, THOMAS W. "Burke and Dodsley's *Annual Register*," *Publications of the Modern Language Association of America*, LIV (March, 1939), 223–45.

COULTER, E. MERTON. "What the South Has Done about Its History," *Journal of Southern History*, II (February, 1936), 3–28.

CUSHING, JONATHAN P. "First Annual Address to the Virginia Historical Society," *Collections of the Virginia Historical Society*, I (Richmond, 1833), 12–30.

DAVIDSON, ALEXANDER, JR. "How Benson J. Lossing Wrote His Field Books of the Revolution, the War of 1812, and the Civil War," *Bibliographical Society of America, Papers*, XXII (1937), 58–63.

DAVIS, JOHN. "A Discourse," *Collections of the Massachusetts Historical Society*, 2d ser., I (Boston, 1838), 1–23.

DAWSON, HENRY BARTON. "Charles Francis Adams' *The Struggle for Neutrality in America*," *Historical Magazine*, IX, 2d ser. (February, 1871), 129–50.

———. "The Motley Letters," *Historical Magazine*, IX, 2d ser. (March, 1871), 163–70.

DEAN, JOHN WARD. "A Memoir of Henry Barton Dawson, Esq.," *Historical Magazine*, IV, 2d ser. (December, 1868), 257–61.

DEBOW, J. D. B. "An Account of the Louisiana Historical Society," ed. B. F. French, *Historical Collections of Louisiana*, II (Philadelphia, 1850), 3–8.

DELAFIELD, MATURIN L. "William Smith the Historian; Chief Justice of New York and of Canada," *Magazine of American History*, VI (June, 1881), 410–39.

DOBIE, J. FRANK. "The Archives Wars of Texas," leaflet (Austin, 1958).

"Domestic Histories of the South," *Southern Quarterly Review*, XXI (November, 1852), 508–12.

"Domestic History of the South," *DeBow's Review of the Southern and Western States*, XXVIII (November, 1860), 509.

ELIOT, SAMUEL A. "Jeremy Belknap," *Proceedings of the Massachusetts Historical Society*, LXVI (Boston, 1942), 102–3.

EMERSON, DONALD F. "Hildreth, Draper, and 'Scientific History,'" *Historiography and Urbanization*, ed. Eric F. Goldman (Baltimore, 1941), pp. 139–70.

EMERSON, RALPH WALDO. "History," *Essays* (New York: Modern Library, 1944), pp. 5–15.

EVANS, JOSIAH J. Untitled speech, *Congressional Globe*, Appendix, 34th Congress, 1st sess. (June 23, 1856), pp. 701–7.

FISHER, SIDNEY G. "The Legendary and Myth-Making Process in Histories of the American Revolution," American Philosophical Society, *Proceedings*, LI (Philadelphia, 1912), 53–75.

FLINT, TIMOTHY. "On History," *Western Monthly Review*, I (1827–28), 543.

FORAN, WILLIAM A. "John Marshall as a Historian," *American Historical Review*, XLI (1937–38), 51–64.

"The Former, Present and Future Prospects of America," *Columbian*, I (January, 1787), 83–86.

GILMER, FRANCIS WALK. "Letters of Francis Walk Gilmer to Thomas Walker Gilmer," *Tyler's Quarterly Historical and Genealogical Magazine*, VI (1924–25), 240–41.

GILMER, THOMAS W. "An Address on the Value of History Before the Virginia Historical and Philosophical Society," *Southern Literary Messenger*, III (February, 1837), 97.

GOFF, FREDERICK R. "Peter Force," *Papers of the Bibliographical Society of America*, XLIV (1st Quarter, 1950), 1–16.

GRAY, FRANCIS C. "An Address before the Society of Phi Beta Kappa on Thursday, the 29th of August, 1816," *North American Review*, III (September, 1816), 288–318.

GREENOUGH, CHESTER N. "New England Almanacs, 1766–1775, and the American Revolution," *Proceedings of the American Antiquarian Society*, XLV (Worcester, Mass., 1935), 288–316.

HAMILTON, J. G. DE ROULHAC. "The Preservation of North Carolina History," *North Carolina Historical Review*, IV (January, 1927), 6–7.

HARDEN, WILLIAM. "The Georgia Historical Society," *Georgia Historical Quarterly*, I (March, 1917), 3–12.

HAWLEY, JOSEPH R. "Report of the President of the Commission," United States Centennial Commission, *International Exhibition 1876* (Washington, D.C., 1880), pp. 2–11.

HAYNE, ROBERT Y. "Dr. David Ramsay," *Analectic Magazine*, VI (Philadelphia, 1815), 204–24.

HELDERMAN, L. C. "A Social Scientist of the Old South," *Journal of Southern History*, II (May, 1936), 148–74.

HENSEL, WILLIAM U. "Dr. David Ramsay," Lancaster County (Pa.) Historical Society, *Papers*, X (November, 1906), 357–67.

HESSELTINE, WILLIAM B. "Lyman Copeland Draper, 1815–91," *Wisconsin Magazine of History*, XXXV (Spring, 1952), 163–76.

———. "Lyman Draper and the South," *Journal of Southern History*, XIX (February, 1953), 20–31.

HESSELTINE, WILLIAM B., and GARA, LARRY. "Draper: Historian Turned Educator," *Mid-America*, XXXV (July, 1953), 131–43.

——— (eds.). "Historical Collecting," *Bulletin of the Historical and Philosophical Society of Ohio* (April, 1957), 141–51.

——— (eds.). "The Historical Fraternity: Correspondence of Historians Grigsby, Henry, and Draper," *Virginia Magazine of History and Biography*, LXI (October, 1953), 450–71.

——— "History Publishing in 1849," *Historian*, XVI (Spring, 1954), 135–41.

———. "Mississippi's Confederate Leaders After the War," *Journal of Mississippi History*, (April, 1951), 88–100.

——— (eds.). "Postwar Problems of a Virginia Historian," *Virginia Magazine of History and Biography*, LXI (April, 1953), 193–95.

HILDRETH, RICHARD. "National Literature," *American Monthly Magazine*, I (July, 1829), 380.

"Hildreth's History of the United States," *DeBow's Review of the Southern and Western States*, X (May, 1851), 599.

"Historical Sketch of the Society," *Collections of the New-York Historical Society*, 2d ser., I (New York, n.d.), 458–70.

HOLT, W. STULL. "The Idea of Scientific History in America," *Journal of the History of Ideas*, I, No. 2 (June, 1940), 252–62.

HUTCHESON, MAUDE MACDONALD. "Mercy Warren, 1728–1814," *William and Mary Quarterly*, 3d ser., X (July, 1953), 380–402.

"I. K. Tefft," *Virginia Historical Register*, II (1849), 176.

"Introductory Address from the Historical Society to the Public," *Collections of the Massachusetts Historical Society*, I (Boston, 1792), 2–4.

IRVINE, DALLAS. "The Archives Office of the War Department, Repository of Captured Confederate Archives, 1865–1881," *Military Affairs*, X (Spring, 1946), 93–111.

———. "The Genesis of the Official Records," *Mississippi Valley Historical Review*, XXIV (1937), 221–29.

JAMESON, JOHN FRANKLIN. "The American Historical Association, 1884–1909," *American Historical Review*, XV (October, 1909), 1–20.

———. "History of Historical Societies," *Seventy-fifth Anniversary Report of the Georgia Historical Society* (Atlanta, 1914), pp. 33–51.

JARVIS, EDWARD. "Some Accounts of the Kentucky Historical Society," *American Quarterly Register*, XV (August, 1842), 77.

JENKS, WILLIAM. "An Account of the Massachusetts Historical Society," *Collections of the Massachusetts Historical Society*, 3d ser., VII (Boston, 1838), 5–25.

JORGENSON, CHESTER E. "The New Science in the Almanacs of Ames and Franklin," *New England Quarterly*, VIII (December, 1935), 555–61.

KEITT, L. M. Untitled speech, *Congressional Globe*, Appendix, 34th Congress, 1st sess. (July 16, 1856), pp. 833–39.

KING, CHARLES. "A Discourse Delivered Before the New Jersey Historical Society, May 7, 1845," *Proceedings of the New Jersey Historical Society*, I (Newark, 1846), 130–45.

"Knapp's Lectures on American Literature," *Southern Review*, VII (August, 1831), 438.

KNEPPER, ADRIAN W. "Obadiah Rich (1783–1850), Bibliophile," *Papers of the Bibliographical Society of America* (2d Quarter, 1955), pp. 112–30

LAW, WILLIAM. "Address to Georgia Historical Society," *Collections of the Georgia Historical Society*, I (Savannah, 1840), 2–23.

LEHMBERG, STANFORD E. "The Divine Art and Its Uses: Some Early English views on the Utility of History," *Historian*, XX (Winter, 1958), 24–38.

LIBBY, ORIN G. "Ramsay as a Plagiarist," *American Historical Review*, VII (July, 1902), 697–703.

———. "Some Pseudo-Historians of the American Revolution," *Proceedings of the Wisconsin Academy of Sciences and Arts*, XIII (Madison, Wis., 1900), 419–25.

———. "William Gordon's History of the American Revolution," American Historical Association, *Annual Report, 1899* (Washington, D.C.: Government Printing Office, 1900), pp. 367–88.

LOKKE, CARL L. "The Captured Confederate Records under Francis Lieber," *American Archivist*, IX (October, 1946), 277–319.

LORING, JAMES S. "Our First Historian of the American Revolution," *Historical Magazine*, VI (February, 1862), 41–49; (March, 1862), 78–83.

MACKALL, L. L. "Edward Langworthy and the First Attempt to Write a Separate History of Georgia, from the Long-lost Langworthy Papers," *Georgia Historical Quarterly*, VII (March, 1923), 1–12.

MALIN, JAMES. "Notes on the Writing of General Histories of Kansas," *Kansas Historical Quarterly*, XXI (Autumn, 1954), 184–223; (Winter, 1954), 264–87; (Spring, 1955), 331–78; (Summer, 1955), 407–44; (Winter, 1955), 598–643.

———. "On the Nature of Local History," *Wisconsin Magazine of History* (Summer, 1957), pp. 227–30.

MASON, JOHN. "Brief History of the Pequot War," *Collections of the Massachusetts Historical Society*, 2d ser., VIII (Boston, 1819), 50–152.

MAYO, LAURENCE S. "Jeremy Belknap and Ebenezer Hazard, 1782–1784," *New England Quarterly*, II (April, 1929), 183–98.

McGIRR, NEWMAN F. "The Activities of Peter Force," Columbia Historical Society, *Records*, XLII (Washington, 1942), 35–82.

MILLER, RALPH N. "American Nationalism as a Theory of Nature," *William and Mary Quarterly*, 3d ser., XI (January, 1955), 74–95.

MONETTE, JOHN W. "The Limited Nature of Human Research," *Southwestern Journal*, I (December 15, 1837), 5–8.

MORGAN, EDMUND S. "The American Revolution: Revisions in Need of Revising," *William and Mary Quarterly*, 3d ser., XIV (January, 1957), 3–15.

MORSE, JARVIS M. "John Smith and His Critics: A Chapter in Colonial Historiography," *Journal of Southern History*, I, No. 2 (May, 1935), 123–37.

MOSSNER, ERNEST C., and RANSOM, HARRY H. "Hume and the Conspiracy of the Book Sellers," *University of Texas Studies in English*, XXIX (Austin, 1950), 162–83.

MURDOCK, KENNETH. "William Hubbard and the Providential Interpretation of History," *Proceedings of the American Antiquarian Society*, N.S., LII (Boston, 1943), 15–37.

"The New York Canals," *North American Review*, XIV (January, 1822), 230–51.

"Papers Relative to the Valedictory Address of President Washington," *Memoirs of the Pennsylvania Historical Society*, I (Philadelphia, 1826), 241–68.

PEMBERTON, THOMAS. "Historical Journal of the American War," *Collections of the Massachusetts Historical Society*, II, 1st ser. (Boston, 1793), 41–246.

PERSONS, STOW. "Progress and the Organic Cycle in Eighteenth Century America," *American Quarterly*, VI (Summer, 1954) 147–63.

"The Philosophy of History," *North American Review*, XXXIX (July, 1834), 36–57.

POTTS, WILLIAM J. "Pierre Eugene DeSimitiere," *Pennsylvania Magazine of History and Biography*, XIII (October, 1889), 341–75.

PRATT, JULIUS W. "Aaron Burr and the Historians," *New York History* (October, 1945), pp. 447–70.

PRINCE, W. F. "An Examination of Peters' 'Blue Laws,'" American Historical Association, *Annual Report, 1898* (Washington, D.C., 1899), pp. 95–138.

PROUD, ROBERT. "Autobiography," *Pennsylvania Magazine of History and Biography*, XIII, No. 4 (1889), 430–40.

"Ramsay's History of the United States," *North American Review*, VI (March, 1818), 331–44.

RAWLE, WILLIAM. "A Vindication of the Reverend Mr. Heckwelder's History of the Indian Nations," *Memoirs of the Pennsylvania Historical Society*, I (Philadelphia, 1826), 268–84.

"Review of Albert J. Pickett's History of Alabama, and incidentally, of Georgia and Mississippi from the Earliest Period," *Southern Quarterly Review*, XXI (January, 1852), 182–87.

"Review of Benjamin Cowell's *Spirit of '76 in Rhode Island*," *Democratic Review*, XXVII (November, 1850), 476.

"Review of Sabine's *The American Loyalists*," *North American Review*, LXV (July, 1847), 138–59.

RIPLEY, GEORGE. "History," *New American Cyclopaedia: A Popular Dictionary of General Knowledge*, ed. George Ripley and Charles Dana (New York, 1859–60), IX, 208–10.

RIVES, WILLIAM C. Untitled address, *Virginia Historical Register and Literary Advertiser*, II (January, 1849), 10–21.

RUSSELL, WILLIAM F. "Early Teaching of History in the Secondary Schools of New York and Massachusetts," *History Teachers' Magazine* (1915) V, 203–8, 311–18; VI, 14–19, 44–52, 122–25.

SCHLESINGER, ARTHUR M., JR. "The Problem of Richard Hildreth," *New England Quarterly*, XIII (June, 1940), 223–45.

SELLERS, CHARLES GRIER, JR. "Andrew Jackson versus the Historians," *Mississippi Valley Historical Review*, XLIV (March, 1958), 615–34.

SHELLEY, FRED. "Ebenezer Hazard: America's First Historical Editor," *William and Mary Quarterly*, 3d ser., XII (January, 1955), 44–73.

"Sketch of the Formation of the New Hampshire Historical Society," *Collections of the New Hampshire Historical Society for the Year 1824* (Concord, N.H., 1824), pp. 1–5.

SMELLIE, WILLIAM. "An Historical Account of the Society of the Antiquaries of Scotland," *Archaeologia Scotica, or Transactions of the Society of Antiquaries of Scotland*, I (Edinburgh, 1792), 1–9.

SMITH, JOSEPH P. "Henry Howe, the Historian," Ohio Archeological and Historical Society, *Publications*, IV (Columbus, 1900), 310–420.

"Southern School Books," *DeBow's Review of the Southern and Western States*, XIII (September, 1852), 259–62.

SPARKS, JARED. "Materials for American History," *North American Review*, XXIII (October, 1826), 275–90.

SPOFFORD, AINSWORTH R. "The Life and Labors of Peter Force, Mayor of Washington," Columbia Historical Society, *Records*, XLII (Washington, 1942), 35–82.

STEPHENSON, WENDELL H. "A Quarter Century of American Historiography," *Mississippi Valley Historical Review*, XLV (June, 1958), 3–22.

SUMNER, CHARLES. "Crime Against Kansas," *Congressional Globe*, Appendix, 34th Congress, 1st sess. (May 19, 1856), 531–36.

THOMSON, C. W. "Notes of the Life and Character of Robert Proud," *Memoirs of the Pennsylvania Historical Society*, I (Philadelphia, 1826), 1–22.

TODD, JOHN A. "Henry B. Dawson," *New England Historical and Genealogical Register*, XLIV (July, 1890), 235–48.

"A Topographical Description of Duxborough, in the County of Plymouth," *Collections of the Massachusetts Historical Society*, II (Boston, 1794), 8–10.

TROUP, GEORGE M. "Address to Georgia Legislature, Nov. 2, 1824," *Journal of the House of Representatives of the State of Georgia for the Year 1824* (Milledgeville, 1825), p. 24.

TUCKER, ST. GEORGE. "Address to the Virginia Historical Society," *Southern Literary Messenger*, I (1836), 259.

VAIL, R. W. G. "The Society Grows Up," *New-York Historical Society Quarterly*, XXXVIII (October, 1954), 384–477.

VAN TASSEL, DAVID D. "The American Historical Association and the South," *Journal of Southern History*, XXIII (November, 1957), 465–82.

———. "Henry Barton Dawson: A Nineteenth Century Revisionist," *William and Mary Quarterly*, 3d ser., XIII (July, 1956), 319–41.

———. "Benson J. Lossing: Pen and Pencil Historian," *American Quarterly*, VI (Spring, 1952), 32–44.

———. "William Rudolph Smith: A Cultural Capitalist," *Wisconsin Magazine of History*, XXXVI (Summer, 1953), 241–44, 276–80.

VAUGHN, MYRA. "The First Historical Society of Arkansas," *Publications of the Arkansas Historical Association*, II (1908), 346–55.

"Von Ranke's Princes and Nations," *North American Review*, XXXI (October, 1830), 291–308.

"Warren-Adams Letters," *Collections of the Massachusetts Historical Society*, Vol. LXXIII (Boston, 1925).

WASHBURN, WILCOMB E. "Sir William Berkeley's *A History of Our Miseries*," *William and Mary Quarterly*, 3d ser., XIV (July, 1957), 403–13.

WEAVER, GEORGE H. "Life and Writings of William Douglass, M.D.," *Bulletin of the Society of Medical History of Chicago*, II (April, 1921), 229–59.

WHARTON, THOMAS L. "Notes on the Provincial Literature of Pennsylvania," *Memoirs of the Pennsylvania Historical Society*, I (Philadelphia, 1826), 107–62.

WHITE, ANDREW D. "Studies in General History and the History of Civilization," American Historical Association, *Papers*, I (1885), 21.

WHITMORE, WILLIAM H. "Life and Labors of Thomas Prince," *North American Review*, XCI (October, 1860), 354–75.

"William Smith's History of New York," *North American Review*, II (January, 1816), 157–67.

WILLSON, MARCIUS. "A Critical Review of American Common School Histories," *Biblical Repository and Classical Review*, 3d ser., I (July, 1845), 517–39.

WINSOR, JUSTIN. "The Perils of Historical Narrative," *Atlantic Monthly*, LXVI (September, 1890), 279–97.

WOODBURN, JAMES A. "Promotion of Historical Study in America Following the Civil War," Illinois State Historical Society, *Transactions* (Chicago, 1922), 38–41.

YOUNG, ELIZABETH. "Juvenile Biographies of the Presbyterian Board of Publication, 1838–1887," *Journal of the Presbyterian Historical Society* (September, 1955).

BOOKS

ABBOTT, JOHN STEVENS CABOT. *The History of the Civil War in America.* 3 vols. Springfield, Mass. 1863–65.

ACTON, LORD. *A Lecture on the Study of History Delivered at Cambridge June 11, 1895.* London. 1895.

ADAIR, JAMES, *History of the American Indians.* London. 1775.

ADAMS, CHARLES KENDALL. *A Manual of Historical Literature.* New York. 1888.

ADAMS, HERBERT BAXTER. *The Life and Writings of Jared Sparks.* Boston. 1893.

ADAMS, JOHN. *Works: With Life, Notes and Illustrations,* ed. Charles Francis Adams. 10 vols. Boston. 1850–56.

ADAMS, JOHN Q. *The Writings of John Q. Adams,* ed. Worthington C. Ford. 7 vols. New York: Macmillan Co., 1914.

AMORY, THOMAS C. *Life of James Sullivan with selections of his writings.* 2 vols. Boston. 1859.

The Annals of the War Written by Leading Participants North and South. (*Century Magazine*). Philadelphia. 1879.

AUSTIN, JAMES T. *A Primer of True Republicanism.* New York. 1796.

AUSUBEL, HERMAN. *Historians and Their Craft: A Study of the Presidential Addresses of the American Historical Association, 1884–1945.* New York: Columbia University Press, 1950.

BANCROFT, GEORGE. *History of the United States from the Discovery of the American Continent.* 10 vols. Boston. 1834–74.

———. *The Office of the People in Art, Government, and Religion.* Boston. 1835.

BANCROFT, HUBERT HOWE. *The Works of Hubert Howe Bancroft.* 39 vols. San Francisco. 1882–90.

BARBER, JOHN WARNER. *Interesting Events in the History of the United States, being a selection of the most important and interesting events which have transpired since the discovery of this country to the present time.* New Haven. 1828.

———. *Incidents in American History.* New York. 1847.

———, and HOWE, HENRY. *Our Whole Country.* New York. 1860.

———. *The Loyal West in the Times of Rebellion.* Cincinnati. 1865.

BARCK, DOROTHY C. (ed.). *Letters from John Pintard to His Daughter Eliza Noel Pintard Davidson, 1816–1833.* 4 vols. New York: New-York Historical Society, 1937–40.

BARLOW, JOEL. *The Vision of Columbus* (*The Columbiad*). Boston. 1807.

BARNES, H. E. *History of Historical Writing*. Norman, Oklahoma: University of Oklahoma Press, 1937.

BASSETT, JOHN SPENCER. *The Middle Group of American Historians*. New York: Macmillan Co., 1917.

BATES, SAMUEL P. *History of the Pennsylvania Volunteers, 1861–1865*. 4 vols. Harrisburg, Pa. 1869.

BELKNAP, JEREMY. *American Biography: or An Historical Account of those Persons who have been distinguished in America, as Adventurers, Statesmen, Philosophers, Divines, Warriors, Authors, or Other Remarkable Characters, comprehending a recital of the events connected with their lives and actions*. 2 vols. Boston. 1794–98.

———. *A Discourse, intended to commemorate the Discovery of America by Christopher Columbus*. Boston. 1792.

———. *History of New Hampshire*. 3 vols. Philadelphia. 1784–92.

———. *Belknap Papers*. (*Collections* of the Massachusetts Historical Society, I, II [5th ser.], IV [6th ser.]). Boston. 1877–91.

BELLOT, H. HALE. *American History and American Historians*. Norman, Okla.: University of Oklahoma Press, 1952.

BENTLEY, WILLIAM. *Diary of William Bentley*. 4 vols. Salem, Mass.: Essex Institute, 1905–14.

———. *True Character of the Past Generation*. Worcester, Mass. 1816.

BEVERIDGE, A. J. *Life of John Marshall*. 4 vols. Boston: Houghton Mifflin Co., 1916–19.

BEVERLEY, ROBERT. *The History and Present State of Virginia in Four Parts*. London. 1705.

BLACK, J. B. *The Art of History*. London: F. S. Crofts & Co., 1926.

BOBBÉ, DOROTHIE. *DeWitt Clinton*. New York: Minton, Balch & Co., 1933.

BONNER, JOHN. *A Child's History of the United States*. New York. 1856.

BOTKIN, BENJAMIN A. (ed.). *A Treasury of New England Folk Lore*. New York: Crown Publishers, 1947.

BRADFORD, ALDEN. *History of Massachussets from 1764 to 1789*. 3 vols. Boston. 1822–25.

BRADFORD, WILLIAM. *A Dialogue, or the Sum of a Conference Between some yonge-men, born in New England, and sundry ancient-men, that came out of Holland and Old England*. Boston. 1648.

———. *History of Plymouth Plantation*. ed. Charles Deane. (*Collections of the Massachusetts Historical Society*, 4th ser., III.) Boston. 1856.

———. *Of Plymouth Plantation*. ed. George F. Willison. New York: D. Van Nostrand Co., 1948.

BROWNLOW, WILLIAM G. *Sketches of the Rise, Progress, and Decline of Secession*, Philadelphia. 1862.

BRYSON, GLADYS. *Man and Society*. Princeton: Princeton University Press, 1945.

BULEY, R. CARLYLE. *The Old Northwest, Pioneer Period, 1815–1840*. 2 vols. Indianapolis: Indiana Historical Society, 1950.

BURK, JOHN DALY. *The History of Virginia, from its first Settlement to the Present Day*. 3 vols. Petersburg. 1804–16.

BURLINGAME, ROGER. *Of Making Many Books*. New York: Charles Scribner's Sons, 1946.

BURR, FEARING, and LINCOLN, GEORGE. *Town of Hingham in the Late Civil War, with Sketches of its Soldiers and Sailors*. Boston. 1876.

BUTTERFIELD, HERBERT. *The Whig Interpretation of History*. London: G. Bell and Sons, 1931.

BYRD, WILLIAM. *The Westover Manuscripts; Containing the History of the Dividing Line Betwixt Virginia and North Carolina*. Petersburg, Va. 1841.

CALLENDER, JOHN. *An Historical Discourse on the Civil and Religious Affairs of the Colony of Rhode Island and Providence Plantations in New England, in America, from the first settlement, 1638, to the end of the first century.* Boston. 1739.

CATER, HAROLD DEAN (ed.). *Henry Adams and His Friends.* Boston: Houghton, Mifflin Co., 1947.

CATTON, BRUCE, *A Stillness at Appomattox.* New York: Doubleday & Co., Inc., 1953.

CAUGHEY, JOHN WALTON. *Hubert Howe Bancroft: Historian of the West.* Berkeley and Los Angeles: University of California Press, 1946.

CHALMERS, GEORGE. *Political Annals of the Present United Colonies from Their Settlement to the Peace of 1763.* London. 1780.

———. *Introduction to the History of the Revolt of the American Colonies.* 2 vols. London. 1782.

CHOATE, RUFUS. *The Works of Rufus Choate with a Memoir of His Life,* ed. Samuel Gilman Brown. Boston. 1862.

COLDEN, CADWALLADER. *History of the Five Indian Nations of Canada, which are dependent on the province of New-York in America.* New York. 1727. Reprinted with introduction and notes by John G. Shea. New York. 1866.

COLLINGWOOD, R. G. *The Idea of History.* New York: Oxford University Press, 1956.

COMMAGER, HENRY S. (ed.). *Documents of American History.* 5th ed. New York: Appleton-Century-Crofts, Inc., 1949.

COULTER, E. MERTON. *William G. Brownlow: Fighting Parson of the Southern Highlands.* Chapel Hill, N.C.: University of North Carolina Press, 1937.

CURTI, MERLE E. *Social Ideas of American Educators.* New York: Charles Scribner's Sons, 1935.

———. *Roots of American Loyalty.* New York: Columbia University Press, 1946.

———. *The Growth of American Thought.* 3d ed. New York: Harper & Bros., 1950.

——— (ed.). *American Scholarship in the Twentieth Century.* Cambridge, Mass.: Harvard University Press, 1953.

CURTIS, GEORGE TICKNOR. *History of the Origin, Formation, and Adoption of the Constitution of the United States.* 2 vols. New York. 1854–58.

DAVIDSON, ROBERT. *The Study of History, an Address Delivered at the Anniversary of the Freehold Young Ladies' Seminary.* Freehold, N.J. 1853.

DAWSON, HENRY B. *The Battles of the United States on Land and Sea.* 2 vols. New York. 1859.

DERBY, JAMES CEPHAS. *Fifty Years Among Authors, Books and Publishers.* New York. 1884.

DOLL, EUGENE E. *American History as Interpreted by German Historians from 1770 to 1815.* ("Transactions of the American Philosophical Society," N.S., Vol. XXXVIII, Part 5). Philadelphia: American Philosophical Society, 1949.

DOUGLASS, WILLIAM. *A Summary View, Historical and Political, of the British Settlements in North America.* 2 vols. Boston. 1747–50.

DRAPER, JOHN WILLIAM. *History of the American Civil War.* 3 vols. New York. 1867–68–70.

DUNLAP, LESLIE W. *American Historical Societies 1790–1860.* Madison, Wis.: Cantwell Printing Co., 1944.

DUNLAP, WILLIAM. *History of the New Netherlands, Province of New York, and State of New York, to 1789.* 2 vols. New York. 1839–40.

DUNNING, WILLIAM A. *Truth in History and Other Essays.* New York: Columbia University Press, 1937.

DURETT, REUBEN T. *The Life and Writings of John Filson, the First Historian of Kentucky.* Louisville. 1884.

EDDY, T. M. *The Patriotism of Illinois.* 2 vols. Chicago. 1865.

EISENSTADT, A. S. *Charles McLean Andrews.* New York: Columbia University Press, 1956.

ELLIOT, JONATHAN (ed.). *Debates, Resloutions, and Other Proceedings in Convention on the Adoption of the Federal Constitution.* 5 vols. Philadelphia. 1861.

EMERSON, DONALD E. *Richard Hildreth.* Baltimore: Johns Hopkins University Press, 1953.

EMERSON, RALPH WALDO. *Essays.* New York: Modern Library, 1944.

FARMER, JOHN. *A Genealogical Register of the First Settlers of New England.* Lancaster, Mass. 1829.

FILSON, JOHN. *The Discovery, Settlement and Present State of Kentucke: and an Essay towards the Topography and Natural History of that Important Country.* Wilmington, Del. 1784.

First Report of the Historical Society of the University of North Carolina, June 4, 1845. Hillsborough, N.C. 1845.

FIRTH, CHARLES. *Essays, Historical and Literary.* Oxford: Clarendon Press, 1938.

FLEMING, DONALD. *John William Draper and the Religion of Science.* Philadelphia: University of Pennsylvania Press, 1950.

FLOWER, MILTON E. *James Parton, the Father of Modern Biography.* Durham, N.C.: Duke University Press, 1951.

FORCE, PETER. *Tracts and Other Papers Relating to the Origin, Settlement and Progress of the Colonies of North America to 1776.* 4 vols. Washington, D.C. 1836–46.

——. *Report made to the Hon. John Forsyth, Secretary of State of the U.S. on the subject of the Documentary History of the U.S. now publishing under an Act of Congress by M. St. Clair Clarke and Peter Force.* Washington, D.C. 1834.

FOULKE, WILLIAM PARKER. *The Right Use of History, Annual Address to the Historical Society of Pennsylvania.* Philadelphia. 1856.

FRENEAU, PHILLIP. *The Miscellaneous Works of Phillip Freneau.* Philadelphia. 1787.

FROST, JOHN. *The Mexican War and Its Warriors.* Philadelphia. 1849.

FROTHINGHAM, RICHARD. *History of the Seige of Boston, and of the Battles of Lexington, Concord, and Bunker Hill.* Boston. 1849.

——. *The Command in the Battle of Bunker Hill.* Boston. 1850.

GARRATY, JOHN A. (ed.). *The Barber and the Historian: the Correspondence of George A. Myers and James Ford Rhodes, 1910–1923.* Columbus: Ohio Historical Society, 1956.

——. *The Nature of Biography.* New York: Knopf, 1957.

GAYARRÉ, CHARLES ÉTIENNE ARTHUR. *History of Louisiana.* 4 vols. New York. 1854–66.

GODKIN, EDWIN L. *Life and Letters of Edwin Lawrence Godkin,* ed. Rollo Ogden. 2 vols. New York: Macmillan Co., 1907.

GOLDMAN, ERIC F. (ed.). *Historiography and Urbanization.* Baltimore: Johns Hopkins University Press, 1941.

GOOCH, GEORGE P. *History and Historians in the Nineteenth Century.* New York: P. Smith, 1959. (Reprint of first edition.)

GOODRICH, CHARLES A. *A History of the United States.* Boston. 1823.

GORDON, THOMAS F. *The History of Pennsylvania from its Discovery by Europeans to the Declaration of Independence in 1776.* Philadelphia. 1829.

GORDON, WILLIAM. *A Discourse Preached Dec. 15, 1774.* Boston. 1774.

――――. *The Separation of the Jewish Tribes, after the Death of Solomon, accounted for, and applied to the present day, in a sermon preached before the general court on Friday, July 4, 1777.* Boston. 1777.

――――. *The History of the Rise, Progress and Establishment of Independence of the United States of America.* 3 vols. London. 1789.

GREENE, EVARTS B. *The Revolutionary Generation, 1763–1790.* ("History of American Life Series," Vol. IV.) New York: Macmillan Co., 1943.

GREENSLET, FERRIS. *The Lowells and Their Seven Worlds.* Boston: Houghton Mifflin Co., 1946.

GRIFFIN, CLARK. *Bibliography of American Historical Societies.* (*Annual Report*, American Historical Assocation, 1905, Vol. II). New York. 1905.

GRIMSHAW, WILLIAM. *History of the United States.* Philadelphia. 1824.

GUERNSEY, ALFRED H., and ALDEN, HENRY M. (eds.). *Harper's Pictorial History of the Great Rebellion.* 2 vols. New York. 1866.

GUILDAY, PETER. *John Gilmary Shea: Father of American Catholic History, 1824–1892.* United States Catholic Historical Society, 1926.

GUY, FRANCIS SHAW. *Edmund Bailey O'Callaghan.* ("The Catholic University of America Studies in American Church History," Vol. XVIII.) Washington, D.C. 1934.

HAKLUYT, RICHARD (ed.). *Divers Voyages touching the Discouerie of America and the ilands adiacent.* London. 1582.

HALE, SALMA. *A History of the United States from their first Settlement as Colonies, to the Close of the War with Great Britain in 1815.* New York. 1822.

HALL, CLAYTON COLMAN (ed.). *Narratives of Early Maryland, 1633–1684.* New York: Charles Scribner's Sons, 1910.

HANSEN, ALLEN O. *Liberalism and Education in the Eighteenth Century.* New York: Macmillan Co., 1926.

HARRISSE, HENRY. *Christophe Colomb.* 2 vols. Paris. 1884–85.

HAWKS, FRANCIS LISTER. *History of North Carolina.* 3 vols. Fayetteville, N.C. 1857–58.

HAZARD, EBENEZER. *Historical Collections.* 2 vols. Philadelphia. 1792–94.

HEADLEY, JOEL TYLER. *Napoleon and his Marshalls.* 2 vols. New York. 1846.

――――. *Washington and His Generals.* 2 vols. New York. 1847.

――――. *Second War with England.* New York. 1853.

――――. *The Great Rebellion.* Hartford. 1866.

Herbert B. Adams: Tributes of Friends. Baltimore: Johns Hopkins University Press, 1902.

HESSELTINE, WILLIAM B. *Pioneer's Mission: The Story of Lyman Copeland Draper.* Madison, Wis.: State Historical Society of Wisconsin, 1954.

――――, and McNEIL, DONALD R. (eds.). *In Support of Clio: Essays in Memory of Herbert A. Kellar.* Madison, Wis.: State Historical Society of Wisconsin, 1958.

HEWATT, ALEXANDER. *An Historical Account of the Rise and Progress of the Colonies of South Carolina and Georgia.* London. 1779.

HILDRETH, RICHARD. *History of the United States.* 6 vols. New York. 1849–52.

HILL, WILLIAM CARROLL. *A Century of Genealogical Progress.* Boston: New England Historic-Genealogical Society, 1945.

HOLCOMBE, JAMES P. *Sketches of the Political Issues and Controversies of the Revolution.* Richmond, 1856.

HOLMES, ABIEL. *American Annals.* 2 vols. Cambridge, Mass, 1805.

HOLMES, GEORGE. *A School History of the United States of America from the Earliest Discoveries to the Year 1870.* New York. 1872.

HOLT, W. STULL, ed. *Historical Scholarship in the United States, 1876 to 1901.* Baltimore: Johns Hopkins University Press, 1938.

HOWE, M. A. DEWOLFE. *The Life and Letters of George Bancroft.* New York. Charles Scribner's Sons, 1908.

HUBBARD, WILLIAM. *The History of the Indian Wars in New England,* ed. Samuel G. Drake. Boston. 1865.

——. *General History of New England from the Discovery to MDCLXXX.* Boston. 1815.

HUTCHINSON, THOMAS. *The History of the Province of Massachusetts Bay from 1749–1774.* London. 1828.

——. *The History of the Colony and Province of Massachusetts Bay,* ed. Lawrence Shaw Mayo. 3 vols. Cambridge, Mass.: Harvard Univesity Press, 1936.

HUTCHINSON, WILLIAM T. (ed.). *Marcus W. Jernegan Essays in American Historiography.* Chicago: University of Chicago Press, 1937.

INGLIS, ALEXANDER J. *The Rise of the High School in Massachusetts.* New York: Columbia University Press, 1911.

IRVING, WASHINGTON. *A History of New York by Diedrich Knickerbocker.* New York. 1809.

——. *Life of George Washington.* 5 vols. New York. 1855–59.

——. *The Life and Voyages of Christopher Columbus.* New York. 1828.

JAMESON, JOHN FRANKLIN. *The History of Historical Writing in America.* Boston. 1891.

—— (ed.). *Original Narratives of Early American History.* 18 vols. New York: Charles Scribner's Sons, 1907–17.

JEFFERSON, THOMAS. *Notes on Virginia in Answer to 23 Queries by M. DeMarbois.* 1st ed., Paris: 1784. New ed., Richmond. 1853.

——. *Writings of Thomas Jefferson,* ed. Paul L. Ford. 10 vols. New York. 1892–99.

——. *The Writings of Thomas Jefferson,* ed. Andrew A. Liscomb and Albert L. Bergh. 20 vols. Washington, D.C.: Thomas Jefferson Memorial Association of the United States, 1903.

——. *The Papers of Thomas Jefferson,* ed. Julian P. Boyd *et al.* 5 vols. Princeton: Princeton University Press, 1950–52.

——. *Catalogue of Thomas Jefferson's Library,* ed. Millicent Sowerby. 4 vols. Washington, D.C.: Library of Congress, 1952.

JENKINS, JOHN S. *History of the War Between the United States and Mexico.* New York. 1854.

JENSEN, MERRILL. *The New Nation.* New York: Knopf, 1950.

JOHNSON, ALLEN, and MALONE, DUMAS (eds.). *Dictionary of American Biography.* New York: Charles Scribner's Sons, 1930.

JOHNSON, EDWARD. *A History of New England from the English Planting in the Yeere 1618 until the Yeere 1652.* London. 1654.

JOHNSON, ROBERT UNDERWOOD, and BUEL, CLARENCE C. (eds.). *Battles and Leaders of the Civil War.* 4 vols. New York. 1884–86.

JONES, HUGH. *The Present State of Virginia,* ed., Richard L. Morton. Chapel Hill, N.C.: Pub. for Virginia Historical Society by University of North Carolina Press, 1956.

JONES, THOMAS. *History of New York during the Revolutionary War and of the leading events in the other colonies at that period,* ed. Edward F. DeLancy. New York. 1879.

KENNEDY, JOHN P. *Memoirs of the Life of William Wirt*. 2 vols. Philadelphia. 1860.

KING, RUFUS. *Life and Correspondence of Rufus King*, ed. Charles R. King. 6 vols. New York. 1894–1900.

KLINGBERG, FRANK J. and FRANK W., (eds.). *The Correspondence Between Henry Stephens Randall and Hugh Blair Grigsby, 1856–1861*. Berkeley and Los Angeles: University of California Press, 1952.

KNAPP, SAMUEL. *Lectures on American Literature with remarks on some passages of American History*. New York. 1829.

KOCH, ADRIENNE. *The Philosophy of Thomas Jefferson*. New York: Columbia University Press, 1943.

KRAUS, MICHAEL. *The Writing of American History*. Norman, Oklahoma: University of Oklahoma Press, 1953.

LALLY, F. E. *As Lord Acton Says*. Newport, R.I.: R. Ward, 1942.

LARNED, J. N. (ed.). *The Literature of American History*. Boston: Houghton Mifflin Co., 1902.

LEAKE, ISAAC Q. *Memoir of the Life and Times of General John Lamb*. Albany. 1850.

LECHFORD, THOMAS. *Plain Dealing; or Newes from New England: a short view of New England's present government, both ecclesiasticall and civil, compared with the anciently-received and established government of England*. London. 1642.

LIVERMORE, ABIEL ABBOT. *The War with Mexico Reviewed*. Boston. 1850.

LONG, ORIE WILLIAM. *Literary Pioneers, Early American Explorers of European Culture*. Cambridge, Mass.: Harvard University Press, 1935.

LONGAKER, JOHN MARX. *English Biography in the Eighteenth Century*. Philadelphia: University of Pennsylvania Press, 1931.

LOSSING, BENSON JOHN. *The Pictorial Field Book of the Revolution*. 2d ed. New York. 1855.

———. *Biographical Sketches of the Signers of the Declaration of Independence*. New York. 1854.

———. *The Pictorial History of the Civil War*. 2 vols. New York. 1866–68.

———. *American Centenary*. New York. 1876.

LUDEWIG, HERMANN E. *The Literature of American Local History*. New York. 1846.

MADISON, JAMES. *The Writings of James Madison*, ed. Gaillard Hunt. 9 vols. New York: G. P. Putnam's Sons, 1900–1910.

MARBLE, ANNIE RUSSELL. *From 'Prentice to Patron*. New York: D. Appleton Century Co., Inc., 1935.

MARCOU, ELIZABETH BELKNAP. *Life of Jeremy Belknap*. Boston. 1845.

MARSH, GEORGE PERKINS. *The American Historical School*. Troy, N.Y. 1847.

MARSHALL, JOHN. *Life of George Washington*. 5 vols. Philadelphia. 1804–7.

MATHER, COTTON. *Magnalia Christi Americana*. 2 vols. London. 1702.

MATHER, INCREASE. *A Brief History of the Warr with the Indians in New England*. Boston. 1676.

———. *A Brief Relation of the State of New England from the Beginning of that Plantation to this Present Year 1689*. London. 1689.

MATHEW, THOMAS. *The Beginning, Progress, and Conclusion of Bacon's Rebellion in Virginia in the Years 1675 and 1676*. Washington. 1835.

MAYER, BRANTZ. *History of the War Between Mexico and the United States*. New York. 1848.

MILLER, PERRY. *The New England Mind: the Seventeenth Century*. New York: Macmillan Co., 1939.

————. *The New England Mind from Colony to Province*. Cambridge, Mass.: Harvard University Press, 1953.

MILLER, SAMUEL. *The Life of Samuel Miller, D.D., LL.D.* New York. 1869.

MINOT, GEORGE RICHARDS. *The History of the Insurrection in Massachusetts in the Year Seventeen Hundred and Eighty-six and the Rebellion Consequent Thereon*. Boston. 1788.

————. *Continuation of the History of the Province of Massachusetts Bay from the Year 1748*. Boston. 1798.

MONETTE, JOHN WESLEY. *History of the discovery and settlement of the Valley of the Mississippi, by the three great European powers, Spain, France, and Great Britain, and the subsequent occupation, settlement, and extension of Civil Government by the United States until the year 1846*. 2 vols. New York. 1846.

MOORE, FRANK. *The Rebellion Record*. 9 vols. New York. 1862–66.

MORSE, JAMES KING. *Jedidiah Morse, a Champion of New England Orthodoxy*. New York: Columbia University Press, 1939.

MORSE, JARVIS M. *American Beginnings*. Washington, D.C.: Public Affairs Press, 1952.

MORSE, JEDIDIAH. *The History of America in Two Books*. Philadelphia. 1790.

MORTON, NATHANIEL. *New England's Memoriall*. Boston. 1669.

MOSIER, RICHARD D. *Making the American Mind*. New York: Kings Crown Press, 1947.

MURDOCK, KENNETH. *Increase Mather, the Foremost American Puritan*. Cambridge, Mass.: Harvard University Press, 1925.

————. *Literature and Theology in Colonial New England*. Cambridge, Mass.: Harvard University Press, 1949.

MURPHEY, ARCHIBALD D. *The Papers of Archibald D. Murphey*, ed. William Henry Hoyt. 2 vols. Raleigh, N.C.: E. M. Uzzell & Co., State Printers, 1914.

MURRAY, JAMES. *Impartial History of the War in America*, 2 vols. London. 1781–82.

NEAL, DANIEL. *The History of New England, containing an impartial account of the Civil and Ecclesiastical Affairs of the Country to the year of our Lord 1700, to which is added the present state of New England*. 2 vols. London. 1720.

NEILL, EDWARD DUFFIELD. *Terra Mariae, Threads of Maryland Colonial History*. Baltimore. 1867.

————. *History of the Virginia Company of London*. Albany. 1869.

————. *English Colonization*. London and New York. 1871.

NICOLAS, NICHOLAS HARRIS. *Observations on the State of Historical Literature*. London. 1830.

NILES, HEZEKIAH. *Principles and Acts of the Revolution in America*. Baltimore. 1822.

NOBLE, DAVID W. *The Paradox of Progressive Thought*. Minneapolis: University of Minnesota Press, 1958.

NYE, RUSSELL. *George Bancroft*. New York: A. A. Knopf, 1949.

O'CALLAGHAN, EDMUND B. (ed.). *Documentary History of the State of New York*. 4 vols. Albany. 1849–51.

————. *Documents of New York*. 10 vols. Albany. 1853–58.

OLIVER, PETER. *The Puritan Commonwealth*. Boston. 1856.

OSGOOD, HERBERT L. *The American Colonies in the 18th Century*. 3 vols. New York: Columbia University Press, 1930.

PAINE, THOMAS. *Letter Addressed to the Abbé Raynal on the Affairs of North America.* Philadelphia. 1782.

PALFREY, JOHN GORHAM. *History of New England During the Stuart Dynasty.* 4 vols. Boston. 1859.

PARKMAN, FRANCIS. *The Journals of Francis Parkman*, ed. Mason Wade. 2 vols. New York: Harper & Bros., 1947.

PARKS, GEORGE B. *Richard Hakluyt and the English Voyages.* New York: American Geographical Society, 1928.

PARTON, JAMES. *Life of Aaron Burr.* New York. 1858.

———. *Life and Times of Benjamin Franklin.* 2 vols. New York. 1864.

———. *Life of Andrew Jackson.* New York. 1861.

PEARCE, ROY HARVEY. *The Savage of America: A Study of the Indian and the Idea of Civilization.* Baltimore: Johns Hopkins University Press, 1953.

PEARDON, THOMAS PRESTON. *The Transition in English Historical Writing, 1760–1830.* New York: Columbia University Press, 1933.

PEASE, OTIS A. *Parkman's History.* New Haven: Yale University Press, 1953.

PERKINS, JAMES H. *Annals of the West.* Pittsburgh. 1857.

PETERS, SAMUEL A. *A General History of Connecticut from its first settlement under George Fenwick, esq., to its latest period of amity with Great Britain.* London. 1781.

PETERSON, CHARLES J. *Military Heroes of the War of 1812, with a Narrative of the War.* Philadelphia. 1848.

———. *Military Heroes of the War with Mexico.* Philadelphia. 1848.

PHILIPS, EDITH. *Louis Hue Girardin and Nicholas Gouin Dufief and their Relations with Thomas Jefferson.* Baltimore: Johns Hopkins University Press, 1926.

PICKETT, ALBERT JAMES. *History of Alabama and Incidentally of Georgia and Mississippi from the Earliest Period.* Charleston, S.C. 1851.

POLLARD, EDWARD R. *The South Vindicated.* London. 1862.

———. *The Rise and Fall of the "Model Republic."* London. 1863.

———. *Southern History of the War.* Charleston. 1865.

POWERS, GEORGE W. *The Story of the Thirty-eighth Regiment of Massachusetts Volunteers.* Cambridge, Mass. 1866.

PRESCOTT, WILLIAM HICKLING. *History of the Conquest of Mexico.* 3 vols. New York. 1843.

———. *History of the Conquest of Peru.* 2 vols. London. 1847.

PRESSLY, THOMAS J. *Americans Interpret Their Civil War.* Princeton: Princeton University Press, 1954.

PRIESTLEY, JOSEPH. *Lectures on History and General Policy; to which is prefixed an essay on a course of Liberal Education for Civil and Active Life.* Philadelphia. 1803.

PRINCE, THOMAS. *A Chronological History of New England in the Form of Annals.* Boston. 1736.

The Proceedings of the Southern Historical Convention which assembled at the Montgomery, White Sulphur Springs, Virginia, on the 14th of August, 1873, and of the Southern Historical Society as reorganized, with the Address by General Jubal A. Early, delivered before the Convention on the first day of its session. Richmond, Va. 1873.

PROUD, ROBERT. *The History of Pennsylvania.* 2 vols. Philadelphia. 1797.

PURCHAS, SAMUEL. *Hakluytus Posthumus; or Purchas, his pilgrimes, contayning a history of the world in Sea voyages and Lande-trauells, by Englishmen and others.* 5 vols. London. 1625–26.

RAMSAY, DAVID. *History of the American Revolution.* 2 vols. Philadelphia. 1789.

RAMSEY, J. G. M. *Dr. J. G. M. Ramsey, Autobiography and Letters,* ed. William B. Hesseltine. Nashville: Tennessee Historical Commission, 1954.

RANDALL, HENRY S. *Life of Thomas Jefferson.* 3 vols. New York. 1858.

RAYNAL, GUILLAUME THOMAS FRANÇOIS. *Revolution of America.* London. 1781.

Report of the Proceedings of the Society of the Army of the Tennessee at the First Annual Meeting Held at Cincinnati, Ohio, Nov. 14 and 15, 1866. Cincinnati. 1877.

RIVES, WILLIAM CABELL. *History of the Life and Times of James Madison.* 3 vols. Boston. 1859–68.

ROBBINS. THOMAS. *Diary of Reverend Thomas Robbins,* ed., Increase Tarbox. 2 vols. Boston, 1886–87.

ROBERTS, DANIEL. *Some Memoirs of the Life of John Roberts.* Philadelphia. 1766.

ROORBACH, AGNEW O. *The Development of the Social Studies in American Secondary Education Before 1861.* Philadelphia: University of Pennsylvania Press, 1937.

ROWLANDSON, MARY. *The Sovereignty and goodness of GOD, Together with the faithfulness of His Promises Displayed; Being a Narrative of the Captivity and Restauration of Mrs. Mary Rowlandson.* Cambridge, Mass. 1682.

SABINE, LORENZO. *Biographical Sketches of Loyalists of the American Revolution.* Boston. 1847.

SANDERSON, JOHN. *Biography of the Signers of the Declaration of Independence.* 9 vols. Philadelphia. 1820–27.

SCHARF, THOMAS J. *History of Westchester County, New York.* 2 vols. Philadelphia. 1886.

SCOTT, R. N., *et al.* (eds.). *War of the Rebellion: A Compilation of the Official Records of the Union and Confederate Armies.* 130 vols. Washington, D.C. 1880–1901.

SCUDDER, HORACE E. *A History of the United States.* New York. 1884.

SEARS, ROBERT. *The Pictorial History of the American Revolution.* New York. 1846.

SHANNON, FRED ALBERT. *The Organization and Administration of the Union Army.* 2 vols. Cleveland: Arthur H. Clark Co., 1928.

SHEA, JOHN GILMARY. *History of the Catholic Church in the United States.* New York. 1856.

SHEDD, WILLIAM G. T. *Philosophy of History.* Boston. 1853.

SHURTLEFF, NATHANIEL B. *Topographical and Historical Description of Boston.* Boston. 1845.

——— (ed.). *Records of the Governors and Company of Massachusetts Bay in New England.* 5 vols. Boston. 1853–54.

——— (ed.). *Records of the Colony of New Plymouth in New England.* 8 vols. Boston. 1855–57.

SIMMS, WILLIAM GILMORE. *The History of South Carolina, from its first European Discovery to its Erection into a Republic; with a Supplementary Chronicle of Events to the Present Time.* Charleston, S.C. 1840.

———. *Views and Reviews in American Literature, History and Fiction.* New York. 1845.

———. *South Carolina in the Revolutionary War.* Charleston, S.C. 1853.

———. *The Letters of William Gilmore Simms,* ed. Mary C. Simms Oliphant, Alfred Taylor Odell, and T. C. Duncan Eaves, 5 vols. Columbia S.C.: University of South Carolina Press, 1952–56.

SMITH, BRADFORD, *Bradford of Plymouth.* Philadelphia: J. B. Lippincott, 1951.

———. *Captain John Smith, his Life and Legend.* Philadelphia: J. B. Lippincott, 1953.

SMITH, BUCKINGHAM. *The Narrative of Álvar Núñez Cabeça de Vaca.* New York. 1852.

SMITH, JOHN. *A True Relation of such occurrences and Accidents of noate as hath happened in Virginia since the first planting of that colony, which is now resident in the south part thereof, till the last return from thence.* London. 1608.

———. *New England's Trials* (1620), ed. Charles Deane. Boston. 1873.

———. *The Generall Historie of Virginia, New England, and the Summer Isles.* London. 1624.

SMITH, SAMUEL. *The History of the Colony of Nova-Caesaria, or New Jersey, containing an account of its first settlement, progressive improvements, the original and present constitution, and other events to the year 1721, with some particulars since; and a short view of its present state.* Burlington, N.J. 1765.

SMITH, WILLIAM. *History of the Late Province of New York, from its Discovery to 1762.* (Collections of the New-York Historical Society, Vols. IV, V.) New York. 1829-30.

SNOWDEN, RICHARD. *The American Revolution Written in the Style of Ancient History in Two Volumes.* 2 vols. Philadelphia. 1793.

SPENCER, JESSE AMES. *History of the United States from the Earliest Period to the Administration of James Buchanan.* New York. 1858.

SPIESEKE, ALICE W. *The First Textbooks in American History and Their Compiler, John M'Culloch.* New York: Columbia University Press, 1938.

STAUFFER, D. A. *English Biography before 1700.* Cambridge, Mass.: Harvard University Press, 1930.

STILES, EZRA. *Extracts from the Itineraries and other Miscellanies of Ezra Stiles, 1755-1794, with a Selection from his Correspondence,* ed. F. B. Dexter. New Haven: Yale University Press, 1916.

———. *Letters and Papers of Ezra Stiles, President of Yale College, 1778-1795,* ed. Isabel M. Calder. New Haven: Yale University Library, 1933.

STITH, WILLIAM. *The History of the First Discovery and Settlement of Virginia.* London. 1753.

STOWE, HARRIET BEECHER, *Uncle Tom's Cabin.* New York. 1852.

STRACHEY, WILLIAM. *The History of Travaile into Virginia Britannia, expressing the cosmography and commodities of the country, together with the manners and customs of the People,* ed. R. H. Major. London. 1849.

STRONG, GEORGE TEMPLETON. *Diary,* ed. Allan Nevins and M. H. Thomas. 4 vols. New York: Macmillan Co., 1952.

SULLIVAN, JAMES. *The History of the District of Maine.* Boston. 1795.

SULLIVAN, WILLIAM. *Familiar Letters on Public Characters and Public Events from the Peace of 1783 to the Peace of 1815.* Boston. 1834.

SWINTON, WILLIAM. *The History of the New York Seventh Regiment during the War of the Rebellion.* New York. 1870.

THARP, LOUISE H. *Until Victory: Horace Mann and Mary Peabody.* Boston: Little, Brown Co., 1953.

THAYER, WILLIAM MAKEPEACE. *The Poor Boy and Merchant Prince . . . the Life of Amos Lawrence.* New York. 1857.

———. *The Poor Girl and True Woman . . . Life of Mary Lyon.* New York. 1857.

———. *The Bobbin Boy.* New York. 1860.

———. *The Pioneer Boy and How he Became President.* New York. 1863.

———. *A Youth's History of the Rebellion.* New York. 1865.

THOMAS, ISAIAH. *The Juvenile Biographer, containing lives of little masters and misses; including a variety of good and bad characters, by a little biographer.* Worcester, Mass. 1787.

——. *The Diary of Isaiah Thomas,* ed. Benjamin Thomas Hill. Worcester, Mass.: American Antiquarian Society, 1909.

THORNTON, JOHN WINGATE. *Peter Oliver's Puritan Commonwealth Reviewed.* Boston. 1857.

——. *The Pulpit of the American Revolution.* Boston. 1860.

THURSFIELD, RICHARD E. *Henry Barnard's American Journal of Education.* Baltimore: Johns Hopkins University Press, 1945.

TODD, CHARLES B. *Life and Letters of Joel Barlow, LL.D.* New York. 1886.

TRUMBULL, BENJAMIN. *A Complete History of Connecticut, Civil and Ecclesiastical, from the Emigration of its first Planters from England in 1630 to 1713.* New Haven. 1797.

TRUMBULL, J. HAMMON. *The Reverend Samuel Peters, His Defenders and Apologists.* Boston. 1877.

—— (ed.). *Note-Book Kept by Thomas Lechford.* Cambridge, Mass. 1885.

TRYON, ROLLA M. *The Social Sciences as School Subjects.* New York: Charles Scribner's Sons, 1935.

TUCKER, GEORGE. *History of the United States, to the end of the 26th Congress in 1841.* 4 vols. Philadelphia. 1856–57.

TYLER, LYON G. (ed.). *Narratives of Early Virginia, 1606–1625.* New York: Charles Scribner's Sons, 1907.

TYSON, JOB R. *Discourse Delivered before the Historical Society of Pennsylvania on the Colonial History of the Eastern and some of the Southern States.* Philadelphia. 1842.

VAIL, ROBERT WILLIAM GLENROIE. *Knickerbocker Birthday: A Sesqui-Centennial History of the New-York Historical Society 1804–1954.* New York: New-York Historical Society, 1954.

VAN SCHAACK, HENRY C. *The Life of Peter Van Schaack, LL.D., embracing Selections from his Correspondence and other Writings during the American Revolution.* New York. 1842.

VENABLE, WILLIAM H. *Beginnings of Literary Culture in the Ohio Valley.* Cincinnati. 1891.

WADE, MASON. *Francis Parkman, Heroic Historian.* New York: Viking Press, 1942.

WALTON, JOHN. *John Filson of Kentucke.* Lexington, Ky.: University of Kentucky Press, 1956.

WARREN, MERCY. *History of the Rise, Progress, and Termination of the American Revolution.* 3 vols. Boston. 1805.

WASHBURN, WILCOMB, E. *The Governor and the Rebel.* Chapel Hill, N.C.: University of North Carolina Press, 1957.

WASHINGTON, GEORGE. *Writings of George Washington,* ed. Jared Sparks. 12 vols. Boston. 1837.

WATSON, JOHN F. *Annals of Philadelphia.* Philadelphia. 1830.

WEBSTER, NOAH. *An American Selection of Lessons in Reading and Speaking.* 3d ed., greatly enlarged. Philadelphia. 1787.

——. *History of the United States, to which is prefixed a brief historical account of our English Ancestors, from the dispersion at Babel, to their migration to America and of the Conquest of South America, by the Spaniards.* New Haven. 1832.

WECTER, DIXON. *When Johnny Comes Marching Home.* New York: Charles Scribner's Sons, 1942.

——. *The Hero in America.* New York: Charles Scribner's Sons, 1949.

WEEMS, MASON LOCKE. *A History of the Life and Death, Virtues and Exploits, of General George Washington, Faithfully taken from Authentic Documents.* Philadelphia. 1800.

———. *The Life of Benjamin Franklin; with many choice Anecdotes and Admirable Sayings of this great man, never before published by any of his biographers.* 5th ed. Baltimore. 1820.

———. *Mason Locke Weems, His Works and Ways,* ed. Emily Ellsworth Ford Skeel. 3 vols. New York: Richmond Mayo-Smith, 1929.

WERNER, MORRIS R. *Tammany Hall.* New York: Garden City Publishing Co., 1932.

WHITEHEAD, WILLIAM ADEE. *East New Jersey under the Proprietary Governments.* Newark. 1846.

———. *The Papers of Lewis Morris, Governor of New Jersey.* Newark. 1852.

———. *Contributions to the Early History of Perth Amboy and Adjoining County.* Newark. 1856.

WILEY, BELL I. *The Life of Johnny Reb.* New York: Bobbs-Merrill Co., 1943.

———. *The Life of Billy Yank.* New York: Bobbs-Merrill Co., 1952.

WILLIAMS, ELLEN. *Three Years and a half in the Army: or History of the Second Colorados.* New York: 1885.

WILLIAMS, SAMUEL, *The Natural and Civil History of Vermont.* 2 vols. Boston. 1795.

WILSON, ROBERT A. *New History of the Conquest of Mexico.* New York. 1859.

WINCHESTER, ELHANAN. *A Plain Political Catechism intended for the use of schools in the United States of America, wherein the great Principles of Liberty, and of the Federal Government, are laid down and explained, by way of question and answer, made level to the lowest capacities.* Greenfield, Mass. 1796.

WINSLOW, EDWARD. *A Relation or Journall of the Beginning and Proceedings of the English Plantation settled at Plimouth in New England, by certaine English Adventurers both Merchants and others.* London. 1622.

WINSOR, JUSTIN, ed. *Narrative and Critical History of America.* Boston. 8 vols. 1884–89.

WINTHROP, JOHN. *A Journal of the Transactions and Occurrences in the Settlement of Massachusetts Bay and the other New England colonies from the year 1630 to 1644.* ed. Noah Webster. Hartford. 1790.

———. *The History of New England from 1630 to 1649.* ed. James Savage. Boston. 1853.

WIRT, WILLIAM. *Sketches of the Life and Character of Patrick Henry.* Philadelphia. 1818.

WOOD, JOHN. *The History of the Administration of John Adams, Esq., Late President of the United States.* New York. 1802.

———. *A Correct Statement of the Various Sources from which the History of the Administration of John Adams was compiled, and the motives for its suppression by Col. Burr, with some observations on a narrative by a citizen of New York.* New York. 1802.

WOOD, WILLIAM. *New England's Prospect.* London. 1634.

YOAKUM, HENDERSON. *History of Texas, from its First Settlement in 1685 to its Annexation to the United States in 1846.* 2 vols. New York. 1855.

ZUNDER, T. A. *Early Days of Joel Barlow.* New Haven: Yale University Press, 1934.

Index